The Achievement of Education

The Achievement of Education

An Examination of Key Concepts in Educational Practice

John H. Chambers
Tasmanian College of Advanced Education

1817

HARPER & ROW, PUBLISHERS, New York
Cambridge, Philadelphia, San Francisco,
London, Mexico City, São Paulo, Sydney

Sponsoring Editor: George Middendorf
Production Manager: William Lane
Compositor: ComCom Division of Haddon Craftsmen, Inc.
Printer and Binder: R. R. Donnelley & Sons Company
Art Studio: J & R Art Services, Inc.

The Achievement of Education: An Examination of Key Concepts
in Educational Practice

Chambers, John H.
    The achievement of education.

    Bibliography: p.
    Includes index.
    1. Education—Aims and objectives. 2. Learning.
I. Title.
LB1025.2.C467 1983   370'.1   82-15640
ISBN 0-06-041237-2

For Alan Chambers,
my first philosopher

Contents

Preface xi

Acknowledgments xiii

Chapter 1: PHILOSOPHY 1

A. Questions of Meaning and Justification *1*
B. Conceptual Questions and Other Sorts of Questions *5*
C. Being Aware of Presuppositions *8*
D. Concepts and Analysis *11*

Chapter 2: ACTIVITIES 15

2.1 Education *15*
A. Educational Activities *15*
B. Cognitive Perspective and Rationality *18*
C. Education or Training? *24*

D. Education of the Emotions   *25*
E. The Justification of Education   *30*

2.2 Indoctrination   *34*
A. Intention   *34*
B. Content   *36*
C. Methods   *43*
D. Misunderstanding   *45*

2.3 Learning   *47*
A. Learning and Content   *47*
B. An Example of Conceptual Implications: Learning and Democracy   *52*
C. Learning and Education   *57*

Chapter 3: CURRICULUM 59

3.1 Needs and Interests   *59*
A. What Are Needs?   *59*
B. Needs and Education   *62*
C. Needs and Motivation   *67*
D. Needs and Wants   *69*
E. Needs Debate   *70*
F. Interests—Psychological and Normative   *70*
G. Interests and Education   *71*

3.2 Growth   *78*
A. Physical Growth   *78*
B. The Importance of a Society   *79*
C. The Content of Educational Growth   *81*
D. Educational Growth and the Forms of Knowledge   *83*

3.3 Interdisciplinary Curricula   *87*
A. What Can Curriculum Integration Mean?   *87*
B. Disciplines and Interdisciplinary Work   *89*
C. Paradigms of Integration   *90*
D. Forms of Knowledge   *91*
E. A Suggested Meaning for the Term *Integration*   *94*
F. The Point of Interdisciplinary Curricula   *96*

3.4 Art   *101*
A. Art Statements   *101*
B. Art's Relationship with Other Forms of Knowledge   *104*

C. Art Concepts   *106*
D. Pedagogical Implications   *108*

Chapter 4: CONTROL   116

4.1 Respect for Persons   *116*
A. What Is a Person?   *116*
B. What Is Respect?   *119*
C. Why Respect Persons?   *125*
D. Schooling and Respect for Persons   *129*

4.2 Freedom   *133*
A. The Meaning of, the Principle of, and Educational
   Implications of Freedom   *133*
B. Freedom Contrasted with Ability   *137*
C. Transcendental Justification of Freedom   *140*

4.3 Discipline   *142*
A. Some Significant Constraints   *142*
B. Discipline and Rules   *144*
C. Discipline and Achievement   *147*
D. The Empirical Situation—The Importance of Context
   148
E. The Gradual Development of Discipline   *151*
F. The Justification of Discipline   *152*

4.4 Rights   *154*
A. The Logic of Rights Talk   *154*
B. The Existence of Granted Rights and the Justification
   of Granted and Claimed Rights   *155*
C. Granted Rights and Duties   *157*
D. Children's Rights   *159*
E. The Right to Education   *165*

4.5 School   *169*
A. The Utopianism of Deschooling   *169*
B. Epistemological Naiveté and the Necessity of
   Instruction   *174*
C. Truths and Half-Truths about Schooling   *176*

Epilogue   *181*

Bibliography   *183*

Index   *189*

Preface

In analyzing key educational concepts, I have tried to provide something written in an uncomplicated manner, which will be of direct and practical use to student teachers, teachers, and school administrators in their work with children. The book derives from ten years as a classroom teacher in elementary and high schools, and ten years of teaching educational theory in a variety of colleges in several English-speaking countries.

In many places I criticize as directly as possible the conceptual and practical fads and fashions of schooling that have had such a debilitating effect on the *educational* practice of teachers. This approach may be too succinct for some tastes, but if readers wish to see finer details of argument and counterargument, they may refer to the admirable work of such writers as Peters, Hirst, Scheffler, Soltis, Dearden, and others.

Any "observer of the American educational scene today must note the chaos of irresponsibility, the inefficiency, the fads, the vested interests, and the confusions that exist in various degrees and various levels" (Lucas, 1969, p. 3). This statement was made over a decade ago, but still applies, I fear. That it still applies may be attributed to the fact that for too many years now educational theory has been dominated by empirical studies. It is my thesis that this emphasis is misguided and that the important issues are equally philosophical. Approaches such as that of psychology have a crucial place, but come in on the back of philosophy. Psychology's job is to help make known the empirical aspects of the issues that philosophy demarcates and clarifies. Similarly, sociology can tell the teacher and administrator about the social context in which the teaching and learning occur, and history can give some indication of the evolution of pedagogical ideas. But, again, these studies have significance because they shed light on the areas that have been philosophically explicated.

The material of the book is arranged in the following way. Initially, the fundamental distinction between philosophical and other issues is considered and the extreme importance of philosophy in talk about schooling is indicated. A case for a special interpretation of *education* is then made and contrasted with other sorts of activities such as training and indoctrination; I also look at what I believe to be the key pedagogical feature of learning. In Chapter 3 an attempt is made to deal with several crucial concepts that bear upon any curriculum that is to achieve education in the sense outlined in this book, such concepts as *interests, growth, needs,* and so on. I then consider issues of social control in schools, keeping in mind the parameters that have already been provided in terms of education and the curriculum, analyzing, therefore, such concepts as *freedom* and *discipline* and arguing for the importance of schools themselves.

Though the content is aimed particularly at students taking classes in foundations of education and philosophy of education (and all of the prepublication reviews have commented upon the book's readability) it should be of use also to classroom teachers, administrators, and supervisors.

The final page of each section lists key statements, which together provide a summary of the argument in the section.

Earlier versions of some of the material of this book have appeared in the following journals: Section 3.3 as "If Art is Knowledge, Then..." in *The Australian Journal of Education,* 23, no. 3 (October 1979): 283–294; Section 3.4 as "Is Curriculum Integration like Miscegenation?" in *The Australian Journal of Teacher Education,* 2, no. 1 (July 1977): 28–39; Section 4.4D as "Children's Right to Childhood" in *The Spectator,* April 28, 1973; Section 4.5 as "Delusions of Deschooling" in *Unicorn,* 6, no. 2 (May 1980): 126–135. I am grateful to the editors of those publications for allowing me to adapt the content of these articles.

My colleagues Dr. John Norris and Dr. Geoffrey Haward, and my sisters Mrs. Joy Chambers Grundy and Mrs. Coral Chambers Garner of the University of Queensland (who also compiled the Index) made helpful suggestions at various stages in the development of the manuscript, and I should like particularly to thank Professor Arnold Rothstein of the City University of New York for his perceptive comments. Several anonymous external readers for Harper & Row also made points that have been incorporated. None of these persons is however responsible for any personal opinions I may express.

J.H.C.

ACKNOWLEDGMENTS

Grateful acknowledgment is made to the following persons and publishers for allowing quotations from the listed publications.

To Routledge and Kegan Paul for: Oakeshott, M., "Education: The Engagement and Its Frustration," in Dearden, R. S., Hirst, P. H., and Peters, R. S. (eds.), *Education and the Development of Reason;* Hirst, P. H., "Liberal Education and the Nature of Knowledge," in Archambault, R. D. (ed.), *Philosophical Analysis and Education;* Hirst, P. H., *Knowledge and the Curriculum;* Field, D., *Change in Art Education;* Popper, K. R., *The Open Society and Its Enemies;* Wilson, P. S., *Interest and Discipline in Education;* Dearden, R. F., *The Philosophy of Primary Education;* Olafson, F. A., "Rights and Duties in Education", in Doyle, J. F. (ed.), *Educational Judgments;* Hargreaves, D., *Interpersonal Relations and Education.*

To Humanities Press for: Hirst, P. H., "Liberal Education and the Nature of Knowledge," in Archambault, R. D. (ed.), *Philosophical Analysis and Education;* Field, D., *Change in Art Education;* Dearden, R. F., *The Philosophy of Primary Education.*

To Princeton University Press for: Popper, K. R., *The Open Society and Its Enemies.*

To George Allen and Unwin for: Francis, P., *Beyond Control;* Peters, R. S., *Ethics and Education.*

To Oxford University Press for: Berlin, I., *Four Essays on Liberty;* Popper, K. R., *Objective Knowledge: An Evolutionary Approach.*

To John Wiley & Sons for: Kneller, G. F., *Introduction to Philosophy of Education.*

To Jacaranda Wiley Ltd. for: Bowen, J., and Hobson, P. R., *Theories of Education.*

To Little, Brown and Co. and Clive Beck for: Beck, C., *Educational Philosophy and Theory, An Introduction.*

To Little, Brown and Co. and the British Broadcasting Corporation for: Bronowski, J., *The Ascent of Man.*

To Macmillan & Co. for: Bradley, A. C., *Oxford Lectures on Poetry.*

To Macmillan Publishing Co. for Lucas, C. J. (ed.), *What Is Philosophy of Education?,* copyright © 1969 by Christopher J. Lucas.

To Cambridge University Press for: Whiteley, C. H., "Love, Hate and Emotion," in *Philosophy,* vol. 54, no. 208 (April 1979).

To the Editor, *Studies in Philosophy and Education,* for: Snook, I., "Indoctrination and the Indoctrinated Society," vol. 8, no. 1 (Summer 1973).

To Random House Inc., Alfred A. Knopf, Inc., for: Olson, R. G., *Ethics: A Short Introduction,* copyright © 1978 by Random House Inc.; Dewey, J., "Education must be both Child-Centered and Subject-Centered, in Silberman, C. E. (ed.), *The Open Classroom Reader.*

To McGraw-Hill Book Company for: Scriven, M., *Primary Philosophy,* copyright © 1966 by McGraw-Hill. Used with the permission of McGraw-Hill Book Company.

To Methuen for: Entwistle, H., *Child-Centered Education;* Oakeshott, M., *Rationalism in Politics.*

To The University of Chicago Press for: Marietta, D. E., "On Using People," in *Ethics,* vol. 82, no. 3 (1972); reprinted from "On Using People" by Marietta, D. E., by permission of the University of Chicago Press. Copyright © 1972 by the University of Chicago.

To the Schools Commission (Australia) for: *Issues in Teacher Education: A Discussion Paper.*

To the Editor, *Cogito,* for: Walters, R. S., "Persons and Non-Persons," in *Cogito,* vol. 1, no. 1.

To the Editor, *Educational Philosophy and Theory,* and the University of New South Wales for: Simons, M., "Marxism, Magic and Metalanguages," in *Educational Philosophy and Theory,* vol. 10, no. 1 (1978).

To Marion Boyars Publishers Ltd., for: Illich, I., *Deschooling Society.*

To Faber & Faber Ltd., for: Macmurray, J., *Reason and Emotion.*

To Professor C. B. Cox and the Critical Quarterly Society for: Bantock, G., "Discovery Methods" in *Black Paper Two.*

To Phaidon Press Ltd., for: Gombrich, E. H., *Art and Illusion.*

To Harcourt Brace Jovanovich, for: Hilgard, E. R., Atkinson, R. C., and Atkinson, R. L., *Introduction to Psychology.*

To Manchester University Press and Professor R. M. Hare for: Hare, R. M., "Adolescents into Adults," in Hollins, T. H. B. (ed.), *Aims in Education: the Philosophic Approach.*

To Professor Lawrence Kohlberg for: "The Child as Moral Philosopher," in C. R. M. Books, *Readings in Educational Psychology Today.*

To Thames and Hudson for: Thomson, D., *The Aims of History.*

To Isaac Pitman for: Haig, G., *Beginning Teaching.*

To The Royal Institute of Philosophy for: Bell, D. R., "Authority," in *The Proper Study.*

To E. P. Dutton for: Holt, J., *Escape from Childhood: The Needs and Rights of Youth.*

To *The Sunday Sun* (Brisbane) for: Robson, F., "Duane Is a Fresh Food Fanatic."

To Appleton-Century-Crofts for: Hull, C. L., *The Principles of Behavior.*

To Associated Press (New York) for: "Toddlers Glorify Red Leader."

To Julian Bach Agency for: Fixx, J., *The Complete Book of Running.*

To Churchill Press for: Jacka, K., and others, *Rape of Reason.*

To *The Los Angeles Times* for: Parrott, Jennings, "Spock Takes the Blame for Nation's Brats." Copyright © 1974 Los Angeles Times. Reprinted by permission.

Chapter 1
Philosophy

A. Questions of Meaning and Justification

Philosophy is a special sort of thinking; it is *clarificatory.* In philosophy we are trying to become clearer about concepts, about meanings that escape our notice, about various assumptions we may be making without being aware of them, about principles and points of view, about why a particular principle or point of view is acceptable or unacceptable, about reasons why, about arguments for and against a position. Taken together, these clarificatory activities help a person to construct an internally consistent and systematic world view that affects what he does.

It is sometimes said that the activity of philosophical thinking can be encapsulated in the two questions—What do you mean? and How do you know?—and the attempts of people to answer these questions. In short, philosophy is concerned with *meaning* and *justification.*

In the search for answers to such questions, philosophy raises further questions, proposes possible answers, develops the implications of the answers, finds the implications suspect in some way, rephrases the questions, reformulates the answers, and so on in a continual cycle. Philosophy cannot take any statement or claim or viewpoint at face value. So philosophers ask such questions as (1) What do you mean?—that is, What is really meant by this? How is this to be interpreted? What type of thing are you talking about? What are you assuming or taking for granted? and (2) How do you know? —that is, what evidence can you produce in favor of your view? What ideas do you have to support you? In what way can this view be justified? How does this view compare with other views? How can you make this part of your argument consistent with the other?

And in philosophy the question is as important as the answer, for philosophy is the only form of knowledge in which no unquestioned assumptions are allowable. As Scriven puts it,

> In philosophy we lift ourselves up by our bootstraps: we begin with problems which we think of, state, and discuss in ordinary language, but we eventually reach a better understanding of the very concepts used in the original question, an understanding which may even lead us to improve or abandon them. We develop our instinct for the sense of words just as a physician develops his instinct for the significance of symptoms. . . . That we sometimes change or abandon our starting language is no reason for thinking that we should, or even that we could, always do so. That philosophy is much concerned with the messy meanings of the terms of ordinary language is just a sign that it is concerned with the complex problems of a life which that language was tailored to describe (1966, p. 6).

I have been talking about philosophy in general, but all these points apply also to philosophy of education, for philosophy of education is merely one branch of general philosophy, the branch that is concerned with meaning and justification in pedagogical[1] theory and discussion, and with developing a self-consistent pedagogical world view based upon this.

In asking the question, What do you mean? we are asking what is called a *conceptual question,* a question about just what is involved in a particular concept. This book deals with such concepts as "education," "integration," "rights," and so on, all concepts that feature importantly in pedagogical debate, and that when considered as a unity, provide us with a complex and interrelated viewpoint on schooling.

A moment's reflection will show us that people's concepts and

---

[1]The term, *pedagogical* rather than *educational* is used deliberately. Pedagogical issues are those that are concerned with teaching and learning. Many issues of teaching and learning are also educational, but not all are, as is shown in the first part of Chapter 2.

arguments are often confused in various ways. This is true in general, and particularly true, I believe, in thought about education and schooling. Because concepts and arguments are so crucial to our thinking, confused concepts and arguments will cause us to think in confused or crooked ways. Such crooked thinking will lead us often into crooked action—that is, we shall be approaching our daily problems in the wrong way—and such mistaken action will often occur in school life.

Now let me provide a short example of What do you mean? and How do you know? questions, or, *What?* and *Why?* questions.

Suppose a schoolteacher in his Christmas holiday begins to think about the curriculum he teaches and the methods he uses. Suppose that he asks himself the interrelated questions, Should I teach history? Why should I teach it? And if I should, what is the best method to use?

It may seem that at least the last question is straightforward. All the teacher needs to do is to test whether teaching machines, or television, or chalk and talk, or rote learning, or some other method or combination of methods gets the best results, and although as a matter of fact this may be complicated, the problem is in principle clear enough.

But it is not as simple as that, for there are prior questions of meaning to be asked. First, what is meant by the word *teach?* Do we mean that someone is trying to bring about learning? Many people will agree that this is correct, that an activity can count as teaching only if one is trying to get oneself or another person to learn as a result of the activity. Suppose this is agreed upon, so that if history has been taught, then there has been an attempt to get some history learned by the pupils or students; isn't there still a second prior question concerned with the meaning of the phrase "teach *history?*" And surely the answer to this question will be tied to the *concept* of "history" as a subject or discipline—that is, it will be concerned with what we mean when we talk about the subject we call history.

In other words, before we can begin to test methods of teaching and learning history, there is the prior question of what counts as historical knowledge and ability, what it is to learn *history.* For just what it is that is to be learned may change entirely the nature of the situation (see Chapter 2.3). Is to learn history to know dates? Is it to gain the ability to gather evidence and to put it together to make a case? Is it to make an imaginative leap by which the pupil or student puts himself in the place of historical persons—Pericles or Queen Victoria or General MacArthur—and by thinking through what he would have done in similar circumstances, comes to an understanding of the motives and thoughts of such persons? Is it to be able to trace chronological developments? How do we decide upon the nature of the subject, history? The only way to decide is to look at the things done by historians; they, if anyone has, have learned and mastered the subject. In other words, it is necessary to examine carefully the books and articles and lectures of former and practicing historians to see what is involved in their historical writing[2] and *to think as clearly as possible about this content* of history.

So the first of the teacher's questions, Should I teach history? cannot sensibly be answered before the *concept* of "history" as a subject is examined. The teacher has to decide what it is he is teach-

[2]This suggestion may appear to be begging the question, because it seems that a person must already know what the discipline of history is if he is to pick history books to examine. However, in order to select history books, a person does not need a detailed understanding of the subject, all he requires is some surface familiarity with its features. By the time someone has become a teacher, he has sufficient knowledge to contrast history and other subjects. What he often does not have is a sufficiently detailed concept.

ing before he can rationally decide whether to teach it, and why and how. The conceptual or meaning issues are crucial for all the questions that the teacher has to ask himself. Answers to the *Why?* question (e.g. suggestions that history is generally educational, that its study is necessary for a person to have a proper understanding of himself and of his place in the world, and so on) can only be sensibly considered when the teacher has a clear concept of the subject, "history." Although this justificatory type of question has to wait for some answer to the meaning question, justificatory questions are equally important to meaning questions in philosophy of education.

Thus, we can ask both conceptual questions and justificatory questions, but the answers to such questions will not be separate. It is indeed interesting to notice how the two sorts of answers are linked, how often the activity of getting clear about a concept helps us to see the justification or lack of justification for the claim or point of view. For instance, when I analyze the concept of "indoctrination" in the next chapter, such issues as intention and content are considered. But it cannot be shown what indoctrinatory intention and content consist of without implicitly showing that the pursuit of such intention and the propagation of such content are morally unjustifiable.

B. Conceptual Questions and Other Sorts of Questions

Once the issues of meaning and justification have been clarified, then the teacher's second question, What is the best method to use to teach history? can be approached. At this point a fundamental philosophical distinction is raised. So far, I have been discussing issues that can be decided one way or another merely by looking at the concepts themselves, and by *thinking* things through as clearly and carefully as possible. But with this question about the best methods to use, we seem to have a rather different sort of question. It is not a conceptual or meaning type of question; it is not a matter of producing a sound and logical argument. It is the sort of question that has to be answered by *doing* something in the world rather than thinking. It is a question about the actual physical facts of the matter, and the final answer to such a question must be decided by experimenting or testing— that is, by going and seeing.[3] This sort of question is called an *empirical* question.

[3]As suggested later (Chapter 2.3) some of the knowledge about methods can be ascertained by thinking carefully about the content to be taught, for to some extent method must follow content. This is not, however, to deny the importance of the fundamental distinction being drawn here between *thinking* questions and *doing* questions.

A further example will emphasize this distinction between questions whose answers can be gained through thinking and analyzing concepts, and those whose answers can be gained through doing and testing. Some years ago I saw an advertisement on the back cover of a magazine. It was attempting to attract people to a particular religious organization and asked the question, WHY DO DOLPHINS GRIN?

At first glance this may look like a *doing* or *testing* question, but it is in fact rather more complex. For although it is probably true that the answers to why dolphins do whatever it is they do can be gained only through some kind of empirical work—by testing or by examining their bodies—whether or not they are indeed grinning is quite another matter, a conceptual matter or question. The point at issue is whether or not we can legitimately call what is going on, on the physiognomy of dolphins, *grinning*. Certainly their features are contorted in a particular way, but is this way similar enough to what happens on a human face to call it *grinning?* It is to be noted that human beings grin when they find something amusing or pleasant. Can we really argue that dolphins find things amusing? Have a sense of humor? I doubt it.[4] And though some people will perhaps argue that a dolphin can find things pleasant, is the experience of the dolphin close enough in its analogy to human pleasant experience for us to be able to use the term *grin* appropriately?

It will be seen then that the question as to how we should *view* what the dolphin does is a conceptual question, whereas the question about *why* the dolphin does it is an empirical one. The second question can be answered only through going to the empirical findings of such sciences as biology and zoology and ethology, where will be found explanations for such dolphin behavior.

In the same way, it is clear that the second part of the teacher's question about teaching history is also an empirical problem: he will need to talk to various colleagues about their methods, go to published findings in empirical research to see what has been said, and *try* various of these methods to discover the most effective for himself and the class in the particular context of their school. Whereas the question, What counts as history? is a *sitting and thinking* question, What is the best method? is largely a *going and doing* question.

---

[4]Some people who train dolphins would disagree. I read recently a claim by one animal lover that because dolphins are so intelligent, the killing of a dolphin should be classed as murder. It is also interesting to note that in a recent court hearing in Honolulu, the prosecution called the unlawful release of a dolphin from its pen, a case of kidnapping. The relationships between the conceptual and empirical issues in this example are also rather more complex than here suggested, but I wish to draw the distinction as directly as possible.

It is difficult to overemphasize how exceedingly important is this general distinction between conceptual and empirical issues if there is ever to be adequate pedagogic practice. Close examination of the theoretical writing about schooling will often show that issues and questions that have been construed in bland empirical terms have a significant but unsuspected conceptual base. For example, as will be seen in the section discussing learning, I believe that for teachers the important questions about learning are basically conceptual ones. Here, at the very heart of what goes on in schools, is a crucial issue that has been to a large extent mishandled since the rise of the empirical movement in schooling in the early part of this century. I am not suggesting that it is always easy to distinguish between conceptual and other matters and questions, however; this will often be exceedingly difficult; nevertheless, the legitimate distinction remains.

I wrote in the last sentence the phrase, "conceptual and *other* matters." The use of the word *other* instead of the word *empirical* was intentional because I wanted to indicate that there are rather more categories of matters and questions than just conceptual and empirical ones. Although I have been drawing the specific distinction between conceptual and empirical questions, not all nonconceptual questions are empirical. However, empirical questions may well be the most common sort, and it is probable that it is conceptual and empirical questions that are most commonly confused by the man in the street, and by people when they discuss questions about schools.

As indicated in the section on educational growth (Chapter 3.2), I agree with Professor Hirst's Wittgensteinian claim that there are seven fundamental ways of interpreting the world, seven fundamentally different sorts of question. One of these seven ways is the conceptual or philosophical way. Another is the empirical or scientific[5] way, but there are also moral and artistic and other ways, and moral and artistic and other issues and questions. For instance, it may have been noticed that the hypothetical history teacher discussed above also asked himself the question, Why should I teach history? In doing so he was asking a moral question, and the answers that might be given fall into the moral category. So now it can be seen that what looked at first like a straightforward set of questions, Should I teach history? Why should I teach it? And if I should, what is the best method to use? involves at least three quite different sorts of issues or questions: conceptual, empirical, and moral. Which is a good indi-

---

[5]See Section 3.2D. I view the scientific category as a subcategory of the empirical. Not all epistemological writing agrees that these two terms are so closely interrelated.

cation of why questions about schooling and education are so contentious, and why it is so difficult to get simple, straightforward answers to them.

C. Being Aware of Presuppositions

It is to be hoped that the analytically critical attitude and approach of the philosopher will be caught by students, teachers, and administrators, and that as a result people in schools, who are building their world view of schooling and education, will be more skeptical of guidance from supposed experts who advocate new methods and changes and from the numbers of pedagogical advisers who make suggestions from outside the classroom. I should like to see a body of teachers who will not just accept, say, "learning by experience" as a supposed panacea, but who will want to question closely just what may be implied by those words and who will be discriminating in their use of *all* methods.

To show some of the complications in what seems to be a relatively straightforward idea, let me concentrate for a few paragraphs on this idea of learning by experience. For instance, in what particular sense can teachers provide experiences for schoolchildren? Is experience very much the result of the child's own doing? Are the contents of experiences relative to the person who undergoes them?

People who know nothing of a foreign language hear only a rapid babel. I used to watch certain Londoners who, knowing little of their history, walked blindly past places of fascinating historical significance. Many people look into an automobile engine and see only a confusion of metal and wires, whereas the qualified mechanic sees a purring, precision instrument. As Bantock makes the point (1970, p. 113),

> I am technically quite inept, and I rely on the good services of mechanics if anything goes wrong with my car... Let us say I suffer a breakdown in a wild and desolate spot. I raise the [hood] and face the engine; I see it, I touch it, I even listen to it; but because I have no idea of the meaning of what I see, my "experience" is null and void; and the car remains stationary.

Bald sense experience may be the common property of all the people of the earth, but experience that has meaning is not.

Our experiences are determined by our concepts and by the knowledge and understanding that these concepts make possible. It is not only that each person has a different set of concepts, it is also that the concepts of any single person are at different levels of awareness and explicitness at different stages of education and life. This point about concepts is stressed to emphasize that experience is not lying about for just anyone to pick up in his own way. Persons simply will not have particular experiences if they do not have the appropriate conceptual background, and it is education that helps make possible the attainment of such a conceptual background.

I believe that experience can be shared, but it can be shared only by those who have mastered the appropriate concepts and knowledge. In this context may be mentioned what Dearden (1968, p. 118) calls the "fallacy of perfect obviousness": the mistake that someone sophisticated in an area of knowledge makes when he imagines that a novice is having a similar sort of experience to himself. Anyone who has preserved a selection of his own school notebooks will on looking into them notice a striking progression in his own knowledge and conceptual equipment with the passing of years, as evidenced by the footnotes, crossing out, words of explanation written in the margin, and so forth. Didn't I *really* know what X meant? we say to ourselves as we flick through the pages. Coming to know and understand is a sort of experience, but bald sense experience is not itself a sort of knowing and understanding.

So when we are being exhorted to let children learn by experience, we should ask ourselves (and, perhaps better still, get our exhorters to ask themselves) What kinds of knowledge are to be acquired, and at what stage in the growth of his understanding of them is the learner? (Dearden, 1968, p. 120). When teachers are trying to get children to master elementary concepts in the early grades of schools, overt experience without much guidance may be an admirable teaching method. But with older children and with the theoretical concepts of the forms of knowledge (see Sections 3.2D, 3.3D) great amounts of explanation, discussion, and guidance from a teacher are required, from a teacher who knows what the end product is and who is himself immersed in the form(s) of knowledge involved.

Much of the learning situation that such a teacher provides will need to be by way of instruction—that is, enlightened telling and explaining that develop knowledge and rational understanding; overt experience should be built into such an approach, of course, but it will be meaningful only to the extent that the student has mastered and is mastering the conceptual and theoretical background. Consider these two examples of teaching, that observers are likely to misconstrue if they do not have the concepts that underpin what they see.

Many mothers of young children just beginning school are perplexed by the to-ing and fro-ing and movement and chatter of the modern infants' classroom; the mothers see the physical activity but do not have the theoretical background to understand what all the movement is about. People who look at television broadcasts on mathematics, but who have a limited mathematical background and are not studying the accompanying course materials, see only a person who manipulates various peculiar symbols in an almost random manner. If either the mothers or the television viewers were asked to describe what they had seen going on, their answers would be superficial and distorted. It is superficiality and distortion that are the dangers with the fads and fashions of schooling, for teachers are forced by their superiors to adopt fashions without a sensitive understanding of the rationale behind them, and sometimes without there even existing a well-worked-out rationale. This concept of "experience" has been considered briefly because it shows how a seemingly uncomplicated suggestion can involve all sorts of traps for the conceptually unwary.

At a conference I once attended in Oxford, some viewpoints put forward by people who taught educational theory in colleges and universities indicate the conceptual confusion among some of those who train and educate teachers. One gentleman, a college principal, spent a considerable time expounding a technique that seemed to me to be a combination of "discovery" from written sources, with appropriate small groupings of pupils and regular reporting to a larger gathering of pupils. He appeared to be trying to persuade the assembly that this was a technique to be adopted above all others, yet he was saved by the break from having adequately to answer a most embarrassing question about how he knew that this method was superior or in what conditions it was superior. It appeared from his egregious hedging, in the short time available for his answer, that he not only did not know, but that perhaps it had not even entered his head to ask himself this kind of question. A second, female, college principal, in answer to my question as to how we might bring about a synthesis between diverse pedagogical theories, replied that a synthesis could come about only through the findings of empirical research—empirical research and more empirical research that would show who was right. But surely this reply was only part of an answer, for before such research can be of any strict use researchers need to do some philosophy to unearth their unexamined assumptions and to clarify the conceptual confusions that underpin their typical approaches; a Baconian inductive accumulation of empirical evidence will not help toward improving pedagogical methods. In order to judge the appropriateness or otherwise of particular practices, data, even when accompanied by conceptual clarity, are not enough. They are not enough because all kinds of choices already presuppose a commitment to a particular conceptual scheme and to particular moral values and ends, all of which ought to be brought into the open and debated.

A further example of confusion occurred at that conference in a group discussion about methods that schoolteachers should be encouraged to use in the classroom. One member of the group suggested that children should gain the idea of scientific method, and to enable this to happen they should be allowed to make observations and build up their generalizations from these observations. Yet a little reflection will show that this view follows a fallacious interpretation similar to that of the principal mentioned above: the interpretation is fallacious to the extent that scientific generalizations are not derived from observations by some chain of logical inference, but in fact come first as acts of constructive imagination from persons intellectually immersed in the particular scientific area, after which are made the observations that can be used as confirmations or falsifications (Popper, 1969). If children are indeed to be able to "make observations," then this act of constructive imagination will already have been done for them by the teacher, and by the scientific tradition in which the teacher has been schooled, in delimiting the children's area of inquiry so that they can actually make observations that are theoretically meaningful. People who imagine that observations somehow speak for themselves misunderstand the nature of scientific knowledge and scientific progress and the crucial place of prior conceptualization in both.

A case can be made that too often teachers suffer in their development as educators through having ill-balanced courses in educational theory. From not being equipped with adequate skills and habits of philosophical endeavor, they are left with an unsuitable background and are unable really to think things through for themselves. This contributes to the situation in which teachers not long out of college come to reject as irrelevant much of their education and training. It seems to me that it is only through clear and rigorous analysis of concepts, viewpoints, arguments, and theories, within teacher-preparation courses themselves, that the situation will be improved substantially, and that teachers will begin to see through the long-standing confusions of educational theory and start, where necessary, to oppose the fashionable fads of school systems.

D. Concepts and Analysis

People are sometimes unclear about what a concept is. For instance, at my own college, I was speaking recently to a mature woman student who said with considerable gravity, that she had not had any concepts until she came to college! What she meant, it would seem, was that she had not been *explicitly aware* of having concepts before she came to college and heard them being talked about. Her comment does, however, point up a rather important fact about concepts; namely, that we are largely unaware of the process of concept formation. Thus, the concept of "school" that we have will depend on such contingencies as the way we have been brought up to regard schools, the types of schools we attended, our present knowledge of what goes on in schools, what we have read about them, our conversations with other people, our impressions of schoolteachers, and so on; in fact, our own concept of "school" will be a complicated mixture of various kinds of knowledge and experience peculiar to us alone. It will be our way of giving unity to that corner of our experience connected with schools in general, for to have a concept is to see sections of the world as displaying a kind of order and sameness that are distinguishable from other parts of the world as viewed by us.

To have a concept is to have an ability to see things as being the same or of the same kind. Our concepts organize those features and aspects that give unity and pattern to our experiences (Dearden, 1968, p. 108). The usual way in which we indicate to other people that we possess a concept is by our use of *words;* we acquire concepts and we get clearer about our concepts by using words; and most (though not all?) of our concepts can be represented by words. But, of course, the words are not the concepts.

Clearly enough, the concepts that we have must affect the way in which we see the world, and in a very real sense our world is made for us by those concepts. The way in which a primitive Jivaro Indian of the Amazon basin sees the world is quite different from the way in which an English-speaking schoolteacher sees the world, and the basic difference between their world views is a matter of their own conceptual schemes. Even with the English-speaking schoolteacher, concepts are more or less firm and clear, more or less explicit, more or less detailed, and they continue to develop. Although we cannot say what the world is like independent of our concepts of it, what it is like and how we conceptualize it are still different questions. I am not arguing for some version of conceptual relativity: one conceptual scheme is not just as good as any other. For it is because conceptual schemes can develop and *improve* that there is the possibility of progress in science and morals and art and in pedagogical theory and practice. It is because conceptual schemes can develop and improve that man has climbed out of the cave and into the spaceship.

Conceptual or philosophical analysis is a way of making us more aware of certain key characteristics of our concepts, that are present in most cases (key characteristics of which we may in fact be largely unaware) and the manner in which such key characteristics contrast with, and relate to, the characteristics of other concepts.

At this point it may be asked: Even though certain concepts are important for pedagogical practice, why should teachers bother with all this suggested *analysis* of them? Why not just look up the meaning of "freedom" or "rights" or "indoctrination" in a dictionary? The answer is that dictionary definitions give the most superficial description by providing the reader with broadly equivalent words. Yet it is only by engaging in conceptual analysis, by way of exploring examples and contrasts, that depth of knowledge results and that the linguistic tools become subtle enough for precise argument and action. It is only through being able explicitly to describe the use and relationships and to tease out the underlying assumptions, that anyone is in a position really to understand what he is arguing in support of, when he uses concepts in building his pedagogical world view.

There is, of course, a sound basis for the procedure of conceptual analysis—after all, we learn our language *in a context.* So when it is necessary to get clear about the meaning of a concept, the best method is the one that brings out the appropriate linguistic features, which consists in the outlining of the whole context, not merely an attempt at a dictionary-type definition (Scriven, 1966, p. 8). This helps to show why discussion with other people is generally thought to be of such importance in philosophy; in the give-and-take of discussion our distinctions can quickly become more refined and our errors are rapidly exposed. The provision of comparisons and contrasts that help to place a concept in a context is what was briefly provided with the concepts of "history" and "experience" in the foregoing pages and what is done in more detail with other concepts in the rest of the book.

However, conceptual or philosophical analysis is approached in various ways. The approach depends very much on the situation in which and the reasons for which the analysis is being made. For instance, it sometimes helps to leave an analysis for a time, and return to it later after the subconscious mind has had a chance to work upon it. The particular analytical steps tend to be chosen somewhat spontaneously as we go along. In general, the way to become adept at such analysis is to read good examples of it and to try to produce our own. This is why educational philosophers assign essays in analysis to their students and hold regular discussions. Conceptual analysis is as much "caught" as "taught," for the ability to analyze concepts is also acquired in a context.

PHILOSOPHY: KEY POINTS

Philosophy is clarificatory. Philosophical thinking can be encapsulated in the two questions: What do you mean? and How do you know?

Philosophy of education is concerned with meaning and justification in pedagogical theory and discussion, and with developing a self-consistent pedagogical world view based upon this.

Because concepts are so crucial to our thinking, confused concepts will cause us to think in confused or crooked ways. Such crooked thinking will lead us often into crooked action; such mistaken action will often occur in school life.

Persons just will not have particular experiences if they do not have the appropriate conceptual background. Coming to know and understand is a sort of experience, but bald sense experience is not itself a sort of knowing and understanding.

It is difficult to overemphasize how exceedingly important is the distinction between conceptual and empirical issues, if there is ever to be adequate pedagogic practice. Close examination of the theoretical writing about schooling will often show that issues and questions that have been construed in bland empirical terms have a significant but unsuspected conceptual base.

In order to judge the appropriateness or otherwise of particular practices, data are not enough, even when accompanied by conceptual clarity. They are not enough because all kinds of choices already presuppose a commitment to a particular conceptual scheme and to particular moral values and ends, all of which ought to be brought into the open and debated.

It is only by engaging in conceptual analysis, by way of exploring examples and contrasts, that depth of knowledge results, and that the linguistic tools become subtle enough for precise argument and action.

It is because conceptual schemes can develop and *improve* that there is the possibility of progress in science and morals and art, and in pedagogical theory and practice. It is because conceptual schemes can develop and improve that man has climbed out of the cave and into the spaceship.

Chapter 2
Activities

2.1 EDUCATION

A. Educational Activities

If we walk about school classrooms, we see various things happening. We see five-year-olds pouring water from small containers into larger ones. We see teenagers typing. We hear teachers telling pupils about the causes of the French Revolution. In one room boys are separating the yolks from the whites of eggs to make souffles. In another room girls are using a lathe to polish a metal ornament. Here students are finding the area under a curve of an irregular plane surface. There infants are tracing the shape of a letter "S" in the air. In a hall a teacher is exhorting pupils of dramatic improvisation to think themselves into a role. In the gymnasium we view students practicing on the parallel bars and the vaulting horse. Nearby in a darkened room we see on a screen a picture of sharp-edged red stones littering the surface of Mars, from a photo sent back to Earth by the U.S. Viking Lander. And so on endlessly.

Is there any easy way of categorizing this variegated mass of activities?

In order to answer this question, let us leave the school context for a while to consider the following examples of things that people do or have done at various times.

Category 1
Learning to read
Hammering in roofing nails
Jogging at 7:00 A.M. on a winter's day.
Filling in a tax return
Washing dishes

Category 2
Playing football
Reading about the last days of Socrates
Telling a joke
Making a mobile
Listening to a Beethoven sonata
Landing on the moon

These are two broad but overlapping categories. Category 1 consists of activities that people engage in, in general, in order to achieve something else that they want. Such activities are often said to be *instrumentally valuable,* or valuable as a means to an end. Category 2 consists of activities that people do for their own sake. Such activities are often said to be *intrinsically valuable,* or valuable as ends in themselves.

There are also activities that are complex mixtures of 1 and 2, ranging across a whole continuum from nearly pure 1 to nearly pure 2. Equally, there may be whole chains of reasons why people do things. We can also perform for ulterior motives the activities listed in category 2 as generally of intrinsic value, in which case they become instrumentally valuable activities; so whether a particular activity counts as intrinsic or instrumental will depend upon the context in which it takes place.

Of course, at any one instant it may be difficult to be exact about why we are doing a particular thing, or our reason may shift from one category to another and back. A person begins a jogging keep-fit run, say, at 7:00 A.M. on a cold winter morning. As he goes up the first hill he feels hardly awake and it is all rather unpleasant, and no doubt he is running at that stage for reasons extrinsic or instrumental to what he is doing—he is jogging to keep healthy. A little farther on he may start to feel warm, he smells the clean freshness of the air, and he begins to enjoy the jog. At that stage his primary reason for jogging may be for his own intrinsic enjoyment of it. Later, if the going gets hard, he may slip back and keep running only because it is good for him.

There are thus going to be all sorts of possible variations and combinations, but I do not think this fact has any effect on the fundamental distinction between intrinsic and instrumental reasons for activities. If someone asks us why we are doing something and he wants the explanation *in terms of reasons,* then we can answer only that it is because of something else that it *leads to;* that we just enjoy, want to do *it;* or that there is a subtle combination of these two. In short, the three categories exhaust the possibilities.

Can the same sort of analysis into categories of instrumentally and intrinsically valuable activities be applied to why children do things in school?

It can, but in a modified way, for we have to bear in mind that the school situation is complicated by the fact that children do not merely have their own reasons for doing things, but that teachers put pressure on children *to* do things for reasons that the teachers have as teachers and as agents of society. So the actual answer to why a particular child is doing a particular thing in class may require an explanation of great complexity, one that has to be traced through a whole series of relationships and reason-giving.

This distinction between the reason-giving of categories 1 and 2 has been introduced because on one level of analysis it is on the basis of one or the other, or on some combination, that teachers must also see the justification for what they teach in schools. In other words, the teachers believe that what they teach will lead to something else important (such as getting a job or becoming socialized) or else that what they teach is in itself something that is worth knowing about or worth engaging in (such as artistic activity or scientific knowledge of the world). Of course, many teachers may teach what they teach because a particular syllabus directs them to, and cynical or indolent or disillusioned teachers may merely keep pupils and students active on what the profession calls "busy work," activities the children do in order to keep busy and to pass the time, rather than for any sound reason.

Bearing in mind that the situation is being simplified in order to discuss things one at a time, it can be argued that there are many school activities that fall into the first category. Teaching children to read and write and calculate has such instrumental aims: literacy and numeracy in general make for a person's better economic viability. Schools are expected to turn out at the end a teenager who can take his part appropriately in the political system, with at least a minimum of skills and understanding that can be of some use in the manpower requirements of the nation. The current disquiet among employers over some of their young employees is an example of this second expectation. Some of these skills are general, such as those that make for democratic behavior, others are quite specific, such as the ability to type or to solder or to bake a sponge cake. This general area of activities in schools can be fairly appropriately called *training*. The justification for training children in these ways is instrumental, whether we see such instrumental value in terms of the later use to the individual or in view of that use to the society as a whole, or both. And it is these sorts of activities that many average citizens see as the job of schools; schools, in their eyes, should produce children with usable and marketable skills and understanding who can fit easily into the social and economic system.

Schools for these people are seen but as a means to some specific end, though they may not state the point that way. Now, to see the activities of schools in this way, in terms of training, in terms of instrumentality, is all very well, for it appropriately describes some of the things that go on, but it is at best only part of a description. For there is a large range of activities that are more usually viewed by teachers in terms of instinsic value—activities that fall within category 2. Many of these activities may be called *education* rather than training, and the reason why they may be so called is that they may be considered to have a particular sort of intrinsic value. Teachers think that such activities and studies are somehow worthwhile in their own way; it is the greater knowledge and understanding of the world and its workings that these studies provide, and the greater rationality that they make possible, that are worth having in themselves. The point may be put alternatively by saying that I and many teachers believe the understanding and insights that such activities provide are in themselves appropriate for human persons. Even to grant this last claim is, however, still in some degree to undervalue these activities, as will be explained later in 2.1E.

B. Cognitive Perspective and Rationality

There is something further to say about these intrinsically valuable activities that I and many teachers take to be educational activities, for not all intrinsically valuable activities are education. Persons may delight in flower arranging or fucshia gardening, in baseball or basketry, in swigging of beer or swimming off boats, but although these activities can have intrinsic value, in their usual forms they will not be education. So it is not just because certain activities in schools are seen by teachers as having intrinsic value that they are called education. In using the terms "education" and "educational activities," I am trying to mark out a special sort of intrinsic value.

By way of example, let us consider what persons have in mind when they say, of an acquaintance at dinner, "It was an education just to be in her presence"; or of the excellent teacher, "He doesn't just teach those kids, he really educates them"; or of the lout, "Though he went to school, he didn't get an education"; or of the quiz king, "He knows a mass of facts, but I wonder if he's educated"; or about an experience that gave us real depth and insight, "That was undoubtedly one of the most educational incidents of my life." What is being emphasized in these examples is not merely the knowledge acquired, but also the broadening effect of certain experiences; what has been learned has wider implications and brings with it some pattern for interpretation of the world. Such experiences and activities give meaning to features of the world other than themselves. Their meaning is not merely tied to the activity or the experience itself. It is general, not specific. It gives comprehension. Education helps people to see the world differently.

Consider for a moment the phrase, "an educated guess," for it helps to make this point about the broadening nature of educational activities. A person may be faced with a situation or question the precise form of which he has never encountered before. In answer to the question, he will say, "Well, I don't really know, but I'll try to make an educated guess"; and in making his educated guess he brings to bear various aspects of his knowledge and understanding of other contexts, questions, and situations. He may draw an analogy; he may make an estimation; he may note a range of individual features and form a generalization; he may use a combination of such approaches; but whatever particular method he adopts, it is characterized by an appropriate and rational adaption of his present quanta of understanding to meet the expectations of the new situation. An educated guess makes intelligent use of present understanding and extends and modifies it to fit within the parameters of the new situation.

To take an elementary example: Suppose a person has to guess the particular distance between his present position and some far point. He thinks about similar experiences in the past, allows for such visual clues as the height of trees nearby and at the far point, estimates the approximate speed of a car and notes how long it takes the car to traverse the distance, or looks at the distance he has already come and then at the far point and makes an estimation, and so on. Educated guesses are possible when a person has the ability and the inclination to put his knowledge and understanding to work in the most appropriate way. Having experienced a range of educational activities, a person is in a position to make educated guesses. The opposite of making an educated guess is epitomized, I think, in the clumsy vernacular phrase, "Wouldn't have a clue."

The special sort of intrinsic value of educational activities that is being alluded to in using a phrase like "an education just to be in his presence" and in talking about educated guesses, is put compactly by R. S. Peters (1966, p. 31) when he writes that educational activities have "cognitive perspective" and when he says that education is something that transforms a person's outlook (1967, p. 9). Another way of describing the last claim is to say that a person has become more rational—the making of educated guesses is the rational thing to do.

As persons become more educated they become more rational. The words *rationality* and *rational* are generalized descriptions; they may apply to a person more at one time than at another. This is why there is some point in the suggestion that mankind is not a rational animal so much as an intermittently rational animal. Rationality, then, is a matter of degree. Furthermore, in talking about rationality we are referring to an interrelated cluster of attitudes, values, beliefs, skills, dispositions, habits, and so on. But though rationality is a matter of degree and involves a complex cluster of features, there are many things that can be said about it. For instance, to be rational a person must have the use of concepts and language, which help him to get purchase upon the real world. He needs to be able to distinguish different sorts of questions and issues; for example, conceptual issues about meaning are not to be confused with empirical issues about happenings or with artistic or moral issues, even though all these may interrelate.

Rationality certainly includes the careful finding of the best means to a particular end or goal, and then making use of these means. When faced with a question, the rational person seeks as much relevant information as time and circumstance permit, for he knows that it is necessary to obtain as many germane facts as possible, not merely a few of them, or only those that are comforting to his present views. He also faces the facts squarely, and because he realizes that human beings are subject to irrationalities of all sorts— bigotries, prejudices, wants, wishes, delusions, fond hopes, biases, dogmatisms, irrelevancies, and unrealities—that warp and distort judgment, he attempts to free himself of these. Allied to this view is the point that the rational person knows that while his thought processes are his own, the standards by which thought is shown to be true or false, precise or clumsy, are public. A person is rational to the extent that he critically analyzes the current and received views of his society, but nevertheless accepts the importance of traditions and stabilities. He is wary of all positions that derive from doctrines (see 2.3), and while he acknowledges a conceptual difference between knowledge and belief, he realizes that it is not always easy to say which is which.

Though rational persons certainly appreciate the rewards of the present, they are not overwhelmed by these; they can postpone gratification, if they calculate a more enduring and intense gratification in the future, or if present gratification conflicts with other ends they seek or with values they hold. They plan ahead: indeed, it is probably not distorting the picture to claim that it is this ability to step outside the concerns and sensations of the present that is the key feature of rationality. Theorizing, rule following, planning, explaining, generalizing, understanding, and the living of a nicely balanced life all involve this feature. Animals and young children singularly lack it, which is why we do not apply the term "rational" to their activities.

Rationality involves not merely the use of the best means to a determined end or value, but also the careful scrutiny of these very ends and intrinsic values themselves. This can only be done in the light of a proper background of history and morality and the various forms of knowledge that together give a sufficiently subtle general education. For the educated state involves rationality *and* cognitive perspective; *the one depends crucially upon the development of the other.* A careful scrutiny of ends also involves clear and logical analysis. By "clear and logical analysis" is meant, for instance, ensuring that the end or value is consistent with a person's other ends and values—that is, it is consistent with equally important other ends he holds, or else helps to achieve a further and more important end or intrinsic value. Peters's suggestions about breadth and fecundity as justification of education as an end (discussed in 2.1D) are interesting in this respect.

The person who seeks to be rational keeps his mind open so that his present viewpoints and positions can be revised in the light of new evidence; he gives due weight to that evidence, is consistent, and makes appropriate discriminations. He tries to be logical at all levels. For example, in noticing that to the extent that the doctrines of, say, Marxism and Mormonism (see 2.2B) involve conflicting and mutually exclusive beliefs about the universe, then both cannot be correct.

Being rational also involves discipline, because it is only through discipline that a person's planned-for ends have the best chance of being realized and that the concerns and sensations of the present can be put in perspective (see 4.3).

Rationality is epitomized in the approach of the good scientist, who is proud of the pet theory that he has produced by mastering the complex content of his scientific field and by making a creative, cognitive leap in an attempt to explain some particular, puzzling phenomenon. At first sight it looks as though the scientist may be expected to hold to the theory at all costs, but what, in fact, happens is that this strength of conviction remains only if, after having expressed it in such a way that it is both clear and precise and can be tested by other scientists, the theory can withstand this sustained critical scrutiny over time (Popper, 1968, 1969). If it does not hold up under scrutiny, he modifies or rejects it, or develops another explanation for the facts as known, and then offers that for criticism. The good scientist realizes that truth depends not upon who says something, but upon public, independent, and replicable activity. Far from being annoyed that his pet theory has been shown wanting, the scientist respects and welcomes the open-minded criticism of other scientists, especially of scientific rivals, as aids in the pursuit of truth. He realizes that freedom of thought and speech, and toleration of diverse views, are first principles in this pursuit. There is no one more useful to a rational person than a critical opponent.

Rationality features crucially in the moral life as well, though this is often forgotten when people incorrectly believe that morals are merely matters of taste or tradition. For moral codes, like any other claims, are not above rational scrutiny. (A brief attempt at a rational approach to the fundamental principles of morality is provided in 4.1C.) It is important to note that such principles of morality may also function as some of the "very ends and intrinsic values themselves" that, it was said a few paragraphs ago, required careful scrutiny. Olson makes a key point about the connection between morality and rationality when he writes (1978, p. 97),

> For example, no matter how much parents may love their children, their love is worth little unless they are sufficiently rational to work effectively for the children's benefit. . . . Rationality is not only a virtue in its own right. It is also an indispensable condition for the proper exercise of all other virtues.

What is more, though it is rarely recognized in the everyday world, rationality is of fundamental importance in the life of the emotions (see 2.1E).

What all this amounts to is that to count as education, the activities of schools must indeed be such that they broaden children's outlooks on life; give perspective to what they do; provide meaning, knowledge, and real understanding; bring encounter with values; and thus help to make children more rational. If the ideas met with in schools are to count as education in this sense of the word, then they must not be inert ideas. They must be ideas that are worked with and upon, ideas that are thrown into combination with other ideas.

Thus it is that science, literature, morality, physical education, and so forth are not education if they are taught in a narrow or limited manner. If history consists merely in learning lots of dates and facts without any endeavor to get children to understand the ways of life behind the pages, or the dilemmas and difficulties faced by men and women in the past; if science involves merely textbook memorization with little time for pupils to apply what they learn or to encounter hypothesis and observation and the scientific way of approaching a problem; if literature is read for grammatical analysis only, or merely because it is a good yarn, with no attempt to involve the pupils imaginatively in the text nor any chance to see its implications for the human condition; if morality is taught as a fixed list of absolute rules rather than as a subtle and developing adjustment to changing contexts; if physical education becomes various skills and knowledge of games, without an attempt at producing a more generalized physiological understanding and kinaesthetic awareness; if this happens, then these subjects are being presented in such a narrow manner that they lose their entitlement to be called education, because they are failing to provide cognitive perspective and they are failing to make children more rational. If after 10 years of schooling all a 15-year-old can do in his visual art is produce a piece of direct but untutored expression that we might admire in a young child, but lacks a more developed artistic way of looking, analyzing, and communicating to others, then despite the spontaneity his art activities have failed to develop cognitive perspective and he cannot use art as a tool of rationality. If a person has studied in detail the history and geography of New York State, but when he first enters the Port of New York is not moved in some way to speculation, questioning, or hypothesis by human achievement in what was once virgin forest, then his studies have been cognitively and rationally inert.[1]

[1]It seems at this point relevant to say something brief about truth. Education is closely concerned with truth. If activities really do throw light on the world, do develop cognitive perspective and rationality, then presumably they have to show concern for truth. A person does not understand *the world* as it is if he holds false beliefs. Of course, such false beliefs will often actually function as principles for guiding a person's conduct. There may be hot dispute about just which beliefs are true or false (see 2.2C), but teachers who are educators want their students and pupils to hold particular positions and to believe particular things only to the extent that these positions and things can be shown to be true or at least acceptable, given the evidence. This situation will be a matter of degree, so educators are concerned that students hold positions with a strength that is in proportion to the evidence or lack of it. Educators, like the good scientist, are concerned with truth and wish to hold a position only insofar as it can stand up to open-minded criticism. If their position does not seem to hold up under criticism, then they change it in the light of the criticism. This approach to the truth is completely opposite to that of indoctrinators and of people who have been indoctrinated, for they believe that in their doctrine they already have the truth, and that all criticism of their position is necessarily wrong (see 2.2).

C. Education or Training?

But to return to what I have called training activities: In this group are those school activities that are seen by the teachers as having instrumental value only. Many activities that go on every day fall into this class, from emphasizing school rules, to chanting tables, to sharpening pencils, to operating a food mixer, to teaching to read. On the wall of an early primary classroom that I recently visited was a large three-dimensional representation of a bright blue shoe. Two thick tape laces dangled from the center of the shoe and the caption underneath in bold gold letters queried, Can you tie your laces? Now, teaching children to tie their laces may be rather useful. It may save parents and teacher from a time-consuming chore. It may stop Johnny from tripping, breaking a leg, and being absent from school for weeks. But it is in general valuable only as a means to various other ends, and does not provide much in the way of understanding. The tying of shoelaces does little to develop cognitive perspective and rationality. This is a simple instance, but there will be, of course, much more complicated groups of knowledge and skills, as occur, for example, in the commercial courses of schools, where training is complex and detailed and where it will often shade off into education. Nevertheless, training always has an object outside itself; it always makes sense to ask, Training in what? Training to do what? Training for what?

In discussing training and education, I have simplified distinctions somewhat, for actual effects and results are naturally matters of degree and depend very much upon personalities, values, and contexts. Such a simplification is justified in that it enables me to put the distinction as directly as possible. On the one hand, there is a concept distinguished by using the word *training,* on the other hand a concept marked by the word *education.* Training has to do with instrumental value and lack of cognitive implications; education has to do with wide cognitive implications and rationality, which I believe have value in themselves for persons. (Notice that severely mentally handicapped people can be trained, but they cannot be educated.)

It was mentioned a moment ago that if science, history, literature, morals, and so forth are taught in a narrow or limited manner, then they fail to be education. This point is crucial. For it is the way a teacher goes about what he is doing and the way a pupil or student responds that in general decide whether or not a period of time spent in a school will be education. Under some teachers and classroom regimes, what might appear to be a program of mere training can become education; under others, a program that appears in the syllabus outline to have considerable educational possibilities is negated. Again, a pupil or student who uses his initiative and imagination can turn a training program into something of an educational one through working out his own connections, implications, and combinations of ideas, while a pupil or student who refuses to do his own mental work on ideas can turn what is education for his classmates into largely valueless timeserving for himself. It is not by chance that education is maximized when an imaginative teacher encounters a thoughtful child.

D. Education of the Emotions

"You can't explain away feelings . . . ," said the heroine of a television soap opera that I was viewing in a Honolulu hotel. Her claim took my attention, because it is representative of a point of view that has eaten deeply into the outlook of Western man, and I want briefly to challenge it here. For some readers may by now have begun to complain of the seeming neglect of the education of what is sometimes referred to as the affective domain of human experience—that is, the life of the emotions.

I have discussed the development of children's cognitive perspective and rationality, and the idea of training, so should schools also educate children emotionally? Train their emotions? Of course they should.

This is a vast and exceedingly complex matter (Kenny, 1963; Wilson, 1971; Harris, 1976), but only one feature will be considered here. Conceptually, I want to distinguish the "knowing" aspect of an emotion from the "feeling" aspect. And because I believe that it is the most crucial aspect and also the most neglected, I want to concentrate on "knowing" in emotions, although I do acknowledge the significance of "feeling." (For similar reasons, a parallel course is followed in Chapter 3, when the arts are considered from the point of view of their knowledge dimension.)

An emotion is a specially complicated group of appraisals and physiological and psychological responses. As Whiteley says (1979, p. 235),

> An emotion—for example fear, anger, anxiety, joy, grief, elation, despair, pride, shame, envy—is a response to situations of one specific type; its components are a belief that the situation is of that type, some characteristic sensations, and an inclination to behave suitably to the situation.

We are pointing to these components when we say that someone is "experiencing" an emotion.

To educate the emotions, therefore, is different from just influencing them. Injecting drugs, carrying out a lobotomy, giving electroconvulsive therapy (ECT), providing electronic stimulation of the brain (ESB), engaging in conditioning, and so on, may all affect a person's emotional reactions, but they are not education.[2] Education is concerned with developing cognition and knowledge and increasing rationality, and the above activities are not. Furthermore, I want to suggest that to develop cognitive perspective and rationality is at the same time to develop and educate the emotions. Far from being on a par with cognitive perspective and rationality in their significance for the development of persons, the feeling side of emotions (the sensations) is secondary and dependent. It is rationally disastrous to imagine that to emote or to feel, irrespective of the appropriateness of the emotion or its context, is an experience worth cultivating. So this means that to educate generally is also to educate the emotions. It is possible to argue this way because it is the case that although emotions certainly consist of particular feelings, involuntary bodily processes, and so forth, they are centrally involved with cognitions or construals of situations—that is, emotions have a fundamental knowledge core. Each emotion is related to a particular way of seeing a situation, or, as Whiteley says above, ". . . a belief that the situation is of that type." Someone is frightened *of,* annoyed *with,* regretful *that.* Thus in normal circumstances a person is angry because he realizes (or believes) that he has been cheated or frustrated; he is afraid because there is danger; he is envious because he sees someone else having the success that he would like for himself; he is proud because he knows that he has succeeded in a particular way; he is saddened by knowledge of man's inhumanity; he is remorseful because of his wrongdoing; and so on.

First there is a construal, or an appraisal and the feeling that comes over a person is a result of this. Indeed, so central is this seeing of a situation in a certain way, that we cannot even distinguish one emotion from another without identifying it. So while it may be true to say that animals experience emotion, only persons (see 4.1A) can experience the range of emotion that rationality, a complex language, and appropriate construal make possible. An angry dog and an angry person are poles apart. Indeed, with many emotions, such as jealousy and compassion, it makes no sense to attribute them to

---

[2]Of course, it may at times be very important to influence emotions in these ways. For instance, it may be necessary for a medical doctor to give a patient a drug to counter a completely debilitating irrational fear in order to be able to do some later psychotherapy of an educational sort. Thus, it is not being suggested here that education is sufficient to deal with certain issues of mental health or with emotional problems and irrational emotions of paranoids and psychopaths. Such conditions are not amenable to education through an increase in rationality or a broadening of cognitive perspective. This section tries to confine itself strictly to the areas of education and training, to activities that *schoolteachers* can do something about.

animals, for such emotions can be learned only by language-using entities.

Thus, I see emotional life both as parasitic upon and as secondary to a person's knowledge and understanding of the world. In developing children's cognitive perspective and rationality, we shall at the same time be developing their emotions in educationally significant ways. How often have we seen young children and uneducated adults reacting in an emotionally inappropriate manner? They often do so because their grasp of the realities of the situation is faulty. Indeed, it is a general truth that to lack proper knowledge is to be a potential victim of inappropriate emotional response—fools do rush in where angels *fear* to tread. People react inappropriately when they mistake the facts, give weight to irrelevant factors and issues, emphasize only partly relevant ones, see only particular aspects of a situation, cannot discriminate, cannot see farther than the immediately pressing present, or get things out of proportion.

One of the great aberrations in the intellectual history of mankind is the widespread acceptance of the belief that emotions are just emotions, feelings about something are just feelings, that rational consideration is therefore irrelevant to them and that is all there is to it. For just as false beliefs can be changed into true beliefs and knowledge, so inappropriate emotional reactions can be changed into appropriate emotional reactions. This is why I was so struck by the wrongheadedness of the statement by the soap opera heroine, "You can't explain away feelings. . . ."

It is not as though this suggestion that the emotions are educable is really new to most of us. Although they do not normally call it education of the emotions, both parents and teachers do indeed try to affect emotional development in this way. For example, they try to get young children to realize the (general) inappropriateness of fear of the dark, or the (general) irrelevance of dislike on the basis of a person's skin color, and so on. What should be encouraged is an increase in the explicit recognition of this activity in which schools already implicitly engage. In developing children's cognitive perspective and rationality, teachers are developing their ability to deal with the world as it is, with objects and events as they are. Children can act only upon what they know; thus such development stops them from being deluded by their subjective lives of wishes, desires, false beliefs, and illusions, and is of crucial importance for appropriate emotional response.

In order to put the idea as simply as possible, it may be argued that education of the emotions will consist in providing knowledge and understanding that *appropriately* lessen or heighten a negative emotion such as fear or hatred, or *appropriately* lessen or heighten a positive emotion such as compassion or admiration. MacMurray introduces this point about appropriateness when he writes (1972, p. 25), "Why should they not be proper feelings when they are in terms of the nature of the object, and improper feelings when they are not in terms of the nature of the object?" And again (1972, p. 33):

> Our feelings may be illusory just as our intellectual ideas often are. Our emotions can be real or unreal. To say that a feeling is unreal does not mean that we do not feel it, any more than to say that an idea is false means that we do not think it. An unreal or illusory emotion may be very strongly felt, and it may influence our conduct profoundly.

MacMurray's terminology may be unusual, but he describes situations of great significance. It is because of such situations that children's emotional lives can be and need to be educated.

As one example of MacMurray's point, consider the case of appropriately lessening the fear of flying. This has been achieved through having the affected person sit in on the crew's preflight briefing sessions, by viewing the preflight procedures for checking instruments and systems, by watching the flight crew in training, by showing the person around the maintenance hangars, control towers, and training carrels, so that the care and thoroughness of service and preparation can be appreciated. The vastly better statistics of safety per passenger mile in the air can be compared with the carnage on the road. Particular worries that have gripped him in the past can be countered: the wing tips flap somewhat in flight because flexibility is necessary, not because the wings are weak or worn; individual noises are attributable to particular, necessary functions— the bang of the retractable undercarriage, the hiss of the ventilators when the air conditioning is switched on, the change in engine noise when cruising altitude is reached, and so on. Between Auckland and Sydney I read a fascinating example of the success of just this sort of well-planned approach in the house journal of Air New Zealand. An irrational fear was replaced by a rational understanding. The passenger, having learned the why of things, now enjoys air travel for he can see it as a pleasant, unworrying, rapid, and instrumentally valuable activity.

What can be done in schools? Teachers can ensure that in such subjects as literature, drama, and history they regularly consider situations that explore the sensitively changing dimensions of the human condition in all its weaknesses and glories, in order to bring about an expansion of children's consciousness through their identification with other people, at a level appropriate to the children's intellectual development. Teachers must show children that children's own reactions influence the way other people in turn react to them, that aggression has a tendency to breed aggression, sympathy to bring sympathy. Through promoting an increase in and a clarity of language, they must try to make children's emotional lives relate to the greater and broader total world of human experience in all its fullness, and also to give them the linguistic tools to think about and educate their own emotions.

Schools should arrange the regular occurrence of situations that help children to understand interpersonal relations and to handle their feelings. They should organize sporting competition, physical education, and "outward-bound" pursuits that bring appropriate feeling to games situations and legitimate rivalry, and allow children to work in challenging situations with others. And the rule-governed approach in schools should allow for children's gradual development of discipline (see 4.3E) in their intellectual and emotional lives.

It must be acknowledged that education of the emotions also involves moral education. Children need to get their ideas into some sort of scale of moral values, so that unlike the young children in the Kellmer-Pringle and Edwards (1964) study, they do not believe that running in school corridors is the next worst act to killing people. Here, of course, teachers need to be careful to avoid indoctrinating (see 2.2) their merely personal moral positions. However, there are dimensions of conceptual distinction that are rationally based and that it is teachers' moral duty to expose. So it is appropriate that as teachers develop children's compassion for, say, the German Jews under the Nazi regime, they should try to ensure that the children see why this may be accompanied by an appropriate disgust for the Gestapo. Children must be helped to recognize things for what they are. It is insufficient for children merely to be able to recognize acts of cruelty; they should also be encouraged into proper reaction. Thus with older children issues such as the confusing modern tendency to view what is actually evil as though it were mental illness (Flew, 1973) should be pointed out, if there is to be correct appraisal leading to appropriate feeling; for instance, the act of murder is only rarely evidence of mental illness.

If this is what it is to educate the emotions, what is it to train them? It may be suggested that training children's emotions is similar to other sorts of training, insofar as it is an attempt to form relatively specific habits and propensities of thinking and action that will come into play fairly automatically. To train the negative emotions is therefore to develop ways of channeling emotional excess or inappropriateness. Parents have done this for generations in their advice to children to count to ten before acting in anger. The very disposition to pause has itself a moderating effect, allowing children to get the issue in better proportion. Something similar but more positive happens when children are encouraged to apologize to the injured party after an unjustified emotional encounter. The institution in the schoolroom of a "quiet corner," where younger pupils go when they feel irritation and annoyance coming on, is a useful technique. To train the positive emotions, teachers must try to foster from an early age appropriate *habits* of generosity and sharing, taking turns, sympathy and consideration for other children and for other persons in the school and the general community. Training of the emotions, like all training, will be of instrumental value; it will lay down right habits and settled dispositions that form a background of behavior upon which teachers can also try to build a proper educated understanding.

Education of the emotions will consequently consist in the development of appropriateness in emotional reaction. This is emphasized again, for while appropriate reaction certainly consists in, say, being angry when anger is justified, and in showing compassion for less fortunate persons, appropriate emotional reaction also includes a developed respect for rationality, and such respect involves such emotion-based content as feeling the importance of consistency, relevance, and critical awareness. In the separate form of knowledge areas (see 3.1D), this becomes delight in mathematical preciseness, concern for the pursuit of truth in the empirical realm, care for human consciousness, passion for individual freedom and a proper anger at disrespect for persons, intense absorption in artistic endeavor, awe at the vastness of the cosmos, and pleasure in precisely expressed ideas. The good teacher is infused with a passionate concern for these things and for the development of the same concern in his pupils and students. Indoctrinators engage in a perversion of this passion, for their feelings for their doctrine outweigh their rationality.(see 3.2A).

E. The Justification of Education.

Just as important in philosophy as conceptual questions, are questions about the reasons why of things—justificatory questions. It is important to know what we mean by the word *education,* what counts as education, but it is equally important to know *why* we engage in educational activities. In liberal democracies such as Australia, the United States, and Britain, millions of adults teach and lecture, millions of pupils and students attend schools, and thousands of millions of dollars and pounds are spent per year on the school system. Why? Is it because people are concerned with national survival? With economic well-being? With turning human beings into full persons? Is it (as philosophers have tended to argue since time immemorial) because it is the pursuit of knowledge that gives the most enduring source of satisfaction? Is it because education helps persons to get their priorities right? Or what? These are crucially important questions. In discussing the concepts of "training" and "education," some discussion of the justification for training and educational activities was implicitly provided. I want now to add to this discussion, particularly as it relates to education.

Although it was suggested that the concept of "education" can be *distinguished* insofar as the activities of education can be seen to be providing cognitive perspective and rationality, which are believed to be of intrinsic value, this does not rule out the possibility that educational activities *also* have functions that are of instrumental value to the persons involved and to society in general. I believe that this is the case. Insofar as it is the case, this will be an additional justification for education. For we often see the justification of something in terms of its use, which is another way of talking about its instrumental value.

Viewed in this way, it should be clear that the range of knowledge and the broad general understanding that help to throw light on the world and to make people rational, which are characteristic of education as it has been outlined above, are generally useful possessions in life. It is of note that many employers prefer people who are generally educated rather than specifically trained, as the educated person proves more adaptable and adjusts better in a changing world, whereas the merely trained person has no resources to fall back upon when his training becomes outdated. An education allows a person to make appropriate choices, to get his priorities in order, to have a framework of appraisal and expectation that allows him to act with a measure of consistency and intelligence, and to have at least some notion of how a novel question may be approached. It is of course also the case that in liberal democratic societies, because of universal adult franchise, it is instrumentally valuable to have voters who are educated.

But, as argued above, educational activities may be justified in terms of their intrinsic value, and this is a reason why many schoolteachers try to educate. Of course, there are many other things and activities in the experience of which Western man finds intrinsic value: freedom, fishing, friendship, sexual activity, art, the thrill of the hunt, and so on. By saying that these experiences have intrinsic value I mean that people pursue them for the satisfaction to be had from them, not because they desire approval, fame, fortune, reward, or because they wish to avoid censure or punishment. Such valued experiences provide their own reason. Such valued experiences themselves help to *constitute* a desirable way of life as seen by the person who values them. Such comments apply equally to the intrinsic value of education, with the intrinsic value of education being instantiated in its provision of rationality and cognitive perspective. But is this intrinsic value of education, the good of the educated state, merely on all fours with other intrinsic values like freedom and fishing, or *does it have some specially significant features of its own?* I think it does. The best recent account of these features has been provided by Peters (1977, p. 97 ff.), and this section is largely a summary of his suggestions.

Quantity and quality are rough categories that we use to estimate the value of experiences. Here educational activities score high, for they transform the nature of activities both by developing them and by altering the way in which people think of them. This last sentence is not merely a description of features of educational activities themselves, but also an indication of how educational activities can affect other activities. There is a certain potential and ever-widening horizon about the pursuit of knowledge and understanding and the development of rationality that are characteristic of education, and that no other type of activity can match—solve a scientific problem and you open up a dozen more, ask a philosophical question and a myriad others manifest themselves. Again, there can never be a scarcity in educational activity and, unlike the situation in other human pursuits, no one can corner the market on ideas. What is more, educational activity is permanent: pets and pastimes pass away; the pursuit of knowledge and understanding continues.

Yet, there seem to be two even more fundamental justifications for the pursuit of cognitive perspective and rationality. As Peters (1967, 1977) and his intellectual ancestors such as Kant have pointed out, the ultimate justification for pursuing such things is that the activity of justification would itself be impossible without such pursuit. The question, Why do one thing rather than another? (which is the more general version of our question, Why educate?) would never concern us at all if we were not already *implicitly concerned* with the importance of knowledge and understanding, with the significance of truth rather than error, with the acquisition of cognitive perspective. If a critic asks us why he should bother becoming rational, we merely need to point out that he is *assuming the importance of rationality* in asking his question, for surely he wants a rational answer to it. What is more, if anything at all is important to him, then rationality must be, because it is by being rational that he achieves the best means to what he thinks important (Scriven, 1967, p. 13).

A further justification lies in the fundamental moral principle of respect for persons (see 4.1). For it can be argued that only by educating human beings can we make them into fuller persons, that anything less is leaving them half developed. Indeed, education can be well expressed in the phrase, "making persons." Educators believe that in educating they are doing what is good for the educatees. In effect, they believe that the educatees will one day be glad that they were influenced in this way. And very few persons who have received an education in the sense in which it has been outlined here ever wish that they had not; indeed, those who do make that claim may be engaging in a sort of conceptual incoherence.

So it is not just that activities which develop cognitive perspective and rationality are appropriate for human persons. It is in this extra, special sense of providing *the very components of a fuller personhood* that the unique intrinsic value of education rests.

EDUCATION: KEY POINTS

Training has to do with instrumental value and lack of cognitive implications; education has to do with wide cognitive implications and rationality, which in themselves have value for persons.

Educational experiences and activities give meaning to features of the world other than themselves. Their meaning is not tied merely to the activity or experience itself. It is general, not specific. It gives comprehension. Education helps people to see the world differently.

To count as education, the activities of schools must in fact be such that they broaden children's outlook on life, give perspective to what they do, provide meaning, knowledge, and real understanding, and encounter with values, and thus help to make children more rational.

It is not by chance that education is maximized when an imaginative teacher encounters a thoughtful child.

One of the great aberrations in the intellectual history of mankind is the widespread acceptance of the belief that emotions are just emotions, feelings about something are just feelings, that rational consideration is therefore irrelevant to them and that is all there is to it. Persons' emotional lives need to be and can be educated.

It is a general truth that to lack proper knowledge is to be a potential victim of inappropriate emotional response: Fools do rush in where angels *fear* to tread.

There is a certain potential and ever-widening horizon about the pursuit of knowledge and understanding and the development of rationality that are characteristic of education, that no other type of activity can match—solve a scientific problem and you open up a dozen more; ask a philosophical question and a myriad others manifest themselves. What is more, educational activity is permanent: pets and pastimes pass away; the pursuit of knowledge and understanding continues.

So it is not just that activities that develop cognitive perspective and rationality are appropriate for human persons. It is in this extra, special sense of providing the *very components of a fuller personhood* that the unique intrinsic value of education rests.

2.2 INDOCTRINATION

A. Intention

It is important to remember that things happen in schools in various parts of the world at the present time and have happened in schools in ages past, that seem to be far removed from education as it has been described in the last section. My present concern is to discuss features of certain antieducational activities, called indoctrination, which certainly occur in many schools of the world, and which unfortunately may be attempted in some degree by some teachers in the state schools of liberal democracies.

In talking about indoctrination, I am talking about degrees of pressure and influence that result from the three interrelated factors of the teacher's intentions, the content of the teaching, and the methods used (White, 1967).

Clearly, teachers at various times and places have different intentions for the content that they wish to teach their pupils or students. Among such intentions will be the following. To get children:

1. To hold that something is the case.
2. To hold that something is the case, and to have some understanding of it.
3. To hold that something is probably the case, and to have some understanding of it, and to have some grounds for holding that it is the case, but to hope that the children will reject it if the grounds later appear to be untenable.
4. To hold that something is the case, when in fact it is the case, and to possess appropriate evidential support—that is, to hold it in such a manner that it is based upon the person's own full and open perusal of the evidence, which itself can stand up to sustained and open public scrutiny.
5. To hold that something is the case, when it is in fact equivocal, and to have some understanding of it and some grounds, but to hope that the children will hold it in such a way that no matter what counter-evidence is produced they will continue to hold that it is the case and not see it as equivocal or false.

Depending upon the age and comprehension of the children, the intentions of teachers may legitimately vary. Where bald facts may be sufficient with young children, appropriate background will be required with older ones. And which of the above intentions is going to be acceptable nowadays in the schools of liberal democracies will surely depend upon just what the content of the teaching is. To teach that $2 + 2 = 4$ or that water is composed of hydrogen and oxygen would seem to be acceptable with intentions 1, 2, and 4. To teach that stars that implode through the white-dwarf and neutron-star stages eventually reach a state of infinite density and zero volume that we call "black holes" seems to be all right if the teacher has intentions 1, 2, or 3. With the claim, King John was a bad king, intention 2 has seemed acceptable in the past, but intention 3 now appears more acceptable because historical research in recent years has been challenging such a contention about John. And so on.

Thus, with some of the possible contents some of the possible intentions will be acceptable, others will not. With some it may be objected that while the claim may be true, it is not good enough merely to teach it as true; more explanation is needed. With others we object that it is not known if the claim is true or not, so teachers should not teach it as though it is, or at the very least they should teach it in a way that shows its equivocal epistemological status. It will be with intentions of the 3 and 4 type that education is most likely to occur. Now, if teachers do teach as true claims that are equivocal, or if they fail to expose disputable status, then they are slipping into what may be called indoctrination, for their intentions have become morally and educationally suspect.

Across the world can be indicated teachers' activities that I and many persons in liberal democracies will call indoctrination in the above sense of intentional implantation of equivocal or debatable content in the hope that no matter what counter-evidence is produced the pupils and students will continue to hold the content as true and never see it as equivocal or false. This is so in the cases of, for example, schools in the U.S.S.R. when the subject is Marxist-Leninist theory, or of Mormon seminaries for 12- to 16-year-olds in the state of Utah when Joseph Smith's claimed discoveries of the golden tablets are being discussed, or when teachers in fundamentalist Christian schools teach about the book of Genesis, or when schools in Fascist countries preach government by the leader and the élite and deny the (general) equality of human beings. The point about such activities is that non-Marxists and non-Mormons and nonfascists and so on see much of the content of Marxism and Mormonism and Fascism and so on as debatable, or equivocal, or downright false, yet in the above contexts it is usually being taught with intention 5. It is significant also that the Marxists would scorn the Mormon content, the Mormons the Marxist content, the Marxists the Fascist content, and so on.

It is this firm intention with such beliefs that helps to make the activity indoctrination rather than sound teaching, indoctrination rather than education; by putting particular viewpoints beyond challenge, there is an attempt to close minds on specific issues rather than to open them; there is an attempt to inculcate doctrines.

Many, perhaps most, indoctrinators have themselves been indoctrinated. Such people hold their claims to be true and believe that nothing can acceptably undermine their position, and if they were asked which intention they held, they would probably claim to be motivated by intention 3. But the extent to which Marxist and Mormon and Fascist and other such teachers actually held a particular intention would of course be shown in their classroom behavior (see 2.2C)—for example, whether they allowed rational discussion of the sort described earlier (2.1B). It may be strongly suspected that as soon as it seemed that they were in fact about to be undermined, the rationality of intention 3 would be dispensed with, deeply rooted feelings for the doctrine would come to the fore, and such teachers would resort to all the authority and power at their disposal to prop up their positions and to influence their classes.

B. Content

It will be noticed that in talking about doctrines the discussion has already begun to consider content. Political, economic, and religious examples have been mentioned because it is in such areas that we can most appropriately argue that content is doctrinal. The concept of indoctrination has to do with doctrines—that is, with interrelated systems of belief, rather than with interrelated systems of knowledge. It does not, for instance, make sense to talk about indoctrination in the multiplication tables or the chemical compounds of sodium, even if the teaching is narrow and uninspired, for these issues are not matters of belief. In purely formal or factual subject matter, to get mere mechanical and automatic performance without proper comprehension is teaching by rote, not indoctrination.

The point about such doctrines as Marxism and Mormonism and Fascism and so on is that they consist of interrelated sets of statements, a number of which cannot be demonstrated to be unquestionably true (i.e., about which there is no well-established and general agreement among intelligent people who have carefully considered the matter), but which, taken together, have immense repercussions for the way the believer deals with other persons, chooses his friends, lives his life, sees the truth, demonstrates his values, views the world, and indicates how society should be organized.

For instance, in the early days of the Mormon church polygamy was practiced. According to Mormon teaching, it was revealed to Joseph Smith in the last year of his life that the practice of having multiple wives was acceptable to God. As the "Revelation of the Eternity of the Marriage Covenant including Plurality of Wives. Given through Joseph the Seer, in Nauvoo, Hancock County, Illinois, July 12, 1843" says:

> Verily thus saith the Lord unto you my servant, Joseph, that in as much as you have enquired at my hand, to know and understand . . . as touching the principle and doctrine of their having many wives and concubines. . . . Therefore prepare thy heart to receive and obey. . . . If any man espouse a virgin and desire to espouse another, and the first give her consent; and if he espouse the second, and they are virgins, and have vowed to no other man, then he is justified; he cannot commit adultery, for they are given unto him . . . and if he have ten virgins given unto him by this law, he cannot commit adultery, for they belong to him, and they are given unto him, therefore is he justified. (Riley, 1967, p. 83).

To many minds this may seem a strange dictate for God to pronounce. Did God in fact say it? Certainly it does not seem easy to demonstrate conclusively that God said it. Yet it has been taught to Mormons that God said it. It was part of Mormon doctrine during the nineteenth century, and thereby had enormous repercussions for the Mormon way of life. Mormons, as I understand it, nowadays argue that there were good reasons why God gave that particular revelation at that particular time—the Church of Jesus Christ of the Latter Day Saints was under attack from secular authorities, there was an excess of women in the church, and so on. But even if these claims are true (and one recent analysis argues that there was an excess of men) there is still the issue of how to establish to the satisfaction of intelligent people of other persuasions (Marxists and Manichaeans, Anglicans and agnostics) that God indeed said it. Merely the most controversial of once-held Mormon beliefs has been discussed here, but the problems of truth status arise with respect to much of the rest of Mormon doctrine, and, naturally, to similar parts of other religious doctrines.

It was said in a previous paragraph that within doctrines there are some statements that cannot be demonstrated to be unquestionably true. However, in claiming that a statement cannot be shown to be unquestionably true, it is not thereby being said that it is untrue. For statements of this sort cannot straightforwardly be shown to be unquestionably false either. (Though perhaps they can be shown to be internally inconsistent, as considered below.) That they cannot easily be shown to be unquestionably false is at the heart of the epistemological difficulty with doctrinal statements; that is precisely the problem.

Thus it is crucial to an understanding of indoctrination that a distinction be drawn between two different sorts of statements. I am distinguishing, on the one hand, statements about which there is no disagreement among intelligent people who have carefully considered the matter, about the kind of evidence which would count as showing that the statements were true or false—potentially provable or disprovable statements—and, on the other hand, statements about which there is disagreement concerning the evidence—potentially neither provable nor disprovable statements (Woods and Barrow, 1975, p. 66). In the first case there is no disagreement among intelligent persons of various persuasions about the sort of evidence that would verify or falsify; in the second case there is no agreement on the sort of evidence that would verify or falsify. The simplest way of making the point is to list a set of typical such statements.

In the first list we have:

1. Human beings need oxygen to live.
2. San Francisco was founded in 1776.
3. Adolf Hitler wrote *Alice in Wonderland*.
4. "Olympus Mons," a volcano on Mars, is fifteen miles high and covers an area about the size of Scotland or South Carolina.
5. The sun consists of burning coal.

These are all statements about which we could get agreement among intelligent persons who had considered the issue of the verifying or falsifying tests, even if a particular individual might not know whether the statement were indeed true or false. We could get

general agreement about the type of evidence needed, even if we
did not happen to have the evidence or any way of obtaining it at
present. Marxists and Fascists and Mormons and agnostics would all
agree about the sort of evidence that counts here. It so happens that
1, 2, and 4 are true, 3 and 5 are false, but that is not the issue. Rather,
the concern here is to emphasize the agreement that exists as to the
type of evidence that would make them true or false.

In the second list we have:

6. God loves all his children.
7. Education involves the realization of the divine potential of
   each child.
8. If parents were on the side of their children, there would be
   no young thieves (claimed by A. S. Neill, 1937, p. 183).
9. The mind consists of the ego, superego, and id.
10. The mode of production of material life conditions the so-
    cial, political, and intellectual life process in general.

With these, among intelligent persons who have carefully considered the issues we cannot get general agreement as to the sort of
evidence which would count for or against. Marxists and Mormons
and so on would not agree about the sort of evidence. A tangential
way of making the point is to say that such statements yield no
predictions that we can test in any simple sense of the word *test.*
This is what makes them different from the first five statements. A
situation or its opposite is equally acceptable to believers of such
statements, for they interpret *all* situations in terms of the statement. Helping to make the test situation so complicated are the
tremendous conceptual and interpretational difficulties embedded
in these sorts of statements. What is meant by "God" and "love"?
What is it to be "on the side of" children? How are we to interpret
entities like "ego"? What counts as a "mode of production" or as
"conditioning"?

I have been discussing examples of doctrinal statements for
which there is no general agreement as to the requirements of evidence. But there are, of course, parts of doctrines for which there is
general agreement—not that believers always see the difference. As
far as purely empirical claims within doctrines are concerned, the
issue of truth or falsity is relatively straightforward. For instance, in
the religious case, either the Mormon leader Joseph Smith was born
at Sharon, Windsor County, in the state of Vermont, or he was not.
This is an empirical statement of the historical sort and we have no
difficulty in getting agreement about the type of evidence that would
count for or against: it would be of the same type as historians cus-
tomarily use. Again, Joseph Smith either did indeed teach the Revelation of the Eternity of the Marriage Covenant, or he is misreported

as having done so. As a practical matter, of course, it may be very difficult to establish truth or falsity of such statements, but there is no difficulty in principle.

It is with statements for which there is no general agreement about the type of evidence needed for proof or disproof, with what may be called the "metaphysical" parts of doctrines, that the great difficulties arise. For instance, in the religious case, parish priests and proselytizers say such things as "God loves all his children," but when the skeptic or agnostic offers evidence to the contrary—for example, that there is massive misery and suffering in the world—most priests and proselytizers, far from abandoning the belief, begin to qualify it in various subtle ways. What seemed at the beginning of the encounter to be discussion of a straightforward statement, "God loves all his children," is progressively modified: "His love is different from human love," "We cannot understand the ways of God," "The ineffable is beyond our comprehension," and so on. The claim is changed until it seems that no matter what contrary evidence the questioning agnostic either assembles or might in principle assemble, the believer will still go on saying, "God loves all his children." But if the believer will not allow any conceivable sort of evidence to count against his belief, even evidence in principle, what sort of belief is it we are here dealing with? (Corbett, 1965, pp. 117–124) After all, for the content of a statement to be claimed to be the case and actually to be the case, then something else is excluded from being the case. In particular, when something is claimed, then at the same time the claimant must at least see the denial of the something as false. A claim that is both conceptually ambiguous and does not by implication seem to deny anything at all for the believer, is not a statement in any normally meaningful sense (Flew & MacIntyre, 1955, p. 96; McPherson, 1974, p. 29). Such statements can account for any phenomenon whatsoever. This is why it was said two paragraphs ago that such statements yield no predictions that we can test. Believers note what they consider to be confirming instances of their doctrinal belief, and because they see the world in terms of their belief, of course they continually see what they take to be confirming instances. This wish to notice only confirming instances is a widespread human trait that reveals a nonrational basis. It is common even in liberal democracies based on mass schooling—witness the tremendous popularity of such intellectual garbage as von Daniken's *Chariots of the Gods* and its sequels, which take into account only what the author sees as confirming evidence and completely ignore all the manifest disconfirmation.

The type of belief discussed in the above paragraph is certainly a problem. So for teachers to teach beliefs of this sort as anything other than equivocal—that is, to teach them as anything more than *mere* beliefs—is to teach more than is epistemologically warranted and is to drift into the realm of indoctrination.

Metaphysical statements of the sort just considered are central to doctrines, and of great importance to believers, because they have the function of, look like, masquerade as empirical statements. But, as has just been shown, they are not empirical, for they do not seem to be testable even in principle. Such statements, however, do provide the followers of the doctrine with a justification and a rationale for much that is done in the name of the doctrine. Often they feature as unchallengeable, axiomatic starting points.[3]

While the presence of interrelated sets of statements of this metaphysical sort may be the best evidence that a set of claims is doctrinal, close analysis of content will show further problems. For instance, there is often inconsistency and contradiction, selective use of evidence, overgeneralization from insufficient instances, and the use of authority as a "stopper" to discussion. At other places the meaning of a key term "slides" from one thing on one page to a slightly different meaning later in the account, in a manner similar to that of the word *love* discussed above in "God loves all his children." It is also common for there to be a use of vocabulary in which concepts are tightly interwoven, mutually reinforcing, self-validating, and circular. As Jacka, Cox, and Marks (1975, p. 40) bluntly put it,

> The trick . . . is to manufacture a range of words (or re-define old ones by statement and repetition) so that a deliberate effort at persuasion and enlistment can be passed off as a neutral description. . . . Independent thought is impossible when using these words; the answers are built in from the beginning.

It may be, of course, that for many persons there are dimensions of the human condition in which it is difficult for them not to make such commitments of feeling, or leaps of faith, in accepting equivocal metaphysical beliefs. At the same time, it must be clearly pointed out that they are in a problematic area. Indeed, it seems that to some extent such persons are behaving in ways opposed to those of the

[3]This is, of course, an immensely complex issue. I am here merely emphasizing a crucial problematic aspect of such statements and its significance for the pedagogy of indoctrination. There is no space here to consider the extremely subtle philosophical work that has been achieved in the religious area in recent years (McKinnon, 1970; Ramsay, 1974). To point to certain logical difficulties in this sort of religious statement is not, therefore, by implication to condemn religion as a whole. As suggested later (3.2D), there may be a case for seeing religion as one of seven logically basic ways of encountering the world.

conscientious scientist whose behavior was considered earlier as a paradigm of rationality. In other words, many persons may find it a psychological necessity to accept doctrinal beliefs in building their world views, but they should admit the controversial status of their positions, and while they may be happy if others come to see the world in the same way, they have no clear justification for forcing such a belief system on other people, or perhaps even for trying to influence others. So it would seem that the teaching of debatable doctrinal beliefs as truths has no place in the school systems of liberal democracies, although teaching *about* such beliefs and the immense effects that belief in them has on the world is important and has considerable educational implications. So if teachers are to achieve education in relation to such beliefs, then open-minded and epistemologically honest methods are called for; thus the methods of teaching will play a crucial part in insuring that their teaching is education and not indoctrination (see 2.2C).

What is more, some aspects of doctrinal beliefs may well become grist for the intellectual mill of liberal democratic societies. Particular statements of doctrines, when approached intelligently, can sometimes be seen as throwing *some* light on man's state in the universe: *some* light, but not the coruscating flash of a supposedly unchallengeable revealed truth. The key tenet of Marxism may be useful in this way. Marx wrote, "The mode of production of material life, conditions the social, political and intellectual life process in general. It is not the consciousness of men that determines their being, but on the contrary, their social being that determines their consciousness." (Marx and Engels, 1962, p. 323) I said that such a belief throws some light on the world, and indeed, when considered to be one important factor, this claim has been seminal in providing historians and social scientists with a refreshing and insightful way of considering historical change. But Marx's claim would seem to be overstated. For to try to untangle the chance happenings and intricacies of historical change and then present merely one feature as the determinant of the whole is surely foreign to the spirit of the expanding, rational human mind. After all, "Causation, like the circulation of the currency, is multilateral and complex, and cannot be traced in lines from A to B to C. Much futile debate can be avoided if these basic facts are kept in mind." (Thomson, 1969, 64)

It must, of course, be asked of this fundamental Marxist claim, How can it be tested? It is not easy to see how we can conceivably get general agreement on the sort of evidence required. It can hardly be seen as a properly empirical claim, for it allows of too great a variety of result: *whatever* form of religion, art, morality, and the like results, it is still to be seen in terms of determination by the means of production of material life, whereas a properly empirical claim must *rule out* at least some possible results. That which seeks to explain everything, explains nothing empirically. Where many Marxists see this ability to explain all as a strength, non-Marxists see it as a fatal weakness. So this claim, like its counterparts in religion, psychology, and pedagogy in the second list provided above, falls into the "not easy to get agreement about a test," or metaphysical statement category.

Also, for a statement (empirical, moral, or whatever) to be testable, it must be internally consistent. Internal inconsistency is a good indication that a claim is doctrinal. Again, the above Marxist axiom is a good example, for if it is merely the development of the mode of production that conditions social, political, and intellectual processes, and not also the other way around, what is it that changes the mode of production? What is more, how is it that Marx's own immense intellectual influence on the modes of production of material life ever happened? (McPherson, 1970, p. 130; Acton, 1973)

C. Methods

The third aspect of this concept of "indoctrination" has to do with the methods used to get pupils and students to accept particular beliefs about which there is no general agreement as to tests of their truth or falsity. It should be clear that if particular methods are used, then a particular intention and some particular content are already assumed. Thus the issue of method is important, because it is by the observation of particular methods in relation to doctrinal content that we become entitled to attribute some degree of indoctrination. Whether or not teachers actually hold the intention to implant unshakeable belief will be shown in what they do in the classroom. "Get them young" is one aspect of much successful indoctrinatory method. It becomes progressively more difficult and more extreme methods have to be used to indoctrinate older people, for children are in the process of developing their basic conceptual schemes, but adults are already relatively developed in that respect. For instance, in North Korea,

> . . . toddlers sing the praises of President Kim Il-Sung before they are two years old. At the age of three, the kiddies have perfected simple songs and dance steps about "eagerly waiting to see the beloved leader of the fatherland." By the time they are four, they are . . . singing about "the train of reunification of the fatherland." As the youngsters get older . . . the devotion to Kim Il-Sung [gets] even stronger. The result is a nation of mini-showmen with a single-minded commitment to glorifying one man in music, paint and song. (*Cape Times*, July 5, 1979)

No doubt the more fanatical proponents of intention 5 would like to resort to the North Korean approach, to the methods of the Hitler Youth Movement, or to "brainwashing" as performed by the Chinese on their own people for some years after the revolution and on United Nations prisoners during the Korean War (Huxley, 1965; Lifton, 1961). But such methods are hardly possible in the schools of liberal Western democracies today, given the influence of other staff members, of parents, and of the community at large with its variety of information media. It should nonetheless be noted that if a teacher is indeed working with intention 5—that is, trying to instill unshakeable beliefs about issues the truth or falsity of which cannot be easily agreed upon—then at least some parts of his methods cannot be fully rational, for to achieve his purpose he must discourage open criticism and he must restrict evidence.

It should also be noted that all teachers have certain opportunities to hammer a line of thinking and to bring to bear upon children various sorts of subtle and not-so-subtle pressures. And some teachers *are* clearly prepared to pervert their educational calling by attempting to get children to see the world in a doctrinal way, through distorting the evidence, choosing it selectively, failing to suggest alternative points of view, and setting loaded questions for homework and for tests.

It was suggested in an earlier section (2.1B) that if teachers are to educate, then they must continually expand, not contract children's mental horizons. In history they must help children to share the ways of life and the thinking of men and women of the past, they must get children to see that morality is a matter of sensitive and subtle adjustments to changing contexts, and so on. It is worth recalling this point here, for presumably the good teacher wishes to educate and not indoctrinate, and thus whenever possible encourage children to find things out for themselves and to think for themselves. On the other hand, there will be many instances when direct telling, instruction, and explanation will be the most educational methods.

There have been some recent suggestions that one way of dealing with controversial matters is for teachers to remain neutral. As Degenhardt (1976, p. 28) points out, this is an impossibility and teachers will be better engaged in drawing to children's attention points of view of which they are ignorant. Indeed, there is a sort of nonsense in the suggestion that *teachers* should be neutral: their job is to teach, not to chair. Of course, in all their work, conscientious teachers should be aware of the potential for influencing children unfairly, and must concentrate on developing and opening children's minds.

Hare sums up much of this when he writes (1964, p. 69),

The educator is waiting and hoping all the time for those whom he is educating to start *thinking;* and none of the thoughts that may occur to them is labelled "dangerous" a priori. The indoctrinator, on the other hand, is watching for signs of trouble, and ready to intervene to suppress it when it appears, however oblique and smooth his methods may be.

D. Misunderstanding

In recent years there have been simpleminded (or deliberately obfuscatory) claims that all schooling is indoctrination, including the systems of such liberal democracies as the United States, Australia, and Great Britain. Such a view argues that the schools are vehicles of the political and social value system of the establishment, and that the schools do not critically study such views, they merely indoctrinate them. But this claim confuses the acquisition of beliefs and values with the deliberate enforcement of beliefs and values, and uses language so loosely as to make the term *indoctrination* almost meaningless. Such writers impoverish the English tongue when they use words so broadly. This impoverishment of language leads to impoverishment of conceptual distinctions, which in turn makes it harder to draw essential epistemological discriminations and easier for the real indoctrinators to go about their vicious business of closing children's minds. As Snook puts the point (1973, p. 60),

> One of the distressing aspects of contemporary political writing is the tendency to make [sweeping] claims. If [the word] "violence" is applied to massive advertising campaigns, how are we to describe the throwing of petrol bombs and the machine-gunning of demonstrators? If all of us are "brainwashed" by the social milieu, what can we say of the activities of interrogators in the cells of police states? If we are all "indoctrinated" because we have undergone a socialization process, what is there left to say about those schools whose avowed function is to inculcate in the minds of the young, unswerving conviction of the truth of various dogmas and unremitting loyalty to the [doctrine] they represent?

If by "indoctrination" is meant the concept that has been outlined above, then to suggest that all schooling is indoctrination clearly misdescribes the general situation in liberal democracies.

Indeed, an observer who looks at the state-supported schools of liberal democratic societies will see that, unlike elsewhere in the world, in most cases it is usual for children to encounter ideas of a wide range of political, economic, moral, religious, and other possibilities. Children meet a range of subject matter, points of view, and methods, of a range of teachers. It would seem to be a not unreasonable generalization to claim that there is in most schools a deliberate attempt to get children to think for themselves. The cases of students affected in an indoctrinatory way by their teachers fortunately remain few. It can be said that most teachers, far from indoctrinating, would feel that they had failed if the schools did not produce critical persons who had cognitive perspective and rationality enough to see various faults in the social system.

Even if readers do not agree with all the substantive claims made here, they must at least concede that statements have various epistemological statuses, and that such differences in status should be brought out in appropriate ways. Where statements and claims are equivocal, children should be made fully aware of their debatable nature. To do anything less with equivocal material may not be to indoctrinate in the fullest sense, but it is certainly to step onto the slippery slope into it.

It rarely or never occurs to indoctrinators to say to themselves, "But what if I am wrong?"

INDOCTRINATION: KEY POINTS

In talking about indoctrination, I am talking about degrees of pressures and influences that result from the three interrelated factors of the teacher's intentions, the content of his teaching, and the methods he uses.

If teachers do teach, as true, claims that are equivocal, or if they fail to expose disputable status, then they are slipping into what may be called indoctrination, for their intentions have become suspect.

By putting particular viewpoints beyond challenge, there is an attempt to close minds rather than to open them.

The point about doctrines such as Marxism and Mormonism and Fascism and so on is that they consist of interrelated sets of statements, a number of which cannot be demonstrated to be unquestionably true. Statements of this sort cannot straightforwardly be shown to be unquestionably false either. Such statements yield no predictions that we can test in any simple sense of the word *test*. A situation or its opposite is equally acceptable to believers of such statements, for they interpret *all* situations in terms of the statement.

Believers note what they consider to be confirming instances of their doctrinal belief, and because they see the world in terms of their belief, of course they continually see what they take to be confirming instances and ignore what is manifest disconfirmation to others.

But a properly empirical claim must *rule out* at least some possible results. That which seeks to explain everything, explains nothing empirically.

There is often inconsistency and contradiction, selective use of evidence, overgeneralization, and the use of authority as a "stopper." It is also common for there to be a technical and esoteric vocabulary in which concepts are tightly interwoven, mutually reinforcing, self-validating, and circular.

"Get them young" is one aspect of much successful indoctrinatory method.

There have been simpleminded (or deliberately obfuscatory) claims that all schooling is indoctrination. Writers impoverish the English tongue when they use words so broadly. This leads to impoverishment of conceptual distinctions, which in turn makes it harder to draw essential epistemological discriminations and easier for the real indoctrinators to go about their vicious business of closing children's minds.

It rarely or never occurs to indoctrinators to say to themselves, "But what if I'm wrong?"

2.3 LEARNING

A. Learning and Content

We can talk about education or indoctrination only if persons are actually learning things. It is learning activities of various sorts that make education and indoctrination possible. So it is necessary now to consider the concept of *learning.*

Many interesting philosophical points can be made about learning (Hamlyn, 1967; Magee, 1971; Komisar and Macmillan, 1976). In this section I shall emphasize but one. Although it has been greatly neglected by educators, it is a feature of learning that is of fundamental importance. Let me begin by asking, Why is it that teachers do not make more use of the empirical findings of psychology and the social sciences in their daily teaching? Why is it that they concentrate as much on *what* they are teaching as on *how?* It cannot be that the whole profession is so obtuse as continually to pass up key tools.

Perhaps the explanation is this: Although psychology and the other social sciences can provide teachers with a set of useful suggestions on procedure and various large-scale theoretical generalizations about human behavior, it is still the case that the *what* (or *what do you mean*) questions remain the key to effective teaching and learning, and teachers in an implicit sort of way realize this. An alternative way of saying this is to claim that what pays greatest dividends in teaching is the *careful analysis by teachers of the content* of curricula; in other words, the conceptual issues.

In claiming that learning has occurred, we are claiming something about any relatively permanent change in mental state or overt physical behavior that is not the result of maturation or of artificial influences such as drugs. How best to bring such changes about is the challenge that faces teachers.

It cannot be said that just any mental change or change in behavior is learning, because some changes are derived simply from maturation of the human organism—changes of adolescence and old age are of this sort—and some changes are interesting combinations of maturation and learning,—for example, learning to walk (feral children do not learn to walk). And we cannot say that learning is just any *behavioral* change, for we sometimes learn things that have no effect on our behavior—that the moon continually shows approximately the same face to our earth, for instance. The result of learning is often that we just see the world differently: we now know something that we did not know, or have an altered sense of appreciation, or are now more sensitive than before we had learned the thing. Indeed, just seeing the world differently may well be the chief result of educational learning.

The initial point to make, and the one upon which all else of importance in this section hangs, is that people cannot be said to learn without learning *something: learning always has a content.* This is the crucial fact. We can categorize this content in various ways. For instance we can talk in terms of general species of learning. Thus we can learn a *concept* such as *mammal* or *camel;* a *language* such as French or Zuni; *factual knowledge* such as that the nodes of cells called the Islets of Langerhans release insulin into the blood, or that there are 100 thousand million stars in the Milky Way; *fictional information* about Daedalus constructing the labyrinth or Gradgrind beating the children at Dotheboys Hall; *beliefs* about Marxism or Mormonism; *a subject* such as topology or American history; *procedures* for solving quadratic equations or crossword puzzles; the *skills* of skiing or of writing on the blackboard; *habits* of covering one's mouth when coughing, or of counting to ten before acting when angry; *attitudes* toward a class of problem adolescents or one's mother-in-law; *dispositions* to be wary of strangers, or to treat children the same until there is a relevant reason for treating some differently; *appreciation* of "blue" jokes or classical music; the *values* of beauty, integrity or education. Such categories overlap and crisscross in all sorts of ways, of course. Alternatively, the content of learning may be seen as exemplifying different forms of knowledge (see 3.2D and 3.3D). Thus we can learn epistemologically different contents: that $4^2 = 16$; that Jupiter has fourteen moons; that we can often detect people's feelings through watching their reactions; to respect human beings as persons; to grasp the point of our seascapes and of other persons' seascapes; to believe in God and the Devil; to recognize that conceptual problems often lurk beneath ostensibly empirical questions.

There are other ways of categorizing the content of learning. Here I have provided but a short list of various examples of learning. Even they, however, should be sufficient to show how complex will be the questions about learning and how simpleminded it must be to believe that there can be just one theory of learning with a set of its own laws that can account for the tremendous diversity of learning accomplishments.[4] How persons learn and the best way of learning must surely be affected by what it is that they are learning; *the different contents make what is going on different.* Learning cannot be sensibly talked about in the absence of some notion of the general or particular content: if we asked someone what he was learning and he replied, "Oh nothing in particular—just learning," the answer would be more than strange, it would be nonsense. This point about the importance of content cannot be overstressed: *Learning is content-specific.*

Just as there is an infinite possible content to learning, so there are innumerable ways in which learning can take place. It can be by way of reading a comic, writing an essay, channeling emotional reaction, painting a picture, praying to God, making love, thinking about a problem, watching a craftsman, listening to a lecture, chanting arithmetical tables.[5] Persons learn by going to school, serving apprenticeships, attending night classes (formal arrangements for achieving some learning content); they also learn by watching television, walking in the park, talking over the breakfast table, playing football (informal ways of achieving some learning content).

But just which of the innumerable ways of learning is the appropriate way in a particular case will depend upon the case—that is,

[4]One of the most preposterous attempts to erect such a theory occurs in C. L. Hull's book *Principles of Behaviour,* where on the basis of certain primitive physiological happenings he hoped to be able eventually, as he says in his summary and conclusions (1943, p. 399), to explain such diverse phenomena as, ". . . the theory of skills and their acquisition; of communicational symbolism or language (semantics); of the use of symbolism in individual problem solution involving thought and reasoning; of social or ritualistic symbolism; of economic values and valuation; of moral values and valuation; of aesthetic values and valuation; of familial behaviour, individual adaptive efficiency (intelligence), the formal educative processes [sic], psychogenic disorders, social control and delinquency, character and personality, culture and acculturation, magic and religious practices, custom, law and jurisprudence, politics and government. . . ."
[5]Educationists who see learning as covered by a limited set of laws, tend to assimilate learning to this type. They see learning as a process rather than as an activity.

upon the content or sort of thing being learned—and the way will in general (and often even in detail) be determined by the case. In other words, the learning outcome being aimed at will dictate that the experiences must be generally so and so. It is at this point that so much pedagogical research has gone astray. Because it is *conceptually* possible to talk about content and experience (or content and method) of learning, many educationists imagine that we are dealing with two things rather than one. This leads them to put the content to one side and then look for the laws or theories that explain learning, as though the method of learning could be independent of the content. But this is a misconception. Even such well-established psychological suggestions as the importance of rest pauses, repetition, retroactive inhibition, and so on depend for their intelligent and precise application on the particular content that is being learned.

When children are learning something they are not doing two things, but one. They are learning-the-concept-*camel,* they are learning-to-ski, they are learning-Euclidean-geometry, they are learning-American-history, they are learning-to-perform-a-forward-roll-from-springboard-onto-vaulting-horse. When teachers and educationists think that there are two things rather than one, this also causes them to indulge in inane pedagogical research to find out such things as whether children learn equally as well in large classes as in small. But this is a nonsense question, because it is obvious that, other things being equal, children must learn better in small classes, and when other things are not equal, whether numbers make a difference depends upon what is being learned by the class. Consider the examples just mentioned.

To learn the concept *camel* epistemologically *must* involve certain ways of classifying and distinguishing one sort of animal from another. A child has learned the concept when he can distinguish camels from horses and other large four-footed animals, when he comes to associate camels with deserts and the storage of fat in their humps, and so on. Such learning can only come through particular experiences that put the child in the way of such distinctions: pictures of camels are perused, visits to zoos are made, the anatomy of camels is discussed, the way of life of desert peoples is told to him or read about.

In learning to ski, actual practice at coordination of various bodily movements will be necessary. In the final analysis, persons learn to ski by skiing. Visits to ski slopes will be required, not visits to zoos, while all the stories in the world about Jean Claude Killy will not help *in* skiing (though these may help to interest persons in it). And the various skills will be gained in practice *on the slopes.* But it is doubtful if such skills can be acquired to a high degree of precision by bald practice alone, without some understanding of the issues and the theory involved—that is, intelligent practice is required, practice informed by theory.

If someone is learning Euclidean geometry, it should be obvious that it is not enough for him to be able merely to reproduce the theorems correctly—learning *geometry* is not just reproducing theorems. If a child has a retentive memory, of course he can duplicate the proofs, but this is insufficient for purposes of learning geometry, he must also be able to understand how the parts of the proofs and the various theorems relate one to another, and how the truth of the theorem is applicable in other theoretical and practical situations. In short, if there is to be the learning of Euclidean geometry, such learning has also to be education.

To learn a humane subject will be different again. Learning a subject such as American history is not just learning a set of true propositions, though it is this also, for there is debate about just which propositions are true: Does the conspiracy theory, the conflict theory, or the revisionist theory best explain the occurrence of the American Civil War? (Dray, 1964, p. 47) A subject is a *how* and *why* affair; there are methods to be mastered, points of view to be acquired, principles to be understood, a particular way of looking at and of trying to solve problems; and there are concepts to be acquired: We do not understand a subject unless we have mastered its concepts. Furthermore, there will be an intimate connection between concepts, principles, true statements, individual cases, and bits of information.

To learn to forward roll from a springboard onto a vaulting horse must involve the learning of subskills such as running up, taking off, placing the hands in a special position on the horse, acquiring a specific back and head posture, and perfecting a position for dismount. These subskills are logically necessary components of the completed skill. It may be that some of these subskills can be learned in any order, but others must follow one another in a logically necessary sequence. It is not just that the final complex skill must involve all the subskills, it is also that the complex skill must involve them in a particular order.

Thus, the sort of achievement that the content of the learning marks out will determine the general form of the learning procedures to be adopted, And the detailed nature of the content of such learning is a philosophical issue rather than an empirical one—it is decided by sitting and thinking, not by going and testing. But, although a philosophical analysis may be able to provide a general outline of what is required, it is not being suggested that philosophers can do all the detailed outlining of content. This may be fully obtainable only from zoologists and Afghan camel drivers, from ski instructors and the author of *Teach Yourself to Ski,* from the high school geometer and the surveyor, from the mildly eccentric local historian and the college lecturer in history, from the gymnast and the specialist in physical education. Nevertheless, such detailed outlining is most definitely *not a matter for empirical research* of the psychological or any other variety, and scientists will certainly be unable to provide it. This seems to be a reason why curriculum planning has to be a team effort. It is of extreme importance to understand this conceptual link between what is to be learned and how to learn it, the complex necessary nature of the relationship, and how to start to demarcate the conceptual base, for this demarcation is one of the key things teachers have to do if they are to get children to learn successfully.

This demarcation will also involve the specifying of what the learner must already understand if the new content is to be meaningfully learned. For there is a crucial link between the content the pupils or students already know and the content they are to know. It is because of this link that things are learned more rapidly and with greater comprehension, when teachers show what it is in the new content which relates to the old, in other words, when teachers *explain.*

At one level of consideration it is merely a truism to say that if a child is to learn to think mathematically, say, or democratically, then he must be exposed to mathematics and to democratic procedures. But because this is a truism, people tend to think that this is all there is to the conceptual implications. They see in an implicit kind of way that the conceptual truth points to an empirical truth and imagine that therefore all the further features that require attention in the learning situation will be of the psychological or generally empirical sort. This is not the case.

Education for democracy will now be considered as a more detailed example of the importance of thinking carefully about content.

B. An Example of Conceptual Implications: Learning and Democracy

To educate for democracy we obviously need to give experience of democracy. That seems uncontroversial enough. But unless we are very careful, at this point all sorts of questions will be begged, for what count as *knowledge* and *experience* of democracy, and what concept of *democracy* are we working with? Even within liberal democratic societies there are different concepts of democracy—

some people stress majority votes while others stress consideration of minority interests; some stress freedom, others stress equality. Again, does all knowledge and experience of democracy have to be acquired in a democratic fashion? Or is a large amount of vicarious experience possible and profitable? I believe that this last is true. Thus, the sentence "I'll force these children to act democratically" is not as self-contradictory as it at first appears. Indeed, here we have touched on what may be called the paradox of democracy; namely, that the democratic behavior of individual persons can only develop out of initial authority-based rules and controls. This is a subset of the paradox of all moral education that too many parents and teachers fail to comprehend, the paradox that if children are to develop rational morality, they have to pass through stages in which they are "moral" for the wrong reasons—that is, in which their morality is external (Peters, 1963).

The extensive researches of Lawrence Kohlberg in various parts of the world (the United States, Mexico, Taiwan, Turkey) claim to show several stages in which general moral development takes place. In a study of 75 American boys, for example, Kohlberg (1970, p. 39) argues that the motive for obedience to rules and ostensible moral action passed through the following six stages:

1. conformity in order to avoid punishment
2. conformity, to obtain rewards, have favors returned
3. conformity, to avoid dislike, disapproval
4. conformity, to avoid censure by appropriate authorities and the resulting feeling of guilt
5. conformity, to maintain the respect of the impartial spectator who judges actions in relation to the welfare of the community
6. conformity, in order to avoid self-condemnation.[6]

And with the same group of boys, views about the value of human life developed through stages in this way:

1. as equated with the value of things
2. as instrumental to the satisfaction of needs and wants
3. as based upon the empathy and affection of family members and associates towards the possessor
4. as sacred in some categorical order of rights and duties
5. as related to community welfare and human rights
6. as a universal individuality and respect for persons.

[6]This is not the same as a feeling of guilt. It is a cognitive awareness of the possibility of infringing rational intellectual principles.

Kohlberg found that development was forward, did not skip stages, but proceeded at various and varying speeds. An individual human being might stop at any stage and at any age, but if he continued to develop his personhood, then he would move in accordance with the stages. In Kohlberg's researches, moral reasoning of the conventional stage 3 or stage 4 sort did not occur prior to the preconventional thought of stages 1 and 2. No adult within stage 4 had passed through stage 6, but all stage 6 persons had gone through stage 4. His major uncertainty was whether all persons at stage 6 actually passed through stage 5, or whether these were two alternative mature orientations.

Now, although Kohlberg's research is in its own way quite fascinating, we do not have to be research psychologists doing empirical field work in order to see that a sequence of *development* could hardly be otherwise, that *something like* a passage through these stages is *conceptually necessary* (although we do need empirical evidence to show that people may regress, or that people may use one stage of thought with one problem and an alternative stage of thought with another, or that people use reasoning that is a blend of stages). How else could children derive an educated and rational notion of moral action and value except from an initial exposure to various developing and gradually more complex ways of viewing situations: as (1) an egoistic confusion of persons and things, orientated to punishment, and confounded by a-rational impulses and aversions, then (2) as a more generalized expediency of want-based reactions involving close associates, then (3) as a more intellectualized and prudentialized approval-based version of this, then (4) broadening into a more widespread but still externally based authority situation, then (5) as a way of viewing social organizations as consensus based, negotiable, and changeable, or (6) as an arguably more refined version of (5) relating to consent, autonomy, reciprocity, and universalizability among rational beings. The levels are progressively more conceptually complex and depend upon an earlier *conceptualizing,* acting and experiencing in situations in terms of less sophisticated notions. And if education is concerned with increasing rationality and cognitive perspective and thus with the ability to make finer distinctions and discriminations, then the later stages exhibit a fuller education in morality, for in them morality is distinguished from custom, prudence, and external authority, a discrimination not conceptually possible in the early stages.

What has gone on in this sequence of development can be seen in simple terms as the interaction of a classifying and experiencing mind with various possibilities in the environment in which the human being is placed. In cultures in which the later stages are not exemplified by some sections of the community, only the occasional genius who is able to make fundamental conceptual leaps by himself will reach the later stages.

There are two reasons for having mentioned Kohlberg's ideas at this point. The first is to provide an example of the unsuspected conceptual content that lurks underneath what is assumed by researchers to be an empirical problem. The second reason is to argue that because a democratic outlook is so closely associated with a general moral outlook and with mature attitudes to rule-following and to regarding other persons as equals, then our present concern, the democratic outlook, will itself also logically have to be developed through stages of the Kohlberg sort. The final stage of universal respect for the equal rights of others—with its complex interrelationships of such moral principles as freedom, respect for persons, persuasion rather than force, toleration, and so forth that characterize the mature democratic outlook conceptually cannot itself be reached prior to concepts and experiences of human regulation in less idealistic terms. But, once again, we do not have to be psychologists to know this; all we need to do is to think carefully about the nature of democracy and the order of conceptually necessary components that would have to be experienced before such an outlook could ever become part of a person's way of seeing the world. Provided that we have clear heads about the outcome we are aiming at, then the outcome we are aiming at will dictate that experiences and knowledge encountered must be such and such at various stages and in a particular order in development. This is why it was said, a few paragraphs ago, that if children are to become moral, they have to pass through stages in which they are "moral" for the wrong reasons.

And as with the examples of the concept *camel,* the skill of skiing, Euclidean geometry, the subject American history, and the forward roll, the details of the experiences and knowledge to be encountered, if there is to be a development of a democratic outlook, have to be *worked out* in a coordinated endeavor by various sorts of people—class teachers, specialists in disciplines, educational and social philosophers, curriculum theorists, psychologists, and so on.

Now, it is of general use, of course, for teachers to know at what ages children typically view the world at the various levels, for they can then adjust their learning situations accordingly. This is where the psychologist can do useful work to help teachers. Researchers such as Kohlberg, and Piaget (1932) in Europe, and Collis (1981) in Australia have done this sort of thing, but it is important to keep their contribution in proper proportion: they provide teachers with quite general age–stage ranges that can be kept in mind as general parameters within which to approach the content that teachers decide upon.

So, in order to know how best to teach for democracy, teachers need to analyze carefully what counts as democratic practice—what they are trying to pass on or develop as learning. They need to be aware of the experiences that children have already had and the approximate stages at which children are likely to be seeing things in which terms, so that they can then provide both experience of the sort appropriate to the stage and also experience of a higher order. Both a philosophical analysis and some general psychological knowledge will be necessary, but the usefulness of the psychology will depend upon the prior conceptual thought and analysis, because learning to be democratic consists in a series of actual achievements that themselves *constitute* democratic understanding and practice. The point of this whole example of the teaching of democracy is that what is fundamental to proper progress is a thorough conceptual analysis. Key features of democratic knowledge and practice are conceptually necessary and follow logically.

Although it is a conceptual truth that only the person himself can do his learning, this does not mean that the teacher has to stand and wait for the learning to occur or for the child to discover the material for himself. The teacher can do all sorts of things to help. After becoming clear about the content to be learned, the teacher can demonstrate, cajole, question, comfort, indicate, hint, feign doubt, and so on. All such actions may help the child to see what is involved, to recognize the concepts and standards immanent in and which constitute the content of the learning. Such actions by the teacher we call teaching. Teaching is the set of actions indulged in by a person who intends by them to bring about learning. And the most economical learning of X is achieved through soundly prepared and appropriately adjusted teaching by those who have already learned X. This is why all advanced societies from Omaha to Omsk deliberately set up schools as formal institutions in which teaching may be achieved (see 4.5).

Thus nothing follows from the conceptual truth that only the students themselves can do their learning to the belief that teachers have to be benevolent child-minders or mere "facilitators"—this latter idea is a most mischievous child-centered fallacy. It is a real irony that indoctrinators recognize this fallacy rather better than some other teachers. But the teacher does have to *know what it is* (what

counts as) learning history, the concept "camel," or being democratic. In short, the teacher has to know the content.

C. Learning and Education

It should be clear that not just any relatively permanent change in
mental state or overt physical behavior that is not the result of maturation or of artificial influences will count as education, or educational learning. For although all education consists in learning, not
all learning is education. Some learning is merely trivial, such as how
to stand on one leg, some learning is just false and misleading, some
learning is indoctrinatory, some learning is conditioning, some learning is training in particular skills, and so on; but the learning that
counts as education is that very special kind of change that is exemplified by a broadened cognitive perspective and an increased rationality. It is because we are dealing with human beings, that analysis
of content becomes important. Human beings come to *understand*
what is learned, and they apply it in new situations. In human learning the matter can be controlled by the person; in animal learning,
the matter controls the animal.

In the section on educational growth in the next chapter, the
importance of society and of the various forms of knowledge are
considered, and in the section on art some detailed suggestions about
educational learning in a particular but neglected form of knowledge
are provided. Chapter 4 describes contexts of control in which it is
argued that education can best flourish: rule-governed situations that
allow for a gradual relaxation of external controls as children come
to master both themselves and the disciplines and forms of knowledge. In all these places, important things are said about the sort of
learning that will be education.

One further point requires making here. It is that the gaining of
an education must involve long periods of serious, sustained, and
systematic learning in the presence of persons who are themselves
educated, using the artifacts that educated persons have produced—
textbooks, television, laboratories, galleries, classic novels, and the
like. From the persons and the artifacts will come the interrelated
learning contents that involve the mastery of conceptual schemes
that can develop and improve and that make the education of children a reality. Judiciously mixed with such artifacts will be experience and encounter with the things of the "natural" world, but this
latter can never be a sufficient condition of education. And unless the
achievement of education is to be a very hit-and-miss affair, teachers
need to be not only educated persons themselves, but also knowledge authorities on their subject matter.

LEARNING: KEY POINTS

In claiming that learning has occurred, we are claiming something about any relatively permanent change in mental state or overt physical behavior that is not the result of maturation or of artificial influences such as drugs.

How persons learn and the best way of learning must surely be affected by what it is that they are learning: the different contents make what is going on different. *Learning is content-specific.*

It is the *careful analysis of the content* of curricula that pays greatest dividends—in other words, attention to the conceptual issues.

So the sort of achievement that the content of learning is will determine the general form of the learning procedures to be adopted. Such aspects of learning are largely philosophical issues, not empirical ones, and they are decided by sitting and thinking and careful analysis, not by going and testing.

The teacher does have to know what it is (what constitutes) to learn history or the concept *camel,* or to be democratic.

Because it is conceptually possible to talk about content and experience (or content and method) of learning, many educationists imagine that we are dealing with two things rather than one. This leads them to put the content on one side and then to look for the laws or theories that explain learning, as though the method of learning could be independent of the content. This is a misconception.

When children are learning something, they are not doing two things, but one, they are learning-to-ski, they are learning-American-history. When teachers and educationists think that there are two things rather than one, this causes them to indulge in inane pedagogical research, to find out such things as whether children learn equally as well in large classes as in small. But this is a nonsense question, because it all depends upon what is being learned.

Provided that we have clear heads about the outcome we are aiming at, then the outcome we are aiming at will dictate that experiences and knowledge encountered must be such and such at various stages in the development.

It is because we are dealing with human beings, that analysis of content becomes important. Human beings come to *understand* what is learned, and they apply it in new situations.

Chapter 3
Curriculum

3.1 NEEDS AND INTERESTS

A. What Are Needs?

One of the more persistent pieces of advice that teachers receive from educational theorists and administrators is that they should try to meet children's needs. Just what are teachers to make of this suggestion, and how valuable for them is it?

It will be best to begin with a close look at the meaning of the word *need*, for the answers to the questions just posed will hinge upon the meaning. Here are some typical *needs* statements:

To read this section, you need time.
If someone is to play poker, a pack of cards is a need.
To be a wife, a woman needs a husband.
If a person is to be good at sport, he will need hard training.
A drowning man needs help if he is to survive.

Children need a certain amount of independence in order to develop properly.[1]

The point to be noticed about such statements is that in their various ways they show that these needs are all really requirements for something else, or, in other words, prerequisites (Wilson, 1971, p. 6). It always makes sense for an observer to retort *Why?* to someone's claimed need. And why should the observer agree to the point or value of the things that the stated needs are prerequisites for? Answers to such questions are going to be all-important. Even when a needs statement involves not so much a prerequisite as someone's intrinsic value (e.g., I need to go fishing), questions can still be asked.

The little boy next door may say that the yellow flowers drooping in the hot sun at the front of my house need watering. I may say that what they need is a dose of MAA or MCPA weedkiller because they are daisies. So "The decision to water or to apply weedkiller depends on prior value judgments about the desirability of daisies on lawn." (Wilson, 1971, p. 6) Now it is at least conceivable that there exists a rational race somewhere out near Betelgeues, Beta Capricorni, or Barnard's Star that thinks that yellow flowers, wherever they be, should be allowed to multiply ("After all, who wants that awful green stuff!") and they would then agree with the little boy that the yellow flowers need water. But it so happens that in liberal Western democracies the culture is such that most persons think that such a viewpoint is crazy. Again, a class teacher may say, "Johnny needs love and care," but the school principal may say, "What Johnny needs is a good, hard talking-to." Thus, until two persons agree in their conceptualization of a situation, there is no chance of their agreeing about what the needs are in that situation. Agreement about needs depends upon agreement in views, values, and objectives.

It is therefore important to look carefully at statements of needs, to see what values are hidden in them, for it is with the values that the crucial issues lie. So I think it is true to say that all needs statements have a value aspect, or that needs statements involve instrumental or intrinsic values in disguise. Thus needs are either prerequisites for something else, and it is the something else that we value, or else they are disguised ways of referring to a thing or activity that we value intrinsically. Shakespeare points to this fact in a poignant passage in *King Lear* (Act II, Scene IV),

> GONERIL: Hear me my Lord; What need you five and twenty [retainers]? Ten? Or five? To follow in a house, where twice so many Have a command to tend you?

---

[1] Needs statements have the same import when put in either a noun or a verb form.

REGAN: What need one?

LEAR: O! Reason not the need; our basest beggars Are in the poorest thing superfluous.

Thus the concept of a need logically implies some norm, objective, assumption, or value. In a sense, needs statements *beg the question* of what is important.

Consider the following statement from an influential paper put out a national schools commission (1979, p. 13):

> Schools will benefit most from a system of school organization that allows a teacher to get to know the individual students so that he can be responsive to individual needs. The Commission can see value in modifying recruitment and training policies so that more teachers particularly at the lower secondary level are capable of performing the "generalized" teacher role.

But if "generalized" is being used as a contrast to "specialized," then whether the generalized teacher role is in fact a need of children at that level is, I think, highly debatable. Indeed, in order for us to agree that something is a need we have to agree about the desirability of the objective, assumption, norm, or value that it involves or is a prerequisite for. This is even so with such seemingly basic needs as those for food and water. For the protester in prison on a hunger strike neither wants nor (from his point of view) needs food. In contrast, the sufferer from anorexia does not want food but does need it.

It should be noticed that there are several epistemologically different components to the concept of *need:* empirical components and a moral component. When the several components are confused, it is easy for people to misinterpret the function of needs statements. For instance, to say that Johnny needs food is to say,

1. Johnny does not have food (empirical claim).
2. Food will change Johnny's state (empirical prediction).
3. It is desirable that Johnny's state be changed in this way (moral judgment).

So to say that Johnny needs food is therefore to say several different things at the same time, two of which are uncontroversial, one of which may be controversial. Thus, as was indicated in Chapter 1, empirical knowledge and conceptual clarity although crucial, are not enough, because all kinds of needs claims already presuppose a commitment to particular moral values, which themselves should be made clear and debated.

B. Needs and Education

Well, a reader may say, All this may be true with respect to general statements of needs, but what about needs statements in the school context? After all, books and articles on schooling often make statements concerning children's needs, such as the one above from the schools commission, or another from the same source, "Preservice training . . . should . . . be concerned with ensuring that trainees are able to adapt themselves and their teaching to the needs of pupils. . . ." (ibid., p. 15) Such statements seem to be implying that provided a teacher can find out what a pupil's needs are, and then try to meet these needs, he will be on the right track. But as Gribble has pointed out (1969, p. 82), the first problem is that there is a great variety of needs statements to be found in books and articles about schooling. Following his approach, let us consider but a few such lists.

In various texts we find Maslow's six:

1. physiological needs such as food and water
2. safety needs such as protection from harm and injury
3. needs for love and belongingness
4. esteem needs, such as self-respect and social approval
5. need for self-actualization in the sense of developing one's potentialities to their limit
6. need to know and understand.

In *Psychology for Effective Teaching*, a work set by the psychologists as a textbook at my own college, Mouly (1972, pp. 66–72) provides the following (what he calls "partial") list. Need for:

7. food
8. water
9. sleep and rest
10. activity

11. sex
12. affection
13. belonging
14. achievement
15. independence
16. social recognition
17. self-esteem.

Jahoda's list (in Peters, 1964, p. 76) is:

18. self-awareness and self-acceptance
19. growth and self actualization
20. integration
21. autonomy
22. perception of reality
23. environmental mastery.

Another well-known list is that of Murray (1938) who among some fifty *(sic)* of his "psychogenic" needs, places these (quoted by Hilgard and others, 1971, p. 316):

24. acquisition: the need to gain possessions and property
25. conservation: the need to collect, repair, clean, and preserve things
26. orderliness: the need to arrange, organize, put away objects; to be tidy and clean; to be precise
27. retention: the need to retain possession of things; to hoard; to be frugal, economical, and miserly
28. construction: the need to organize and build
29. superiority: the need to excel, a composite of achievement and recognition
30. achievement: the need to overcome obstacles; to exercise power; to strive to do something difficult as well and as quickly as possible
31. recognition: the need to excite praise and commendation; to command respect
32. exhibition: the need for self-dramatization; to excite, amuse, stir, shock, thrill others
33. inviolacy: the need to remain inviolate; to prevent a depreciation of self-respect; to preserve one's "good name"
34. avoidance of inferiority: the need to avoid failure, shame, humiliation, ridicule
35. autonomy: the need to resist influence; to strive for independence
36. contrariness: the need to act differently from others; to be unique; to take the opposite side

37. play: the need to relax, amuse oneself, seek diversion and entertainment
38. cognizance: the need to explore, ask questions, satisfy curiosity
39. exposition: the need to point and demonstrate; to give information, explain, interpret, lecture.

Further textbooks advocate further needs. A teacher can read three or four different texts and be faced with the puzzle of what to do with such a plethora of needs proposals. There appear to be two ways of overcoming this problem (Gribble, 1969, p. 82). The first is to suggest that a list of forty or fifty needs can on closer examination be reduced to a relatively manageable number, because they actually overlap or coincide. There is something in this suggestion—for example, 1 and 7-8 seem the same; 3 and 12-13 are the same, as are 5 and 19; 4 and 16-17 and 31 are similar, as are 15 and 35. But even if we do this, the list can still be long and there is still the issue of value judgments. The second way out is to say, "No we do not have to satisfy all these so-called needs; all we have to do is to satisfy some of them." But, of course, to say this again merely puts the issue back on stage, for it is the same as saying that there must be some *other* criterion by which we are to choose which needs are to be met, which needs are needed! Statements of needs are not sufficient in themselves, so we must look behind the statements of needs to the instrumental or intrinsic values underlying them (Dearden, 1968, p. 16) in order to gain a proper understanding of the statements. It is no good pretending that teachers can sidestep the value judgments that they have to make, or that they are forced to accept from superiors and educationists, on behalf of their pupils and students.

But for the purposes of this book, there is a further and crucial issue to be considered with respect to these lists of needs. Consider the ones from Mouly. His list comes from a book called *Psychology for Effective Teaching.* The needs listed are therefore supposed to be needs that if met will help persons to teach and educate their children more effectively. Now, as suggested at the beginning of this discussion, needs are either prerequisites for something else, and it is the something else that is being valued, or they are disguised ways of referring to a thing or activity that is valued intrinsically. Presumably the needs listed by Mouly are supposed to be prerequisites for helping to meet or for achieving teaching and educational values and objectives, for that is why they are discussed in a pedagogical textbook. When fulfilled, such needs are supposed to help in achieving or even to achieve teaching and education. But *are* they prerequisites for achieving teaching and reaching educational values and objectives, or in meeting them do teachers either find help for achieving or actually achieve teaching and education?

Suppose all food, water, sleep, and rest needs are met, how does this help teachers to *teach* and *educate?* Suppose children's sex needs are met (whatever that means), have teachers *in meeting* such needs been helped to teach and to educate them? Suppose children receive affection from their teachers and begin to feel affection for their teachers and a sense of belonging, is *the meeting* of these needs helping to achieve or actually achieving teaching and education? Are the achieving of social recognition and self-esteem *ways of* getting children to be taught and educated? My own reply to all these questions is in general either, "No," or, "Not much." Of course, teachers may thereby be helping to give children particular prerequisites for mental stability and mental health, but these have little to do with the actual provision of teaching and education or the actual achievement of learning.

It may be, however, that in meeting needs for achievement and independence teachers will at least have to do things *connected* with teaching and education, because we can foster achievement by way of an educational program, and if teachers actually do help children to become independent in a truly autonomous sense, they will in doing so have to have helped them to become educated. Again, in meeting a need for (physical) activity, especially with younger children, there will be possibilities for actual teaching and perhaps education to occur. But generally these lists of supposed needs seem *in themselves* shallow in their help for those who want to learn something about teaching and education.

Furthermore, various psychologists may wish to argue that their lists (or similar lists) of items are indeed needs of children, and I will agree with most of their values and with much of what they have to say. It is noticeable, for instance, that some good sense in our relationships with children can come from the sort of hierarchy of needs that Maslow describes, but I still wonder about how much such needs have to do with the activities of teaching and education.

However, it is probably true to say that psychologists and professional advisors of teachers introduced needs talk because they felt that identification of needs would positively help teachers in their teaching and educating. And I do think that they have been of some help to teachers, but not much help in the way of teaching and educating! For if what I have been saying is true, then these so-called needs, while valuable in their own way, are mostly merely prerequisites for getting children into an appropriate physiological and psychological state *from which teachers can then start* to teach and educate them.

The only exceptions to this last point are those listed needs that are actually alternative ways of talking about the *need for education,* though I doubt whether the compilers of such needs lists usually recognize this point. By this I mean that such listed needs as "achievement" and "independence" (Mouly), "achievement," "construction," "autonomy," and "cognizance" (Murray), and "self-actualization" and "to know and understand" (Maslow) are themselves largely *redescriptions* of educational achievements: they are really tautologous ways of saying that children need education! And such claimed needs as "social recognition" and "self-esteem" may or may not be redescriptions of particular educational achievements, depending upon the content of what is recognized by others or esteemed by oneself. So what these lists of needs actually offer are general physiological and psychological *prerequisites* to teaching and education on the one hand, and *alternative ways of describing* education, on the other.

I argue that the greatest of children's needs that teachers should concern themselves with is indeed the *need for education,* but this should be said straight-out, not as a roundabout tautology. The point is that much of the textbook literature that discusses children's needs skirts around the actually important issue. It either discusses supposed needs that although important in their own right, are more the concern of other people such as the parent, the psychologist, and the social worker (and that, even when they become the concern of the teacher, have little to do with teaching and education), or it dresses up the need for education in a misleading way. In a sense, the common needs literature is putting things the wrong way around. It is listing needs (usually quite justifiable ones) and saying that meeting these will help the teacher to do his job. Whereas the situation is more realistically and accurately described in terms of, first, the need for education—a need that can be established by moral arguments to do with respect for persons (4.1C), with the duty of parents and society and the rights of children (4.4E), and with the general requirements and values of a liberal-democratic society—and then seeing what can be done to meet this need for education. Of course, there will then be "subneeds" that are prerequisites having to do with how teaching and education are to be achieved, and it is here that empirical practitioners such as psychologists and sociologists may do useful work in diagnosing the best ways of actually achieving the teaching and education. But it is misleading to believe that teachers can gain much pedagogical guidance from statements about needs prior to thinking carefully about just what is to count as education.

What thus seems crucially to be missing in all this talk about needs and education is a clear concept of education. This is where the concern should be focused, not on supposed general needs. The concept of education described in Chapter 2 is that education is concerned with intrinsically valuable activities that broaden and deepen people's understanding of the world and increase their rationality. Just what particular activities will count in this way is, naturally, the subject of further debate. (Some suggestions about these are made in Section 3.2D.) And if a reader disagrees with the view that it is the need for education that is paramount, I shall answer that he is doing one of two things: Either the reader is making this section's more fundamental point very well—for he is demonstrating implicitly that it is the values that underpin needs statements that require looking at, as was argued at the beginning; or he is showing that he is not actually considering the point of this whole section—namely, the connection between needs talk and education and teaching—he is showing that his thinking has drifted on to views of what is of value in life in general.

In the terms of the various components of needs statements that were described earlier, we have a situation that can be described in something like the following way:

1. Johnny does not have education.
2. Education will change his condition.
3. It is morally desirable that his condition be changed in this way.

In more detail this becomes:

1. Johnny has not passed through a series of learning experiences that have intrinsic value and that broaden and deepen his understanding of life and make him more rational.
2. Such learning experiences will turn him into a person who can make up his own mind about things, is adaptable, can bring his learning to bear on new situations, is tolerant, open-minded, and so on.
3. It is morally desirable that he become this sort of person.

This is actually the core of real significance that can be teased out of all the various lists of needs that teachers are subjected to.

C. Needs and Motivation

It was said earlier that many books on schooling seem to imply that provided a teacher can find out what a pupil's needs are, he will be on the right track as a teacher and educator. This belief has often been taken to mean that the satisfaction of such needs will help to *motivate* children to engage in learning activities—that is, meeting pupils' and students' needs will get them going. But this idea is misconceived. As Gribble (1969, p. 85) points out, there are numerous children who are well looked after (whose physiological and psychological needs are satisfied) who show scant interest in learning, while on the other hand neglected children may show extreme interest. Of course, this is not to claim that this always happens, it merely points to the fallacy of tightly connecting needs satisfaction with motivation. The fact that children whose physiological and psychological needs are met may not show any desire for learning indicates that fulfillment of needs is not a *sufficient* condition for motivation. The fact that children whose physiological and psychological needs may not be met may show desire for learning, illustrates that fulfillment of such needs is not a *necessary* condition for motivation. It is because this is true that the Chinese aphorism "sandals to sandals in three generations" or its American variant, "three generations from shirtsleeves to shirtsleeves," can be a correct empirical generalization about the fortunes of some families in this world.

It is not being denied that severe physiological and psychological need deprivation may well lead to ineducability, but even then, as Gribble (ibid.) says it is not clear why this should be thought to be a matter of motivation in *education*. It is rather the case that it is also true that such a claim is somewhat equivocal or presumptive. In actual fact—as for instance Dearden (1972, p. 56) and Gribble (ibid.) indicate, the only way in which a teacher can with reasonable certainty connect actual satisfaction of the commonly listed needs and actual motivation to do schoolwork is to do exactly the opposite of what is often advocated in the needs literature: it is to make the satisfying of the needs depend upon the children's *first* achieving the learning—that is, don't let the children go out to play, don't let them have any food or water until they get the work completed! I recall this kind of thing occurring occasionally in my own schooldays, but it will generally be considered to be an immoral and inefficient way of achieving learning today. A further irony is that those who have argued that meeting needs will motivate children see this as being a variety of intrinsic motivation, whereas the points just made show that the only foolproof way of connecting needs and motivation occurs as an extrinsic feature of the learning situation.

Perhaps the equivocal or presumptive nature of the claim that meeting physiological and psychological needs will motivate derives from the following situation, for at first glance it looks plausible. It looks plausible because of the inherent ambiguity in the word *need*. The person who makes such a claim unknowingly confuses two quite different categories of need. He mixes up fundamental physiological and psychological needs, such as the need for food and the need for companionship, with the logically quite different need for education. Now, giving food to a hungry child will usually be enough to motivate him to eat it, and when a lonely child encounters a new playmate he will usually be motivated to play with him; but though it can be said that an illiterate child needs to learn to read and an ignorant child needs broadening, the provision of appropriate educational fare may or may not motivate. What is more, such fare may still not motivate even when these are *felt* needs—that is, even when children recognize such needs. In the history of ideas many apparently plausible cases have been established by using ambiguous terms.

D. Needs and Wants

Some of the difficulties in beliefs about needs and education arise because people are unwittingly confusing needs and wants, for of course wants are usually motivating. But to imagine that if someone finds that a child wants something then this is also one of the child's needs, or because the child needs something then the child will also want it, seems rather bizarre. Only people who have not done their conceptual homework can make this kind of conflation. The kind of confusion between needs and wants can be laid to rest by taking an extreme case (Dearden, 1972). Johnny may want to pull the legs off live frogs or to hang the cat, and given half a chance his want may be motivational! But what he *needs* is more likely to be a belting from dad, or psychiatric treatment. Happily for teachers, needs and wants sometimes coincide, as in a situation in which a child needs to learn to read, wants to learn to read, and enjoys the method the teacher uses. In such a situation there is motivation, but not because the need as such is motivational.

To say that a person *wants* something is merely to describe his state of mind; to say that a person *needs* something is to claim that he will not reach *an agreed norm or standard or value or objective* until he gets it (Benn & Peters, 1959, p. 165). Wants only become needs when there is agreement that something further should be reached or met, or when there is agreement on the intrinsic value in a particular needs claim.

So it seems to me that most of the needs literature that teachers are forced to suffer is confused and confusing. Instead of concentrating on the key problem of getting clear about education, many educationists who write about needs lead teachers into a world of pseudosophistication about the issues.

E. Needs Debate

Philosophical analysis appears to some persons to be too often merely critical of what other educationists, researchers, and thinkers have established. Certainly one function of philosophy is criticism, but it is criticism with the purpose of clarifying concepts, issues, arguments, and theories, and thus rejecting suggestions that are confused and misleading and indeed deserve rejection. When such a procedure has occurred in talk about schooling, we can be more certain that what is left is worth bothering with. The residue that is left after philosophical criticism will also point the way to what to do next and what to take action upon. In the present instance, the consideration of the relationship between needs and education has shown that most needs statements are either pedagogically misleading, question-begging, or merely superficial ways of getting a consensus in pedagogical talk. It has also exposed the crucial point that the various social sciences are of most use in needs talk when we are deciding on means to meet agreed-upon needs, not in specifying what the needs are with which teachers should concern themselves.

What we have to do to approach schooling in the most rational manner is first to engage in vigorous and *openminded debate about needs* (with changing circumstances, this will be a continuing debate), and only second to seek scientific and social scientific help. These latter disciplines will be of help either in providing guidance about physiological and psychological prerequisites, or in making suggestions about methods of teaching and learning. Vigorous and openminded debate will often revolve around the principle of respect for persons (see 4.1). Education is a need of persons, and, given that persons function in a particular society, training and socialization may also be needs.

F. Interests—Psychological and Normative

It is often claimed that interests are important in pedagogy, but in what way are they important? Well, any teacher who has his wits about him must realize that reference to needs is unhelpful in pedagogical planning prior to further debate, and I should wish to argue that unfortunately this lack of precision in people's concepts of *need* is repeated in their concepts of *interest* (which is perhaps why the two terms seem to go so well together in the often-heard slogan "to meet children's needs and interests").

But my concern at the moment is with interests, and if we are to get anywhere at all, it must be pointed out that just as there is a distinction (usually unacknowledged) between stated needs and objectively agreed and assessed needs, so we get a distinction between two meanings of *interest*. First there is, of course, a psychological use, and second there is a normative or value use. Psychologically, the word *interests* carries the idea of "what I like to do or take notice of" —that is, *felt* interests. Here interest is being contrasted with *un*-interest (not *dis*interest) or boredom. Evaluatively, the word means "that which is for a person's good," "that which is *in* his interests." Psychological interests may themselves be usefully divided into oc-current interests and dispositional interests. Occurrent psychological interests are those in which persons are actually interested at a par-ticular moment. Dispositional interests are continual and are those in which persons are predisposed to show an interest in the appropri-ate circumstances (White, 1967, p. 82). For instance, many persons have a dispositional interest in a hobby or a sport, but their interest in the evanescent items of the news media is only occurrent.

Teachers are often exhorted to begin from children's (psycholog-ical) interests. But why, it may be asked, should it be thought that children's present psychological interests are fit bases for *educational* beginnings, that is, fit bases for what is in their interests? In the situation being discussed here, something like this is being said: The children are interested in X, Y, and Z, therefore we ought to let them pursue X, Y, and Z in school. But teachers cannot know whether they are fit bases and have proper educational possibilities prior to explor-ing just what they are. The chief danger in beginning from children's interests is made clear by substituting arguably undesirable things for X, Y, and Z. For instance, the children are interested in bullying younger children, sailing boats in the toilet, and drawing penises and female pudenda on the illustrations in the school geography books. Indeed, for both moral and educational reasons, many of children's interests must be ignored by the teacher. If psychological interests were all that were in children's interests in schools, much of the time schools would be reduced to mere places of entertainment, or places of mere play.

G. Interests and Education

In the previous chapter a case was made that education is in the interests of children. Because of its exemplification and instantiation in cognitive perspective and rationality, much of education consists in bringing children into *new* awareness and understanding. Such propensities can scarcely be among things children will be interested in, before even having met them! Of course, other things being equal, and whenever educationally possible, teachers should allow children to pursue X, Y, and Z. From common sense, philosophical analysis, and pedagogical research we know that people learn best when they are interested in what they are doing. Perhaps the point should be put more strongly: Felt interest *can* be a most positive and educationally fertile way of going about schooling. A little thought on the part of teachers will often reveal the educational possibilities in a child's present situation and psychological interests; all too often teachers reject the possibilities out of hand. Teachers should not allow their own particular interests to blind them to the educational possibilities inherent in the world of the child.

There is also to be noted the moral presupposition of freedom, in Western democratic societies, the presupposition of allowing persons to do what they want to do or are interested in as long as this does not interfere unduly with the wants and interests of others. In our type of society, the onus is always upon him who wishes to interfere with others to show why he should be so allowed, not the other way around. The present concern is merely to indicate that this presupposition must be a background consideration even in relation to children within the compulsory parameters of the school situation. I say "a background consideration" because, as argued later (4.1), children are on the way to becoming persons in a fuller sense, and the school situation is a special case in which pedagogical and educational concerns must be paramount.

Despite the remembrancers about the pedagogical importance of psychological interests and the moral presupposition of freedom mentioned in the two previous paragraphs, teachers also need to be aware that even when children's present interests are morally unexceptionable they may not be able to lead on from them to educational endeavors:

> One of the most difficult of the boys was a hulking lad called Kevin. Star of the school soccer team, his interest was sparked only by football and ferrets. Faithful to my training, I endeavoured to pursue these interests but Kevin remained hostile. (Francis, 1977, p. 40)

The teacher whose words these are tried every possible trick to develop education out of football and ferrets, but without success. She might have succeeded better by introducing Kevin to something completely different that would have startled him out of his intellectual inbreeding. The point seems to be that the situation is not like that relating to the general population on a Saturday afternoon, when whatever people's psychological interests are, they ought, other things being equal, to be indulged. In that situation, one interest is more or less as good as another. But here we are dealing with schools that are specifically set up to educate and train. It was said a moment ago that, "the onus is always upon him who wishes to interfere . . . to show why he should be so allowed." Why teachers should be so allowed resides in their duty to educate and train in order to develop children toward a fuller personhood.

This includes introducing children to concepts and ways of seeing of which children have never dreamed. It is sometimes suggested, as a counterexample to what has been said, that in fact in kindergartens and infant schools children are given a wide freedom to follow their felt interests. But kindergartens and infant schools are special cases brought about by the educational immaturity of the children. For to the extent that teachers indeed allow children to follow their interests in such schools, this is because at that age one psychological interest is usually pedagogically as good as another.

From what has been written, it seems clear that to say that something is "in children's interests" means "for the children's good" or "for their welfare." When it is interpreted this way, the question must be asked, Who is likely to be the best judge of what is for the children's good? The children? Their young friends? The parents? The teachers? Or who? Teachers may wish to say that the children are sometimes (perhaps often) the best judges of their own good, but they will almost certainly not wish to say that they are always so. Surely the moral principle of benevolence rules that out, because with their limited conceptual and experiential background children often are just not aware of the possibilities and thus are unaware of what we as adults and as teachers see as their real interests. The exercise of responsibility by adults on behalf of children may be called "vicarious prudence." This is a phrase of G. C. Lewis (1849, p. 124). As Bell says (1971, p. 200),

> Lewis called the authority of moral norms grounded in a utilitarian justification which could not be grasped or understood by all men, "vicarious prudence". The authoritative guidance of a child by a parent is a form of vicarious prudence and is vicarious because, in view of the natural incapacities of the child, first-hand prudence is not possible. Much the same applies in the educational field where the situation is defined by the inequality between those who know and understand on the one hand and on the other those who do not know or understand but (one hopes) wish to.

But judgments of what is good for others are not always easy to make. Parents and teachers agonize over such decisions. It is therefore simple to see why some parents and teachers and educational theorists take the seductive, short way out and claim that children know best, and so derive curriculum content from the immature impulses of the children themselves (Olafson, 1973, p. 180). But this short way out ignores our duty to implement vicarious prudence, for there are many things that children are not cognizant of. How many children, for example, will without adult pressure and advice eat nutritious food? Or learn to treat others as ends, not merely as means? Or lay some plans not merely for today or for tomorrow, but also for their future lives? Or get an education? In considering children's good, we are considering their long-term capabilities and potentialities, their fundamental welfare as creatures who live in a time continuum, not merely their ephemeral interests of today. Though the point and detail of this argument for vicarious prudence naturally varies with the age and experience of children, it is of general validity.

Indeed, even when teachers try to explain to children why adult impositions are necessary, the children often enough are unable to comprehend the reasons fully. As Dearden notes, this is why we so often have problems of motivation and why the task of educating children is often difficult. As he goes on to suggest, it is only after we have been educated that we are even in a position to evaluate education and to see where our real interests lie (1968, p. 19). As was said earlier, few people who have been educated ever wish they had not; in fact, most of them argue for education as a right of all.

It is important to realize that what is for the children's good is to quite an extent already decided by societal requirements and by the long history of mankind's search to know. I am not suggesting, of course, that adults and teachers are infallible in their decisions or that our culture should remain stagnant; in a continually changing world it will be rare for the education and training provided by one generation to be just right for the requirements of the rising generation in its actual future. But I cannot see any morally valid and educationally viable alternative to considerable adult decision and compulsory provision. It will be argued later (4.1D) that in educating children teachers are in fact meeting the moral principle of respect for persons. It therefore seems that there is a moral priority of normative interests over psychological interests in the area of schooling. After all, one reason why teachers allow children to follow their psychological interests in schools is that they implicitly agree that such felt interests have in some way educational possibilities—that is, are in children's normative interests.

So when teachers do take some educationists' advice and start from the children's present psychological interests, they should be aware that pupils' and students' existing interests have derived from what they have experienced to date, and from the environment in which the children have been brought up. And there are times when such experiences may not be merely noneducational, but even antieducational. In such situations, to start from children's existing interests may make schooling either trivial or worse. This means that some advice (like the following from a Schools Commission) must be handled with discrimination, for it is surely an "other things being equal" issue: "Good teaching entails adapting the curriculum to the interests and cultural and social experiences of the individual student . . ." (1979, p. 14).

Other things being equal, there is often a case for following children's present interests in order at least to get them started on something, but in itself and *without further development* on the teacher's part, this kind of approach will usually be limited in its educational possibilities. As John Dewey writes (1973, p. 524),

> Nothing can be developed from nothing; nothing but the crude can develop out of the crude—and this is what surely happens when we throw the child back upon his achieved self as a finality, and invite him to spin new truths of nature or conduct out of that.

What I mean by "further development" is this. When teachers do allow the child to follow his felt interests in the classroom, or to "learn through interest," it must be realized that the child, as Wilson says (1971, p. 61), ". . . cannot simply see what to do in the furtherance of his interest, as though its cognitive and practical implications were somehow written on it" like details on a packet of pills. The child has to discover just what these further implications are, and it is the teacher's job to help him to do this. For the child's interest to be retained and sustained, ". . . he must make progress in *learning* how to pursue his interest, and, in doing so, learn more of what is involved in that interest itself" (ibid.).

The distinction drawn earlier between occurrent and dispositional interests becomes important at this point. Teachers can often get children started into educational activity through attractive presentation of aids or ideas at the beginning of a lesson or a piece of work. Such a procedure creates an occurrent interest in the aid or the idea. But to produce educational development the teacher has to lead away from such occurrent interest into a continuing dispositional interest in a topic, problem, or subject. In talking about motivation, too many educational theorists are really focusing on occurrent interests. In so doing they are largely missing the point and merely touching the surface of this extremely complex issue. Acquiring an interest in this sense is something like coming to see the point in it, coming to see what is involved and where it will take someone. So the child must be shown how to pursue an interest so that it becomes dispositional, after the initial and superficial appeal of occurrent interest has faded. Otherwise many so-called interests will be

ephemeral and sporadic. Unless a child's interests are developed in this way, they will do little to develop his cognitive perspective or to make him more rational. In home economics, for instance, certainly the part between mixing the cake and the eating of it has to be sustained by the teacher, but more than that, an attempt must be made to involve the student in the chemistry and physics and the artistic dimension of cake making.

The summary account of the situation, then, is this: teachers ought to base their teaching on children's psychological interests (occurrent or dispositional) only when they judge that it is or will be in the general educational interest of children to do so, and they should give children more freedom to choose what they will do in school as the children acquire more knowledge and ability to use. Though these statements may seem platitudinous to some, they are of signal educational importance and cannot be said too often.

In the complex society of a late-twentieth-century industrialized liberal democracy, it is therefore often necessary for teachers to exercise vicarious prudence and to make decisions on behalf of their pupils and students regardless of whether pupils and students actually show interest. There is no moral escape from such decisions, though, assuredly, there are confused teachers who do refuse to make such decisions and immoral educationists who advise them so to do. Teacher decisions are inescapable because our society is continually changing and developing, yet teachers must give children the tools to deal with such change. It is because the teacher has to ensure that children are receiving as full an education as possible that decisions on their behalf are required.

NEEDS AND INTERESTS: KEY POINTS

In order to agree that something is a need, we have to agree about the desirability of the objective, assumption, or value that it is a prerequisite for.

It is no good pretending that teachers can sidestep the value judgments they have to make (or to accept from superiors or educationists) on behalf of their pupils.

Such listed needs as "achievement" and "independence" (Mouly), "achievement" and "autonomy" (Murray), and "self-actualization" and "to know and understand" (Maslow) are themselves *redescriptions* of educational achievements: they are really tautologous ways of saying that children need education.

What these lists of needs actually offer are, on the one hand, general physiological and psychological *prerequisites* to teaching and learning and, on the other, *alternative ways of describing education.*

What seems to me crucially to be missing in all this talk about needs and education is a clear concept of education.

The person who claims that meeting physiological and psychological needs will motivate unknowingly confuses two quite different categories of need; he mixes up fundamental physiological and psychological needs, such as the need for food and the need for companionship, with the logically quite different need for education.

What we have to do to approach schooling in the most rational manner is to engage in vigorous and *openminded debate about needs,* and only secondarily to seek scientific and social scientific help in providing guidance about physiological and psychological prerequisites, or in making suggestions about methods of teaching and learning.

Why should it be thought that children's present psychological interests are fit bases for educational beginnings?

The situation is not like that relating to the general population on a Saturday afternoon, when whatever people's felt interests are they ought, other things being equal, to be indulged.

The child cannot simply see what to do in the furtherance of his interest as though its implications were somehow written on it like details on a packet of pills. The child must make progress in *learning* how to pursue this interest.

To produce educational development, the teacher has to lead away from occurrent interest into a continuing dispositional interest in a topic.

It therefore is necessary for teachers to exercise vicarious prudence, to make decisions on behalf of their pupils and students, regardless of whether pupils and students actually show interest. There is no moral escape from such decisions, though certainly there are confused teachers who do refuse to make such decisions and immoral educationists who advise them so to do.

3.2 GROWTH

The word *growth* and its cognates continue to be used by teachers and educational theorists. Growth is by no means a passé notion. But the problem with the use of a term such as *growth* is that unless its users have carefully examined its possible meaning, ramifications, and implications in the context of education, they give the appearance of talking good sense when they may in fact be talking banalities, or even gibberish. For words such as *growth* are surely the sorts of terms that the Plowden Committee in England had in mind when it wrote (1967, ¶550) that,

> Free and sometimes indiscriminate use of words . . . has led some critics to the view that English primary education needs to be more firmly based on closely argued educational theory. . . . What is immediately needed is that teachers should bring to bear on their day to day problems astringent intellectual scrutiny.

A. Physical Growth

It should be clear that the idea of growth in education derives first from the idea of physical growth. Plants and animals show sequences of development in their growth, pass through various stages, and reach a relatively determinate end state (i.e., we have a reasonable idea of what they should look like at the end). Physically human beings also show sequences in their growth through the infant stage, through childhood and adolescence, and into adulthood. But is there as relatively determinate an end state to the physical growth of human beings? Perhaps the answer is both yes and no, in different ways.

Physical growth is not, for example, equatable with every change in the physiological organism; obesity and the results of malnutrition are not considered an appropriate end toward which physical growth should move. Perhaps it may be thought that there must therefore be some *ideal* type toward which physical growth proceeds and that there will be some sort of educational equivalent. But a short spell of historical and anthropological research will quickly reveal that what is to be considered physically optimum in this case is relative to time and culture. The prize females who adorn the centers of magazines like *Playboy* would be much too mammary for a seventeenth-century painter like Rubens, while even he would be appalled by the steatopygous buttocks of a bushwoman of the Kalahari Desert. Nevertheless, such "perfections" of bodily growth are not arbitrary, but are tied up closely with the economic and social realities of their time and place and also with the contemporary knowledge of the sciences of physiology and diet. Though medical doctors may make some use of lists of normal height–weight scales, full provision is made for individual differences and particularities, so it is only ignorance that could imagine that there is ever some inflexible or uncontroversial standard by which ideal human physical growth may be assessed. Indeed, modern scientific developments and information about diet and exercise have opened up previously undreamed-of possibilities for physical development and fitness. The concept of physical human growth then is as directionless, on the one hand, or as full of explicit direction, on the other, as any particular person's own knowledge makes it. I am claiming then that not even human physical growth has an absolutely unequivocal end state, so it is only to be expected that the end state of the metaphorical idea of educational growth will be controversial, and thus the statements of the desired end state of educational growth will only be as good as the reasons that can be produced in support of them.

When we let plants grow, we water them and nurture them in order to "lead out" what is within. This same sort of idea would seem to be involved in the unsophisticated concept of educational growth. This is the idea underpinning the claim that the root of the word *education* is *educere* which means "to lead out." Implicit in this idea of "leading out" what is within is that what is within must be worth leading out, must be naturally good, that there must be some sort of basic naturally good essential order within, otherwise we should not bother to lead it out. Just as the acorn and the butterfly pass through stages, each of which has its particular appropriate appearance and perfection, so too does the child, or so the implication runs.

Thus, as Dearden points out (1968, p. 32), this would mean that children ought in a sense to be looked upon as perfect children rather than as imperfect adults. This last idea, apart from being mere sentimentality (since children are neither), helps to push into the background the fact that most children eventually become adults and spend the greater part of their lives as adults. Rational consideration therefore requires that these future lives get as least as much consideration in what goes on in schooling as do their present lives as children.

B. The Importance of a Society

Notions of the natural and of natural goodness often spawn themselves in distinction to notions of convention or of what is environmentally or culturally conditioned. This is the idea that early child-centered theorists such as Rousseau seem to have had in mind, and it is usually the distinction that present-day advocates of growth are thinking about. To them growth is something that develops best when free from a society's influences, for they see society as constricting and constraining people's basic talents and drives.

But if we consider for a moment just what this thought entails, it seems that in general it must be rejected, for without the influences of a society, any society, what can a human being be? Certainly not a person in any developed sense. Suppose we hypothetically remove all the effects of upbringing, socialization, training, and education, what do we get back to? We do not "get back to some core of being which is the essential person [but to] crude and undifferentiated basic desires and appetites" (Dearden, 1968, p. 33). Human beings free of societies are not able to grow in their own way, they scarcely grow at all; consider, for example, feral children.

It is only by partaking of the collected mores and accumulated knowledge of a society that a human being is able to develop into a person. Any human being so unfortunate as to grow up outside a society would not be (to use the contemporary idiom) "doing his own thing." To "do his own thing" a person requires not merely the type of society that *permits him the freedom* to do it, but the type of society that both makes persons aware of their individuality and potentialities and also *provides the cognitive wherewithal.* The very concepts of "individuality" and "freedom" are local in time and place and precious because of their rarity.

It is indeed extraordinarily difficult to step free from a society's influence, and people who make great play of having "dropped out of society" are usually naive about their real relationship with it, their dependence upon it, and the intellectual inheritance it provides them. For example, a few years ago, I read a revealing article, which described the lives of some Californian "hippies" who boasted of their commune's freedom from Western industrial society and its values, but their commune *leader* made a big issue of their *cleanliness* and of burying their refuse with a Massey-Ferguson *tractor!*[2]

---

[2]Simons (1978, p. 34) makes a similar point:
People who join such groups often believe themselves to be opting for something quite different but it is nearly always apparent that they are only exercising one option within our system that they are fortunate enough to find open to them. It is a kind of option that has, in various forms, often been taken up before. One of the earlier instances was the Pythagorean commune in Southern Italy; but the Pythagoreans remained Greeks. Although they may have seen themselves as breaking away from the Aegean rat race, their thought and rituals grew out of the Greek tradition and were quickly re-absorbed. In much the same way it is because certain sets of ideas within our developing tradition have been seized on, that our drop-outs depart. Some of them are less resolute than the Pythagoreans were, for they take with them not only their language and their ideas, but also their medical cards and their social security cheques. Often enough, too, they realise before very long that the lifestyle they have adopted, which seemed attractive from within the greater, more complex tradition, becomes impoverished and even sterile when it is cut off from its origins.

Another possible candidate for the root word of *education* is *educare* which means "to bring up or to rear," bringing up and rearing were being talked about in the previous few paragraphs.

I have been indicating the implicit difficulties in the idea of leading out, and have been emphasizing the importance of rearing. Nevertheless, some kind of synthesis of these two ideas can be achieved, for it was mentioned a moment ago that people who push the concept of *growth* tend to see society as constricting children's natural instincts. Now to the extent that unimaginative teachers can stifle children's spontaneity, scientific curiosity, musical and artistic talents, and so on, to that extent do I agree that education should be seen as growth and growth should be seen as "leading out." But at the same time it should be noticed that skills and abilities that are "led out" always manifest themselves *in specific ways*—scientific curiosity, musical talent, and so on can be "led out" only in a society where such excellences are already going concerns. They can be "led out" only in a society that makes provision for such skills and abilities and values them, and that makes possible their development in even the most economically disadvantaged children by having schools that emphasize their importance for everyone (see 4.5).

What is being suggested is that we can look at education in a particular manner by engaging in the metaphor of growth, but that the metaphor does useful work in an educational context only when it is seen to be growth in particular ways and that these ways will be provided by society. But no society can agree with the outlandish ideas suggested by Holmes (quoted in Dearden, 1968, p. 25) to "Let the end of the process of growth be what it may. Our business is to grow." The end product does matter to a society, especially to a society posited on rationality, freedom, and the democratic way. Furthermore, the end product must also matter enormously to the individual person, for it makes his life what it is. Teachers in our society are placed in authority to get children to grow through encountering the accumulated intellectual and social wisdom of the culture, through understanding it, adding to it, criticizing it, and changing it where the pursuit of truth and value show this to be appropriate.

C. The Content of Educational Growth

It seems from the foregoing that the metaphor of educational growth makes positive sense only when given specific content. Earlier it was said that education consists of intrinsically valuable activities that broaden people's outlook on life and make them more rational. The metaphor of growth is interesting when we think of it in relation to such activities. For just as in physical growth there are broad general sequences from infancy through childhood and adolescence to adult-hood, so I think there are in educational growth.

The Swiss psychologist Piaget (in his work that has some antece-dents in that of Kant) discusses such growth in terms of the meta-phors of *assimilation* and *accommodation*—when a child encounters a new concept he assimilates it to his existing conceptual scheme, but if the concept is too radically different to fit into the existing scheme, the child accommodates by *changing* his conceptual scheme so that the whole scheme, including the newly acquired concept, is self-consistent. Discussions of these activities of assimilation and accom-modation may be seen as alternative ways of discussing educational growth. Educational growth will consist of the acquisition both of new content at a particular level (new quantity of understanding) and of new sophistication at a higher level (new quality of under-standing).

Piaget has discussed this sort of growth in the areas of mathemat-ics and physics and in morality. As mentioned earlier, Kohlberg, the American psychologist, has done some work in morality that embod-ies the idea that I am trying to develop in this section.

As I am discussing human educational growth and am claiming that Kohlberg's work supports my views, it is worth looking at a piece of his writing in some detail. In the following passage (1970, p. 40) he discusses the growth of a young man, Richard, through the last three moral stages. Richard is talking about the value of human life in relation to euthanasia.

> At sixteen, he said, "I don't know. In one way, it's murder, it's not a right or privilege of man to decide who shall live, and who should die. God put life into everybody on earth and you're taking away something from that person that came directly from God, and you're destroying something that is very sacred, it's in a way part of God and it's almost destroying a part of God when you kill a person. There's something of God in everyone."
>
> Here Richard clearly displays a Stage-4 concept of life as sacred in terms of its place in a categorical moral or religious order. The value of human life is universal, it is true for all humans. It is still, however, dependent on something else, upon respect for God and God's author-ity; it is not an autonomous human value. Presumably if God told Rich-ard to murder, as God commanded Abraham to murder Isaac, he would do so.
>
> At age twenty, Richard said to the same question: "There are more and more people in the medical profession who think it is a hardship on everyone, the person, the family, when you know they are going to die. When a person is kept alive by an artificial lung or kidney it's more like being a vegetable than being a human. If it's her own choice, I think there are certain rights and privileges that go along with being a human being. I am a human being and have certain desires for life and I think

everybody else does too. You have a world of which you are the center, and everybody else does too and in that sense we're all equal."

Richard's response is clearly Stage 5, in that the value of life is defined in terms of equal and universal human rights in a context of relativity ("You have a world of which you are the center and in that sense we're all equal"), and of concern for utility or welfare consequences.

The Final Step

At twenty-four Richard says: "A human life takes precedence over any other moral or legal value, whoever it is. A human life has inherent value whether or not it is valued by a particular individual. The worth of the individual human being is central where the principles of justice and love are normative for all human relationships."

This young man is at Stage 6 in seeing the value of human life as absolute in representing a universal and equal respect for the human as an individual. He has moved step by step through a sequence culminating in a definition of human life as centrally valuable rather than derived from or dependent on social or divine authority.

In progressing through these stages, Richard has been growing educationally. He has continually been developing his cognitive perspective and he has been taking a progressively more rational approach to the subject matter of morality. Such educational growth in the moral realm shows a progression along a public mode of understanding and experience through stages that can be distinguished by reference to the form of the experience rather than to its content, though it is the content, of course, that will give particular meaning to the experience. Such educational growth will be a coming to understand the point of and a gradual mastery of the different levels, together with various sorts of content. For instance, a person is not in the later stages of moral growth if he cannot work with such concepts as "freedom," "fairness," "respect for persons," and so on, see their interrelationships, and interpret in terms of them the specific moral experiences that he and other persons undergo. For someone in this stage of moral understanding the language of morals is used in a generalizing way and a vast variety of experiences can thus be assimilated. The person's growth has been by way of progressive assimilation of new interpersonal experiences, and accommodation to new ways of construing these, so that he can now view dispassionately, less sophisticated early ways of looking at moral questions, though he does not now agree with them.

D. Educational Growth and the Forms of Knowledge

The work of psychologists such as Piaget, Kohlberg, and Collis indicate that the sort of growth just discussed in the moral dimension occurs in various areas of understanding. It may be suggested that such psychological argument, when combined with the philosophical argument of P. H. Hirst, provides the educator with a pregnant model by which to interpret the metaphor of educational growth. Following a path traced out by Wittgenstein, Hirst (1965, 1966, 1970, 1974) has made claims that there are seven fundamental and mutually exclusive ways of interpreting the world, one of which is the way of morality.[3]

In order, these seven "forms of knowledge," as Hirst calls them, are: pure mathematics and logic, science, knowledge of minds, morals, artistic knowledge, religion, and philosophy. Such forms of knowledge can be distinguished on the basis of the concepts and the structure of conceptual relationships peculiar to a form, together with the tests that are used to establish the truth or acceptability of the statements of the forms. It will be seen that the epistemological situation varies considerably from form of knowledge to form of knowledge. Whereas the truth tests of maths and science are well established, there is hot debate in morality, art, and religion, while even the meaningfulness of some religious statements can itself come under questioning, as I earlier tried to demonstrate briefly (2.2B). What appear to be *further* sorts of knowledge will then be, according to Hirst's argument, complex mixtures of these fundamental types, and all human knowledge and understanding will necessarily presuppose such basic types, as will all human inquiry that goes in search of knowledge and understanding.

Hirst is not referring only to organized or disciplined knowledge; the thesis applies to knowledge of everyday affairs and common-sense knowledge. After all, any item of knowledge, whatever its level of sophistication or abstraction, must involve a conceptual structure of some sort, and it will be this conceptual structure and the truth criterion for making claims about it that give it its special quality. It is just because we accept common-sense knowledge so easily and without question that makes it seem different in type from the knowledge categorized in Hirst's seemingly more abstruse and academic forms. But the taking of common-sense knowledge for granted does not make it any different, nor does its unorganized appearance, since any particular aspect or proposition will still lie within a form (Hirst, 1974, p. 142). Quite esoteric and complex claims of science can become as though they were common sense for the

---

[3]Some philosophers see these forms of knowledge as more problematical than is suggested in this book. Nevertheless, despite any debatable features it may have, Hirst's scheme still provides an immensely valuable conceptual net in which to catch life's experiences and meanings and to reduce them to a manageable number of categories. (See Brent, 1978.)

researcher at the fringes of his discipline, and can be taken just as much for granted by him as things assumed true by the first-year nursery-school child. Five-year-old Johnny may say that the red stone is hard and the white rubber is soft, while Professor Herbert Dingle (1972) may argue that Einstein "got some of his sums wrong" in the theory of special relativity, but they are both making claims about the empirical world and *to that extent* they are in the realms of natural science. Scientific knowledge begins with the simple language of description and explanation; it begins with everyday language formulations, which it then makes progressively more subtle and sophisticated.

Similar claims about a continuum between everyday knowledge and more sophisticated knowledge can be made with respect to the knowledge of the other forms. In view of the usual claim that teachers of young children are not concerned with the disciplines, it is revealing to look at what goes on in the early primary-school class in these terms: when they are manipulating Dienes rods, children are working within the form mathematics; when watching a plant grow from a seed in wet cotton, or when engaging in sand and water play, they are beginning to develop scientific understanding; when watching a friend's actions to try to decide his intentions, or when making a decision of his own, a child is beginning to have knowledge of minds; when learning to take turns, children are in the moral realm; when they act out a nursery rhyme or do finger painting, they are in their childish way laying the foundations for later artistic development (for details of this view see 3.4D), and when they say a prayer they are engaging in at least some sort of elementary religious exercise. The children themselves will not make such distinctions explicit, of course, and perhaps neither will the teachers. Nevertheless, the children will be working within these forms of knowledge. Education and life are not divorced; rather, it is education that helps make life what life is. The marriage of education and life is continually being consummated.

Hirst's analysis seems to make a good case for the existence of a number of irreducibly distinct forms of knowledge. Such learnings just are epistemologically different: it *is* possible to be morally very sophisticated without having any mathematical knowledge whatsoever, or to be a mathematical wizard and a moral cretin. And the disciplines as usually understood, such as botany and history, will be either branches of a form (botany is a branch of science) or else complex mixtures of two or more forms (history, it is argued later [3.3E], is a mixture of knowledge of minds and of science). There are, naturally, some questions of detail. By this is meant that we can ask questions about the nature of the truth criterion for our knowledge of minds, and about in just what way works of art make artistic statements that are analogous, say, to scientific statements; I do not mean that Hirst's thesis can be questioned in the way some writers in the sociology of knowledge have somewhat simplistically questioned it by saying that all knowledge is culture-relative (Berger and Luckmann, 1966; Young, 1971).[4]

What is more, it is not being said that there exist minds that are independent of the forms of knowledge and then somehow assimilate these various ways of seeing the world. Rather, it is that the various ways of seeing the world make the human mind what it is. To put it bluntly, to have more ways of seeing the world is to have more mind, just as to have more sophisticated and complex levels of grasping the world within these ways and more details within them (recall the example of moral growth) is to have more mind, which is why language development is so crucial for education. The growth of mind is the growth of these ways. As Hirst puts this point (1965, p. 125),

> . . . to have a mind basically involves coming to have experience articulated by means of various conceptual schema. It is only because man has over millenia objectified and progressively developed these that he has achieved the forms of knowledge, and the possibility of the development of mind as we know it.

And Oakeshott makes the same point in this manner (1962, pp. 89–90),

> Mind as we know it is the offspring of knowledge and activity; it is composed entirely of thoughts. You do not first have a mind, which acquires a filling of ideas and then makes distinctions between true and false, right and wrong, reasonable and unreasonable, and then as a third step, causes activity. Properly speaking the mind has no existence apart from, or in advance of, these and other distinctions. These and other distinctions are not acquisitions; they are constitutive of the mind. Extinguish in a man's mind these and other distinctions, and what is extinguished is not merely a man's knowledge (or part of it), but the mind itself.

Several ideas run together at this point and mutually illumine one another: Educational growth is the development of mind; expanding cognitive perspective and rationality are educational growth; growth in the forms of knowledge is both educational growth and development of mind; and educational growth and development of mind are crucial aspects of the development of the person.

[4]For accounts of why relativism is simplistic, see Trigg, 1973; Flew, 1976; also section 3.3D.

GROWTH: KEY POINTS

We can construe education in a particular manner by engaging in the metaphor of growth, but the metaphor does useful work in an educational context only when it is seen to be growth in particular ways, and these ways will be provided by society.

Human beings free of societies are not able to grow in their own way, they scarcely grow at all. To "do his own thing" a person requires not merely the type of society that *permits him the freedom* to do it, but the type of society that both *makes persons aware* of their individuality and potentialities, and also *provides the cognitive wherewithal.* The very concepts of "individuality" and "freedom" are local in time and place and precious because of their rarity.

Educational growth will consist of the acquisition both of new content at a particular level (new quantity of understanding) and of new sophistication at a higher level (new quality of understanding). Educational growth in the moral realm shows a matter of progression along a public mode of understanding and experience through stages that can be distinguished by the form of the experience, rather than its content, though the content will give particular meaning to the experience.

Hirst has made claims that there are seven fundamental and mutually exclusive ways of interpreting the world. In order, these seven forms of knowledge, as Hirst calls them, are: pure maths and logic, science, knowledge of minds, morals, artistic knowledge, religion, and philosophy. To have more ways of seeing the world is to have more mind, just as to have more sophisticated and complex levels of construing the world within these ways and more details within these is to have more mind. The growth of mind is the growth of these ways. It is precisely these ways of developing that educational growth consists in.

Education and life are not divorced; rather, it is education that helps make life what it is. The marriage of education and life is continually being consummated.

Rational consideration therefore requires that these future lives of students get at least as much consideration in what goes on in schooling as do their present lives as children.

Growth in the forms of knowledge is both educational growth and development of mind, and educational growth and development of mind are crucial aspects of the development of the person.

3.3 INTERDISCIPLINARY CURRICULA

A. What Can Curriculum Integration Mean?

The dean of a college in which I once worked suggested one day that various high schools in the city were already engaged in interdisciplinary and integrated studies. He said that our college should not only be preparing student teachers for the actual world of schools, but should be leading in new ideas, and that therefore it was high time for the college to be teaching integrated material to its students. His suggestion was that one of the subjects we offered for students' personal development should be of an integrated nature. To be called European Studies, it would enable us to draw upon the discipline-knowledge and the staff that the college already possessed. The historians could teach European history, the philosophers European philosophy, the literature lecturers European literature, the geographers European geography, the artists European art, and so on. We would, he thought, by this approach be getting the best of all possible worlds.

His suggestion was received enthusiastically enough by most of the staff and got duly underway, despite some reservations I expressed. There were four-week units on European history, European art, European geography. By semester's end there were distinct rumblings of discontent from the students, and the staff involved were having misgivings. Prior to a meeting to review the progress of the course, I asked some of the students about their feelings and received answers of the sort, "We get a bite of the cherry and they take it from our mouths," "The work is too superficial," "What is the real point of this course?" In truth, there was much disillusion and muddle, and in the middle of the muddle the dean left for a position at a famous university while the staff struggled to give life to his premature pedagogical infant.

The moral of the story is that an important idea is liable to be ruined by superficial understanding and misdirected enthusiasm. After all, *what* was being "integrated" in that European Studies course? In what sense were the studies *inter*disciplinary? Is Europe an educationally unifying concept that has its meaning and significance written on its face? What content was there in common to the different parts of the course? In what epistemologically useful way is a continent by itself a unifying feature? There is little in the way of cognitive perspective or rationality to be gained from the fact that "all these things happen to relate to the geographical entity called Europe." The college might as well have had a subject called Wednesday Studies, presenting all those things that just happen to have occurred on a Wednesday. The fault with this particular European Studies course was that it was never made clear either what was to be brought together with what possible results, or what was supposed to be the educational and pedagogical point of it all.

This college example has been by way of introduction to the sorts of issues to be discussed here. There will be an attempt to answer the question, "In the organization of a school curriculum, what do the words *integration* and *interdisciplinary* mean?" and to examine certain fundamental epistemological issues in doing so.

Let it be emphasized that I am talking about *curriculum* integration—that is, about the content of the courses, the variety of learning it is planned children will acquire in school—rather than about the methods used, or Dewey's integrated problem-solving approach (1938), or the flexible time organization of the so-called integrated school day. Neither am I talking about the integrated understanding of the world that it is hoped children will acquire as a result of studying the various contents of the curriculum, an understanding that may also be gained from an intelligent approach to a traditional subject-centered curriculum.

B. Disciplines and Interdisciplinary Studies

The term *interdisciplinary* (I-D) despite its complexity, has meaning. It may be understood as bringing together different disciplines (see the next paragraph) to focus on a topic of interest or to help solve a problem. In the I-D parts of a curriculum various disciplines will be used to solve a problem or to throw light upon a topic of interest. An I-D problem will be a problem that requires an answer in the world of practical application and that requires more than one discipline to be brought to bear to solve it; an I-D topic will be a topic that is interesting in its own right and that requires more than one discipline to understand it. Typical I-D problems will be abortion, creating government foreign policy, town planning and urban renewal, bridge building, and educating children—indeed, in educating children there will be an unlimited number of problems whose solutions can only be achieved through an I-D approach. Typical I-D topics will be pollution, poverty, the environment, nuclear energy.

By the term *discipline* is meant something like a well-established, relatively-discrete area of study with a recognizable conceptual scheme, a particular pattern of enquiry and an accepted name. It is probably simplest to define a discipline denotatively, by suggesting that history, literature, botany, psychology, philosophy (or a subdivision of these, for example, American history, Australian literature, marine botany, Freudian psychology, philosophy of mind) as studied in colleges and universities are disciplines. Many disciplines will fall within a form of knowledge, for example, algebra within mathematics, botany within science, literature within the arts, but some will be inter-form (geography and history). (See 3.3E below.)

In I-D work the nature of the claims and statements from the disciplines will remain the same in the suggested solution to the problem or in the attainment of understanding of a topic, so that an analysis of any conclusions reached or points of view held after an I-D study will show various disciplinary facts and assertions meshed or woven in some way, but still retaining their original character.

For instance, the finished town plan will be a complex mixture of statistics, economic claims, philosophical analyses, moralizing at various levels of sophistication, claims about the historical worth of buildings, scientific statements of a physical, botanical, biological, geological, and other sort, and so on. Official educational reports are also I-D in content, consisting of claims about morality, economic assessments and assumptions, statistical tables of population distribution and growth, historical accounts of school development in the area, sociological evidence hypotheses and arguments, psychological claims about children's development, and so on, brought together somehow. Furthermore, the statements that may be labeled pedagogical will themselves be mixed and I-D, for they will be complex meshes of philosophical, psychological, moral, sociological, and similar considerations. So there is I-D content on at least two levels in educational reports—just one cause of their usual contentious and equivocal nature.

I-D work and curricula are complex and difficult, but at least we can understand something of the conceptual basis, the basis and structure contributed by the various disciplines. To the extent that we can understand the contributory disciplines, to that extent we have some possibility of understanding an I-D approach. To the extent that we can understand the moral judgments, the statistical projections, and so on, to that extent we can follow the evidence and understand the recommendations, though the logic of the connections between the evidence and the recommendations is a more problematical matter.

C. Paradigms of Integration

However, can the same sort of claim just made for I-D work be made for so-called integration? It certainly sounds as though whatever it is that is integrated is more permanently combined or fused than whatever is achieved in an I-D fashion. But *what* is being integrated in a so-called integrated study or integrated curriculum? It is clear what entities are being integrated when mathematicians use integration in the calculus: many small movements become a large movement, many infinitesimal changes in position become a curve. It is clear what is meant by racial integration: South Africa's Cape Coloreds provide a good instance, for miscegenation between slaves, Hottentots, early Dutch inhabitants of the Cape, and sailors on the town in Capetown has produced a unique racial mixture, or has achieved racial integration; while the opposite of racial integration would be the South African apartheid policy, with races being segregated rather than integrated.

What is meant by the word *integration* in these sorts of contexts can be understood because of the things being integrated and the resulting product—a curve or a new racial type. Yet, just what is to be made of suggestions about curriculum integration? Equivalent to the infinitesimal changes, the different racial types, there will be various pieces of knowledge drawn from such various disciplines as botany or history; but in place of the large curve, the new racial type, what is there supposed to be? New knowledge that can be acquired? A new unity? A new discipline? In short, the crucial question is, *What is the epistemological thesis underlying talk about school curriculum integration?* Can we, logically can we, provide children with a new sort of knowledge and understanding through doing something called *integration* in the curriculum? Or do we in fact have precisely the same sort of learning and end product as we have when we approach the school's curriculum problems and topics in what we say is an I-D curriculum, but we give it a new and fancier name, *integration* or *integrated curriculum"*?

D. Forms of Knowledge

Perhaps the issues can be made a little clearer by recalling Hirst's thesis about the fundamental sorts of knowledge (discussed in 3.2.) Hirst's thesis can be put quite succinctly in the claim that all human knowledge and understanding can on analysis be reduced to a number of fundamental, discrete, and mutually irreducible types, distinguishable on the basis of concepts unique to them and of tests for the truth or appropriateness of statements within them. Hirst nominates seven such basic forms: pure mathematics, science, knowledge of minds, moral knowledge, artistic knowledge, religion, and philosophy, some of which can themselves be subdivided into various disciplines.

Hirst's analysis has been mentioned in an attempt to answer the question, "Do we, in short, have in schools the same learning from the same sort of curriculum as with I-D work, but we give it a new and fancier name, *integration?* Now, if the term *integrated* in *integrated studies* or *integrated curriculum* had a meaning in a school curriculum distinct from the meaning that can be attached to the term *I-D,* such meaning would have to attach to the new *unity* of the learning content that was to be derived or achieved, a new unity that would be analogous in at least some way to the new unity produced from disparate racial types through miscegenation, or to the unified curve that integration produced from small movements in the calculus. I suggest that there is no such analogy in the curriculum of the school.

Of course, it is not fundamentally important whether we use one name or two for the learning that is acquired in an I-D curriculum. What is important is that we be aware of the epistemological foundations of the things we teach in schools, so that teachers can have a proper basis for decisions they make about content. But names can lead us astray in our expectations and in our beliefs about the foundations, and (more importantly, perhaps) in our beliefs about the possible curriculum arrangements that can be made—that is, in the arrangements of the things that are to be learned. It may be suggested that the term *integration* leads us astray in just these ways. This is why it may be better to use only the term *I-D* and to drop the term *integration* from school curriculum talk, with perhaps the possible exception of a special use suggested below (3.3E).

Hirst's thesis has for the curriculum further important implications that should be discussed. This is because of the belief held by a number of advocates of curriculum integration that any curriculum organization is as acceptable as any other. Hirst's thesis would seem to give the lie to such a claim, for it indicates that it is not possible to reconstruct the curriculum just as anyone likes, because in a sense the nature of the fundamentals of knowledge is a given and cannot be disregarded, if we are to be concerned with the acquisition of knowledge rather than with indulgence in fancy or irrationality. All knowledge occurs within a structure of one kind or another—this must be so if it is to be *knowledge.* The meaning of the term *knowledge* in the present discussion may be taken to be "justified true belief" (as it is often put), knowledge being connected with objectivity, truth, and rationality. For example, someone possesses knowledge when he says that the earth is spherical. He knows that the earth is spherical and it can be agreed that he is in possession of knowledge, not because any particular person has said so, but because it is so, because it can be shown so by a myriad of both independently established and mutually supporting experiments tied to the world of experience. The "flat-earthers" are just wrong. Their flat-earth thesis can be sustained only through the introduction of the most preposterous ad hoc auxiliary hypotheses such as "the higher our altitude, the stronger our eyesight," hypotheses that can be quickly shown—to any person interested in truth, objectivity, and rationality—to be false. This example of knowledge was introduced because I said that it is not possible to reconstruct the curriculum just as we like if we are actually concerned with knowledge. The fact that the earth is spherical is not an isolated fact, but one that interrelates with a host of other empirical truths that fall within the fundamental form *science*. Thus, to know that the earth is spherical is to know something that is basic to a rational understanding of our place in the universe, and on Hirst's analysis all knowledge is thus traceable to its place within one of the forms.

There are several fundamental forms of knowledge because, in order to deal with the real world, conceptual structures have had to be separated out alongside the truth or appropriateness tests that both support the structure and help to inform the structure. There must be both units with which to grasp reality and ways of testing statements that involve the units. When we reorganize the curriculum we merely reorganize the ways in which the fundamental structures of knowledge are acquired; we delude ourselves if we believe otherwise. What needs to be acquired is not just bits and snippets of knowledge, but detailed and patterned knowledge drawn from the forms that structure our understanding and upon which we necessarily draw from day to day.

So while an attack upon the structure of the curriculum may be completely acceptable, it will have certain epistemological limits. But an attack on the knowledge foundations that underpin any curriculum will be misplaced. Some curriculum theorists have mistakenly thought that the first is possible only by way of the second (Hirst, 1974, p. 139.) Indeed, under the influence of the simpleminded suggestions of some sociologists of knowledge, some curriculum theorists have argued that everything that we call knowledge is culture-relative. This has led them to tell teachers that there is no such entity as knowledge and that teachers therefore have no right to teach particular things as though they are true. But their claim is nonsense. Even for their claim itself to have meaning and not be entire gibberish, it must rely on nonculture-relative concepts of knowledge and truth (Warnock, 1977, p. 107). It is only because it is possible to distinguish in principle between what is indeed true about the world and what some people mistakenly say about it that there can even be *disagreement* about what is the case about the world.

It is not being suggested, of course, that the development of one form of knowledge never makes use of another form. Of course it does. Indeed, one form may be necessary for progress in another form, as is argued later with respect to the arts, but to be *necessary* is not to be *sufficient* (Hirst, 1976, p. 169). It may be that no serious progress in physical science could have occurred without an appropriate development in mathematics, but that does not mean that scientific knowledge and understanding *are* mathematics. For instance, the physicist may idealize a mechanical problem by putting it into purely mathematical terms; the idealized problem can then yield a solution, but the solution must be verified by experiments in the actual physical world. Again, it may well be that we cannot draw moral conclusions without reference to various empirical facts about the world, but this does not turn our moral judgment into an empirical one. These kinds of interrelationships between our knowledge of different forms are manifest and multitudinous, but they are not evidence for any supposed integrationist thesis about the school curriculum. It may be suspected that it is the use of one form of knowledge in another form that has helped to bring about belief in the false epistemology of so-called integration.

E. A Suggested Meaning for the Term *Integration*

There is perhaps a way in which the term *integration* can be given another quite meaningful use at the level of school curriculum talk. It might be suggested that it be used when general reference is being made to some of those studies that are already well-established in schools, but which are not as epistemologically basic as Hirst's seven forms of knowledge or of the divisions within the forms, which were referred to above as "well-established and I-D." Hirst calls these studies *fields of knowledge* and *practical theories of knowledge* (1965, 1966).

Fields of knowledge are grouped around some common interest or topic, while *practical theories of knowledge* have the additional unifying purpose of a set of practical problems or concerns. On this categorization "Our Neighbourhood," "Modern Man," "Pollution," geography, and history are fields; medicine, home economics, and educational theory are practical theories. My present suggestion is that teachers could perhaps call the well-established fields such as history and geography *integrated studies* rather than just I-D studies. Such subjects have a long tradition of maintained study, well-established names, and the man in the street has some notion of what they are, but they are different in epistemological type from forms or from disciplines that are divisions of forms. I think that the term *integration* may be appropriate in their case because they are meaningful psychological wholes unified around the methodological concepts of time and space, of happenings through time on the one hand, and of organization across space on the other.

That a study such as history can perhaps be regarded meaningfully as an integrated study because it is a psychological unity can be shown by briefly analyzing its features. History studies historical events. Historical events take place across periods of time. Historical events include the Battle of Waterloo, life on the California gold fields, Mohammed's Hegira, Captain Cook's discovery of eastern Australia, Galileo's scientific experiments, World War I. Broad or narrow, these are historical events to be explained in an historical way. Historians describe, explain, interpret, and relate events, attempting to see them as wholes and to outline the circumstances and causes surrounding, and the reasons for, actions taken by human beings in the past. In history, the individual pieces are also important for their own sake as objects of knowledge. The historian is distinguished from other scholars not only because he is interested in happenings through time, but also because of the emphasis he places upon the role of individual motives, actions, accomplishments, failures, and contingencies. It is these that give historical events their "inside"; it is these that make history different from a mere empirical or scientific study and give it the dimension that in Hirst's terms lies within the form *knowledge of minds.* Historians, whenever it is suitable, give explanations in terms of motives and reasons, not in terms just of causes. In history it is often appropriate to ask why certain persons acted as they did and to answer at a level different from that at which the phenomena of rocks and animals are explained. We understand what it is to have purposes of our own, what it is to strive, what it is to be a person at that particular moment in time.

The second dimension to history is, of course, the scientific and empirical one. While it is true that historians describe past events and in that sense there is not anything "there" in the way the scientist's material is (usually) there, in principle there is no difference between this aspect of the historian's work and the work of scientists. Certainly the historian deals with the past, but *the past* is not an epistemologically fundamental category. It has to be interpreted from the evidence that remains, but to the extent that it has left evidence that is accessible, the past is accessible to the historian in the way that the present is accessible to the scientist. The historian, like the scientist, has an hypothesis in mind. To explain the appropriateness of his hypothesis, he refers to reasons and causes. Both sorts of explanation are derivable from such primary and secondary sources as letters, newspapers, cabinet records, and so on, which discuss both human decisions such as a dynastic marriage, and impersonal forces such as monetary inflation and earthquakes. When he has to rely upon less overt evidence he makes use of archaeology, numismatics, palaeography, sigillography, economics, chemistry, and so on, through both their procedures and their established laws and theories, to draw his historical conclusions.

In brief, the argument is that history is a complex interrelationship of the more epistemologically fundamental forms, knowledge of minds and science. The historian's final output of article or book is a largely ordinary-language kind of description and explanation using these more basic forms of knowledge.

This is why I think it may perhaps be suggested that the term *integration* be appropriately applied to a subject such as history at the school curriculum level. It seems that a similar case for calling geography at the school level an integrated study can be made, and perhaps a case for some of the other well-established fields of knowledge that have traditionally featured as school subjects. However, the same sort of case cannot be constructed for such curriculum groupings as "Our Neighborhood," or "Modern Man." Studies such as these are fields in Hirst's sense, but they lack the psychological and methodological unity provided in history and geography. "Our Neighborhood" and "Modern Man" are I-D studies consisting of statements, claims, arguments, and assumptions of the sort earlier suggested as characterizing town plans or educational reports. They will themselves involve the more "integrated" statements and arguments of history and geography.

The point of this section has been to expose the epistemological errors of a curriculum concept that, because of such errors, has been widely misused and has led to mistaken expectations. However, although the usual use of the term *integration* has been here rejected as redundant and misapplied, it is important that it be emphasized that I am in no way opposed to properly directed I-D studies in schools. Indeed, certain I-D work in the school curriculum, as in moral and sex education, and education for democracy is of extreme importance (see below). But a superficial understanding of the epistemology, a misdirected enthusiasm, and a glib use of the term *integration* may do more harm than good to the important cause of I-D studies in schools, the sort of harm indicated in the college example of European studies mentioned at the beginning of this section. For unlike the issues with which, say, educational theory has to deal—issues that can only be approached in an I-D way—the European studies course had no problem to solve, no issues to decide, not even an organizing focus or real center of interest; its reason for existence was the worst of all pedagogical reasons—pedagogical fashion.

F. The Point of Interdisciplinary Curricula

As I write, I look out the window and see the snow on the distant mountains. I remember I want to ski this weekend, which reminds me of meteorology and the necessity of watching the weather reports in the newspaper, at which I recall that I must pay the paperboy shortly; this thought causes me to speculate upon the economics of the present rate of inflation, which I believe has at least some connection with the law of supply and demand, which draws my attention to oil supplied by the Arab countries, and I wonder about the moral status of women in such countries, and then bring to mind the psychological state of the harridan down the road who's always shouting at her children. But the more I consider these things, the less I am able to concentrate on writing this section.[5]

So while there is a sense in which it is true to say that we are living in an interdisciplinary world, we should be careful not to beg any general questions about what this may mean for our understanding of life and in particular about what implications it has for the planning of curriculum content. We may be living in an I-D world, but this does not necessarily mean that in order to master it, we have continually to be dealing with it in an I-D way.

So why have I-D studies in a curriculum? The first and most obvious reason for moves toward I-D work has been dissatisfaction with previous curriculum arrangements. Clearly there has been something wrong with some of the teaching in the traditional subject-centered curriculum, and it has therefore been assumed by many teachers and curriculum theorists that alternative curriculum units might work better. It has been thought that I-D approaches might provide such alternatives. Well-planned and properly thought out I-D approaches can provide a realistic educational alternative for parts of school curricula, but not for all, for it is only knowledge and understanding of discipline structures that provide the tools that give sufficient cognitive perspective, and I seriously doubt whether enough understanding of disciplines can be achieved if pupils encounter all ideas in an I-D way. This is because discipline knowledge consists of patterns of interrelated concepts and explanations; later concepts and explanations presuppose earlier ones, and they together form a structure or pattern that can be used to give meaning to the continual new experiences that have to be assimilated and accommodated to in life.

It is important to emphasize that dissatisfaction has been with *teaching,* since *teaching* is a word with more than one meaning. It may mean the activity of a teacher or the content of his teaching (the curriculum), or the end products of his work (the learning that has taken place). As Hirst has indicated (1970, p. 73) confusions between ends and means, aims and methods, curriculum organization and teaching methods, have at times made the supposed cures worse than the disease. For instance, to recognize a need for the introduction of new types of learning and teaching *activity* may or may not expose a need for an I-D *curriculum.* Whatever way our curriculum units are constructed, it is equally possible to use a wide variety of modern methods. Depending on our requirements, we can have

---

[5]The idea for this example has been taken from Entwistle (1970, p. 104) and for much of this section his suggestions have been used.

changed curriculum content, or we can have changed methods, or we can have both.

The point seems to be that when people produce reasons for changes in the curriculum, they should be quite clear that it is *curriculum* changes they are talking about, and that they are clear why these changes are supposed to be for the better. That there have been things wrong with the traditional subject-centered curriculum is scarcely *in itself* an argument for I-D curricula. It is merely an argument for making that subject-centered curriculum better in some way—more up to date, more relevant to "life," more applicable to problems, more meaningful to children, more imaginatively taught, and the like.

A second reason for I-D studies is that some of the knowledge, skills, traditions, attitudes, and values that ought to be encouraged in education in the late twentieth century were being neglected in the traditional curriculum. I-D areas of great importance were being glossed over or omitted entirely until recently. Sex education, education for democracy, education of the emotions, and moral education were four such. Now it may be that these areas can be effectively covered in a discipline-based curriculum, but I think this possible, if at all, only with the most careful planning and cooperation among many teachers in the one high school, and with the most careful planning, extra study, and organization by a particular elementary or primary-school teacher. John Wilson (1967, 1970), for instance, has suggested that with respect to moral education a proper curriculum organization will need to do the following things: enable children to see that the feelings of other people count as much as their own, develop an ability to understand how other people feel in various sorts of situations, provide children with sufficient concepts and factual knowledge to be able to assess reasonably the various possible consequences of actions, promote the ability to communicate socially and verbally, produce a capacity to form general principles that can carry children through a range of moral situations, strengthen children's resolve to act upon these principles, and make them aware of the irrationality that often lurks below the surface of human behaviour. Clearly, such concepts, values, facts, skills, and propensities can come only through a study of relevant sections of a whole range of content. The study of geography, history, and literature and the engagement in drama help children to internalize the idea that other people's feelings count; the factual knowledge that allows people to assess consequences rationally comes through a proper study of the various branches of the science form of knowledge (biology, physiology, physics, etc.) and the lessons of history and geography; games and physical education activities of various sorts help clarify the concept of rules and indicate the importance of rules and discipline in life; and so on. Though some of Wilson's argument may be problematic, I-D study does seem to be essential in the moral education area. (It would *also* seem that, in relation to the present example, children need to become directly acquainted with the form of moral knowledge itself. They will have to engage in moral talk and moral reason-giving of a type appropriate to their stage of moral development.)

The discussion of moral education leads into the third reason why I-D approaches have been justifiably advocated. Many of the interests and problems that people encounter in life are I-D; such things do not come labeled under a discipline name. It has been argued, therefore, that children should have experience of dealing with such problems and interests. This suggestion is sensible, but at best it indicates that there should be some provision for I-D pursuits in the curriculum, not that the whole curriculum should be I-D; for, as suggested earlier, only discipline knowledge and understanding give sufficient cognitive transferability. Furthermore, even I-D pursuits and interests have to be approached through large measures of activity drawing upon individual disciplines.

It has sometimes been suggested that I-D approaches encourage children to learn more readily and apprehend knowledge more easily. This claim is a very sweeping generalization that would seem very difficult to test, but common sense would suggest that its truth will surely vary from topic to topic, problem to problem, child to child. Such claims for universal panaceas in pedagogy have consistently been shown to be conceptually confused, exaggerated, or false. A parallel way of putting this point is to argue that I-D study is more natural in the sense of being more geared to the ordinary procedures of finding out that children actually use. Such finding out, it is claimed, does not respect discipline divisions, but surely this is true only at an elementary level when children are quite young—interests of young children are promiscuous across disciplines (perhaps across forms of knowledge) because of the children's limited intellectual development. If, say, children really want to find out why a butterfly develops as it does, or how a battery works and why, they will have to remain squarely within biology on the one hand and physics and chemistry on the other. Children's finding out, as with adult finding out, can, I suspect, get detailed answers only by pursuit in depth within discipline or form-of-knowledge boundaries. Thus, a child may encounter knowledge of music or the Mississippi River or monetary value; each of these may provide him with truly educational activity, but to be educational the three do not have to be linked together in any way.

It is also argued that what teachers should be seeking in constructing a curriculum is not discipline knowledge and understanding, but certain qualities of mind or person—qualities such as imagination, integrity, creativity, thoughtfulness—and that such qualities are in some way I-D. Now, it can be agreed that particular qualities of mind help to make a person what he is, but we must be very careful how this suggestion is understood. Certainly the educated person manifests these sorts of excellences in various ways; he shows that he is thoughtful, imaginative, or creative in what he does. But it is difficult to see what could possibly be understood by the claim that a particular person manifested such qualities in the absence of knowledge drawn from the disciplines and forms of knowledge, for what could he then be imaginative, thoughtful, or creative *in?* The disciplines and the forms of knowledge provide the content for such potentialities: people can be imaginative in their paintings and sculptures, produce a creative mathematical solution, show great moral integrity, be cleverly critical of someone's religious beliefs, be suitably thoughtful about a scientific theory, and so on. Thus, it is entirely too superficial to argue that the development of such excellences in children is important if it is forgotten that such excellences are merely formal and require a content from a discipline or a form of knowledge to make them actual.

Certainly we are living in an I-D world, but this does not mean that in order to master or manipulate it we have continually to be dealing with it in an I-D way. In schools today all too often there is a straining, a deliberate search for ways of getting I-D studies into being, when teachers would be better off striving for the real educational potential to be derived from an established discipline area of study. The most trivial and inane poetry and song I ever hear in schools is produced when teachers are told that they have to integrate all their curriculum content around such themes as hats or rocks or bats or clocks.

As was suggested earlier, there are good reasons for having I-D work, but it is important that we do not accept I-D work for the wrong reasons, for the wrong reasons may cause teachers to undervalue the fundamental importance of subject or discipline study, or else to trivialize their teaching.

INTERDISCIPLINARY CURRICULA: KEY POINTS

In the I-D parts of a curriculum, various disciplines will be used to try to solve a problem or to throw light upon a topic of interest.

I-D areas of great importance were being glossed over or omitted entirely until recently. Sex education, education for democracy, education of the emotions, and moral education were four such.

Any conclusions reached or points of view held after an I-D study will show various disciplinary facts and assertions meshed or woven in some way, but still retaining their original character.

While there is a sense in which it is true to say that we are living in an I-D world, we should be careful not to beg any general questions about what this may mean for our understanding of life and for our curriculum planning.

Certainly we are living in an I-D world, but this does not mean that in order to master it we have continually to be dealing with it in an I-D way.

Only disciplinary knowledge and understanding give sufficient cognitive transferability.

All too often today there is a straining, a deliberate search for ways of getting I-D studies into being, when teachers would be better off striving for the real educational potential to be derived from an established discipline.

If the term *integrated* in *integrated studies* or *integrated curriculum* had a meaning distinct from the meaning that can be attached to the term *I-D*, such meaning would have to attach to the *new unity* of the learning that was to be achieved, a new unity analogous in at least some way to the new unity produced from disparate racial types through miscegenation, or to the unified curve that integration produces from small movements in the calculus. I suggest that there is no such analogy.

Superficial understanding of the epistemology, a misdirected enthusiasm, and a glib use of the term *integration* may do more harm than good to the important cause of I-D studies in schools.

There are several fundamental forms because, in order to deal with the real world, conceptual structures have had to be separated out, alongside the truth or appropriateness tests that both support the structure and help to inform the structure. There must be both units with which to grasp reality and ways of testing statements that involve the units.

3.4 ART

A. Art Statements

So that the interrelated concepts of cognitive perspective and rationality will not be too narrowly conceived, I want to consider education in the arts as a more detailed example of educational growth in one of the forms of knowledge. Education, as it has been described in this book, will include knowledge and experience of the arts.[6] As Hirst (1974, p. 152) puts it in a significant passage, within the arts,

> . . . the physically observable features of shape, colour, sound, etc., have a significance that parallels the shape and sound of words and sentences we use in making statements about the physical world. In the arts . . . the observable features are used as symbols, have meaning, can be seen as making artistic statements . . . .

There are statements in each of the forms of knowledge. Running through the forms in turn, we may have such examples as:

1. $2 + 2 = 4$; $(a + b)^2 = a^2 + 2ab + b^2$.
2. Water is composed of hydrogen and oxygen; $2NaCl + H_2SO_4 \rightarrow Na_2SO_4 + 2HCl$; $E = mc^2$; force $=$ mass $\times$ acceleration
3. "I am in pain," "She is happy"; an actual groan of pain, an actual laugh.
4. We ought not to cause pain; Justice is fundamental.
5. (various art statements).
6. God is love; God made the world in six days.
7. The necessary and sufficient conditions for the application of the concept of *teaching* are merely that the teacher has the intention of bringing learning about; There are seven forms of knowledge.

The general nature of the statements in the other forms of knowledge is obvious enough, but what are these "various art statements"? These various art statements are made by the works of art themselves. They are made by *Guernica* and Beethoven's *Fifth Symphony* and *Moby Dick* and *Swan Lake* and *Star Wars* and Shakespeare's *Sonnet CXVI*. And they are made every time someone encounters the work of art.

If this claim about works of art making statements is to be more than a pleasant metaphor, then the features that can be seen as normally characteristic of statements will in various ways also have to be characteristic of art statements. Just as ordinary language statements about the empirical world or in putting a moral case can be simple or abstruse, original or hackneyed, clear or confused, so will art statements be, and the work of art, if simple, will make a state-

[6]The word *art* is sometimes used here to mean visual art, sometimes to refer to the arts in general; the meaning should be clear from the context. By *the arts* is meant the whole range of artistic endeavors: painting, opera, drama, music, ballet, etc. While most of my examples refer to visual art, similar points can be made about the other arts.

This section draws considerably upon Chapter 10 of P. H. Hirst's book, *Knowledge and the Curriculum.*

ment equivalent to a single ordinary language sentence, while if it is very complex it will be more akin to a book.

The general situation that is art is well summed up by A. C. Bradley, when he writes (1973, p. 248),

> Poetry in this matter is not . . . different from the other arts; in all of them the content is one thing with the form. What Beethoven meant by his symphony, or Turner by his picture, was not something which you can name, but the picture and the symphony. Meaning they have, but what meaning can be said in no language but their own.

And again (1973, p. 244),

> Just as there is in music not sound on one side and a meaning on the other, but expressive sound, and if you ask what is the meaning you can only answer by pointing to the sounds; just as in painting there is not a meaning *plus* paint, but a meaning *in* paint, or significant paint, and no man can really express the meaning in any other way than in paint and in this paint; so in a poem . . . .[7]

When an adult artist paints a representational picture of, say, a wheat field, he is not making a generalization. The statement of the picture is not "This is what wheat fields look like, so by looking at the picture you need not bother looking at the real thing." Rather, it says something like "I the painter have encountered this wheat field and this is the significance of the thing-in-itself as it is revealed to me" (Macmurray, 1972, p. 59). Such art statements are efforts at becoming cognizant of and of expressing the significance of individual things-in-themselves "in their own right." These things-in-themselves may

[7]What Bradley is saying is true of the entity in the empirical world, but *conceptually* we can to some extent separate the meaning from the paint and the content from the form. Indeed, this is what art critics try to do, as is pointed out below.

be objects or scenes or ideas or colors or forms. The art of older children and of adults expresses that impulse in persons to take notice of "the things that are real individuals in the world just because they are there and reveal themselves to us" (ibid., p. 60). That this is so is shown by the fact that the artist recognizes at last when he "has got it right." For there is with most works of art an incremental development of the work over time, with progressive modification of a schema; though he has a general idea, the artist knows not fully what the art statement is to be until he has stated it. When finally he has stated it he has exposed the thing-in-itself. Whereas the point of the empirical claims of science lies in generalizing, the point of art lies in individuality. Science makes general statements, art makes individual ones. Art statements are concerned with the object or idea or form for its own sake, and it is this crucial realization that art teachers must eventually enable children to grasp. Though they will, of course, have to convey this in ordinary language—ordinary language of the empirical, philosophical, and so on kind.

B. Art's Relationships with Other Forms of Knowledge

Although I am arguing for the uniqueness of art as a form of knowledge, the autonomous epistemological status of art, art can, of course, as Hirst says, still be very much interrelated with and very dependent upon other forms. Artistic knowledge will *presuppose* knowledge from other forms, not in the way that different sorts of knowledge in, say, home economics or in educational theory presuppose one another and are interrelated to form a logically mixed composite, but in the way argued in 3.3D, that knowledge in one form necessarily *assumes* and relies upon the existence of knowledge in another form. By this I mean that just as it is the case that there could have been no elaborated progress in science had there been no development of subtleties in mathematics, so there could have been no refinements in visual art had there not been things, forms, happenings, objects, actions, and so on in the empirical world to provide some content for the minds of artists, and also the actual possibilities and the gradual developments in the chemistry and physics of colors and materials; there could have been no great dramatic tragedies unless there were actual persons with minds and the development of knowledge of minds and of the human moral condition; and so on. This is merely to say that just as knowledge of mathematics makes possible the scientific statement $E = mc^2$, so knowledge of the chemistry and physics of colors and direct visual experience of the ordinary empirical world make possible the artistic statement *The Fighting Temeraire Towed to Her Last Berth To Be Broken Up*, and knowledge of mental anguish and moral cowardice make possible the artistic statement *Hamlet*. But the artistic knowledge of statements such as *The Fighting Temeraire* and *Hamlet* will still be irreducibly artistic. It is merely that other forms of knowledge "provide simply the occasion for all that is distinctive and irreducible in the arts" (Hirst, 1974, p. 162). For although art certainly deals with things-in-themselves, the things-in-themselves are in their various ways related to things of the world.

I have said that art will *presuppose* other forms of knowledge. It is also the case that, as well as offering their own unique contributions to knowledge, the arts will throw light upon other areas of life and, in so doing, further develop rationality and cognitive perspective. Thus, a classic novel like *Anna Karenina* may help us to understand how people's minds work; a masterly painting such as *Guernica* may have been caused by and may induce moral indignation at man's inhumanity; posters may be informative about far-flung places; and so on. But this does not indicate that works of art are really making other sorts of statement, it merely shows that art activity can be engaged in because of and be used as a vehicle for other than merely artistic purposes. Of course, art activity can be used to throw moral, religious, and scientific light on the world; it can be used to sell deodorant or to proffer propaganda; it can be therapeutic, recreational, or instrumental; but these in various degrees are limited and limiting insights, and are as epistemologically untenable as a way of grasping art statements as their equivalents would be for any of the other forms of knowledge. Indeed, it appears that Picasso produced *Guernica* not only as a revelation of "war-in-itself," but as a sort of political tract; yet the *art* statements of *Guernica* are still unique and particular, and Picasso is saying visually something like "I see war like this!" and Picasso did not know precisely what he visually would state in *Guernica* until he visually had stated it (Wertenbaker, 1980, p. 134). So such purposes and such light and understanding as art makes possible in other areas, although important in their own way, are not the point or core of art and are not concerned with *artistic* rationality.

Most of the statements we encounter in life are made in ordinary language. They are most commonly of the empirical/scientific sort, such as, There are words on this page, or, The earth traces an ellipse with the sun at one focus. They may also be of the moral sort, such as, We ought not to cause pain, and so on. Works of art also make statements, but, except in the literary arts, these are not made in ordinary language. In the visual arts and in the arts of movement and music the art statement is *analogous* to ordinary language statements. Such art statements are on the same ontological level, but are epistemologically not the same, as the ordinary language statements. Similarly, in the form *knowledge of minds* a scream of pain or a laugh may *reveal* a person's state of mind, or will itself be making statements that give knowledge of minds, but not in ordinary language terms in the way my *saying* "I am in pain" or "I feel happy" will give knowledge of minds. Equally $(a + b)^2 = a^2 + 2ab + b^2$ is a statement, but not in ordinary language terms.

The fact that such arts as opera, drama, and literature use ordinary language as a *vehicle* is confusing only at first sight, for there the ordinary language is to the operatic, dramatic, or literary statement as the canvas and pigments are to the painting statement. The novel, the spoken part of drama, the libretto of opera, and other such aspects involve ordinary language in *making* art statements, not instantiations of language in the everyday ordinary language world or in making statements in the other forms of knowledge. Ordinary language is not itself a form of knowledge, it is merely a widely pervasive tool for the communication of the statements of the various forms of knowledge.

In short, art statements depend upon the possibility of knowledge of other sorts. It is only because we have an empirical world that we can make empirical/scientific statements or hear someone laugh or see paintings by Picasso, but the scientific statement is a statement about the way the empirical world is, the laugh is a statement directly revealing of a personal state of mind, and the Picasso is a nonverbal, nonauditory, direct visual statement revealing artistic meaning and insight about a thing-in-itself.

C. Art Concepts

Something should now be said about the extraordinarily complex issue of art concepts. As mathematical statements embody mathematical concepts characterizable in the special language of mathematics, and scientific statements embody scientific concepts characterizable in the special language of science, so artistic statements will in some way embody artistic concepts. But due allowance must be made for the fact that there will be both similarities and differences between the way concepts are embodied in mathematical and scientific statements and the way they are embodied in art statements. Just as our understanding and experience of the empirical world depend upon the concepts we have acquired in empirical talk about the world, so our artistic knowledge will be determined and limited by the art concepts we have learned in our encounters with the meaningful public language *of* art itself (art statements) and in the meaningful critical language *about* art (statements in the other forms of knowledge) (see below). The art critical language and the language that is art will in tandem enable persons to acquire the art concepts.

Just as human beings learn to understand the empirical world by using ordinary language in ordinary language contexts, just as they learn to understand specific scientific language in scientific statements by using it in particular scientific contexts, so they learn to understand art. Art statements get purchase in the world, are meaningful, because we are encountering art *in* the world, in a context that is part of the world. It is not that there is a world out there and art statements here; rather, as is the case with statements in the other forms of knowledge, it is that art is in the world, art statements help to make the world what the world is for any person. As Paul Klee is reported as saying, "Art does not reproduce the visible, it makes visible." Or as Gombrich says (1977, p. 73), "the artist will therefore tend to see what he paints rather than to paint what he sees."[8] In the way that mundane empirical language statements and their concepts shape the world, so art statements and their concepts shape the world: the grasp is on the world once the engagement has started at all. We do not know the world and then somehow superimpose art statements on it; we know the world by way of the art statements about things-in-themselves. In the same way we do not understand the world and the equation $E = mc^2$ and then bring the two together; rather, we understand the world through $E = mc^2$. If a child is made more educated through encountering the formula $E = mc^2$, he is made more educated through encountering Rembrandt's *Risen Christ*. The point can be put slightly differently by saying that art statements, therefore, have their own way of helping persons to know the world. The world cannot be known independently of the symbolization involved in the various forms of knowledge, and among these the artistic conceptual symbolization that art provides gives its own knowledge of the world.

Consider the art concept *balance*. It can be discussed in words (indeed, it probably has to be discussed to be acquired), and it can be mentioned that the art concept is somewhat analogous to the balance of weights in scales, and examples of balance in painting can be indicated, but a person does not grasp the concept *balance* until he is able himself to see examples of balance in works of visual art that make their statements directly, and/or to use it in his own painting. A necessary condition for his mastering the concept will be exposure to art statements that employ it. Hogarth's *Life School* employs it. If we remove the statue on the right in *Life School* through masking, the balance is also removed, for balance *is* the subtle concatenation of various visual elements. Thus the art concept *balance* is embodied

[8]This point is perceptive, but it should be noted that the first *see* is a conceptual seeing and the second *see* refers to bald sense experience.

in art statements, in the instantiations of various works that make use of balance.

Possession of the concept, shown in recognition and use of the concept, makes possible a more sophisticated artistic knowledge when the statements of art are encountered or made, just as possession of scientific concepts like *light year* or *symbiosis* make possible a more sophisticated knowledge than that made possible by the mere concepts of the ordinary everyday empirical world. So, although the thing-in-itself is mediated directly to someone whatever the work of visual art and whatever his level of artistic sophistication, the mediation can become increasingly complex and meaningful. The art statements in *Life School* use the concept *balance,* they involve balance in a directly presented way; but though the unsophisticated and the children see the desks and the art students and the nude model in *Life School,* they do not see the balance. Yet they have to see the balance if the art statement is to be fully mediated to them. But when someone has mastered the concept *balance,* the mediation will be by way of that concept and by way of any other visual art concepts— *dissonance, contrast, repetition, symmetry, alternation*—that he has in his artistic understanding. It is not that his eyesight was defective before he had grasped the concept, it is rather that his artistic intellect was less developed. Parallel things happen in the other forms of knowledge. Consider the following examples. Of the geologically unsophisticated: He saw the strata but he didn't see the igneous rock, or, He saw the rocks but he didn't see the moraine. Of the mathematically unsophisticated: He saw the numbers but he didn't see the Fibonacci sequence, or, He saw that the numbers were getting larger but he didn't see the geometrical progression. Similar examples from the various forms of knowledge are encountered all the time in everyday life. I once met a clerk who had spent part of a vacation in Venice, but claimed that Venice was just a lot of smelly old houses and dirty water. How very different his encounter with that subtle city would have been had he had a depth of conceptual equipment in history, science, and the arts. So the mature artist and the art critic have different encounters with works of art than do the novice, the Philistine, or the child, because they have a more complex range of artistic concepts that mediate directly in the viewing, hearing, and other experiences of art.

D. Pedagogical Implications

The purpose of the present section is to discuss implications for schools. Now just as children make childish or childlike statements in ordinary language about the empirical world, or in making moral points, or in saying their prayers, so their art statements in their own special way will be childish or childlike too. Here it is crucial to recall the pedagogical truism that children pass through stages in their development. It should be noted, then, that art for younger children and art for older children are rather different entities. From art activity used largely for the mental solution of, or accommodation to, personal problems, it becomes art as a quite specific, rational, and cognitive activity.

Mature art statements are not some poor relation of statements in ordinary language about the empirical world, or of the statements of mathematics, but rather are constituted in their own sort of language, a language that can be finally specified in no way other than through its own unique instantiations in works of art (though it can be alluded to in words).

It is perhaps because teachers and school administrators have too often not realized the unique epistemological status of the arts that they have underestimated their importance for education and the curriculum. Too often they have seen art merely as an adornment, or as a vehicle for use in other subjects, or as the poor relation in a vaguely interdisciplinary grouping of work. But such an approach to art is entirely to miss the point that art statements have their own way of making the world what it is for each person. Teachers who use art activities for pedagogy in the other forms of knowledge are not giving art education, for no longer are they dealing with individual things-in-themselves as such. When teachers use art activities as a means to other learnings, such as in history or geography, the special nature of art is either distorted or destroyed or being ignored. This is also usually the case in so-called integrated approaches to the curriculum.

So what is being claimed here is that there is (or ought to be) in schools both art education in its own right and art activity as a means to other sorts of education, and both will have their place in the school curriculum, the first because artistic knowledge is important for a proper grasp of the world, the second because the other forms of knowledge are important also.

Having claimed that artistic knowledge consists in making and grasping art statements that involve art concepts, and that art statements are efforts at becoming cognizant of and of expressing the significance of individual things-in-themselves in their own right, and taking into account that there is development through stages whatever the form of knowledge, it seems that some pedagogical implications follow if it is intended that schoolchildren are to attain artistic knowledge.

Coming to know in any form of knowledge is a slow and incremental experiential and conceptual development. At the appropriate age, there must be creative art encounter. We must oppose the pedagogical myth that there is artistic value in self-expression for its own sake, without any attempt to solve an artistic problem. As Field puts it in his own insightful discussion of these issues (1970, p. 108):

> The need is for the pupil to experience a total creative process in art, from the uncovering of a starting point through problem-formation, exploration and move towards solution, as part of a sequential programme spread over a period of time.

Older children must be given the chance to replicate the activity of the adult artist in this sense of being given an artistic challenge and then encouraged to find their own individual statement as a result. This involves the experience of grasping that they did not know fully what it was they were artistically trying to state until they had finally stated it. If the arts are to become a normal way in which the world mediates itself to children, then children must gradually become self-consciously aware of art as art, and begin to grasp their involvement with things-in-themselves.

This is but an analogous requirement to development in other forms of knowledge, which attain their full meaning in person's lives only when persons become self-consciously aware of them as ways of giving pattern to the world. Compare knowledge of science: children are not expected just to be able to state finished scientific facts and laws, but to have encounters with science at school in the laboratory and the field so that they regard the world with a scientific view that they continually carry with them and that enables them to grasp new empirical situations intelligently. But the encounters with science in early primary school are very different from those in the sixth grade, as are those in turn from encounters in senior high school. And so, of course, must it be with art. Furthermore, scientific and mathematical statements come in various guises. So too do art statements. So if art is to fill a proper function in children's lives, children must be given experience in a range of arts; painting, drama, music, and so on.

As is probably the case with mastery in any other form of knowledge, certain amounts of freedom for a child to experience for himself and to explore a personal line of interest will be necessary conditions for the development of artistic knowledge. Especially will this be so with younger children, who will be engaged in activities that are really preparatory to full art activity. But it has been learned through hard experience and at the expense of many children's artistic lives that freedom is only a necessary condition, not a sufficient one. The teacher, as well as encouraging individuality, must gradually and at the proper age introduce children to the techniques, approaches, ideas, and insights discovered by others, if children are to develop their work and multiply their artistic options for doing, seeing, hearing, and so on.

> . . . if they are merely surrounded by attractive materials and then "allowed to develop on their own" they fail to develop but rather repeat a performance ad nauseam and with diminishing effort and sincerity. (Ministry of Education, 1959, p. 221)

Those educationists and artists who argue against this last point, by saying that young children do not need to be taught visual art but produce it spontaneously, misunderstand what is going on. For it is not so much that young children do not need to be taught visual art, but rather that they *ought* not to be taught art. This is because at their then stage of psychological development, young children are not really engaged in art. Picasso, for instance, is quoted as saying, "All children paint like geniuses. What do we do to them that so quickly dulls this ability?" But Picasso also misunderstood. Young children are certainly not primarily and perhaps not at all concerned with the production of visual art statements, but in various degrees are concerned to state visually problems about themselves and their surroundings and to reach towards *psychological* solution, not artistic solution. The young child is not an artist, for he does not use his gift; his gift uses him (Malraux, 1974, p. 285).

The much-lauded spontaneity is thus not *artistic* spontaneity so much as, in various degrees, the spontaneous expression of a desire to come to terms with the world and to have problems with the world solved. When this occurs, what is really going on is more accurately to be seen not as activity within the form of knowledge *art*, but as activity within the second form of knowledge *empirical knowledge/ science*, or as activity within the third form of knowledge *knowledge of minds.* Young children are then indirectly indicating what they know of the empirical world, or what their current mental state is, in a way equivalent to what they might show in more intense instances through laughing or crying. They are not, then, with their art-like activities making artistic statements about a thing-in-itself. Psychologists seem to be aware of this fact (though it appears to have been overlooked by curriculum theorists) and use children's painting activity as part of their play therapy, in order to allow children the opportunity to say visually what is troubling them. The children are using the pictures that they paint as a language in place of ordinary language, for their ordinary language is either not sophisticated enough or not appropriate enough to do the job required by the psychologist.

It is crucial to note that this sort of art activity is, therefore, a surrogate for ordinary language that makes empirical and mental-state statements; it is not, in such cases, art language making art statements. Young children are then getting to grips with the empirical and mental worlds in their own specially childlike way.

> Their art is a kind of instant surrogate life put together out of experience and hopes and fears, with the help of whatever materials and techniques and motor skills they happen to be given. (Brook, 1978, p. 28)
>
> Young children drawing or painting must follow a track trodden by all their peers; they cannot help themselves. Their procedures are common to all, their development through schemata shows in all countries; their work has common attributes from China to Peru. . . . they are developing means of structuring present reality. (Field, 1970, p. 116)

Young children are not creating art statements in the sense of art that is being used in this book. Rather, they are using art-like activity as a vehicle for making statements of other kinds.

So although it is true that there is little place for the art "lesson" with young children, this is not because the art of young children is in some mysterious way already sufficient. And though there is little place for "lessons," young children should still be encouraged to engage in art activity, and paintings and other art objects should be a normal part of their world. For it is important that the way is prepared for a later fuller grasp of things-in-themselves, and children

should be able to experience in an embryonic way that art is a significant aspect of the world as a whole. What is more, it is not, as Picasso
says, that children's ability "so quickly dulls." It is rather that older
children are at last capable of becoming cognizant of the significance
of things-in-themselves and this brings with it a changed artistic
stance to the world. It is now that the teacher can become not just
as he was, a teacher who understands art, but also an art teacher
(Field, 1970, p. 117). The stage has been reached where children
must be helped through the teacher's inspiration, through encounter
with elementary aesthetics theory, through mastering art techniques
and art concepts, and through their own burgeoning awareness, to
make and grasp art statements in the full sense. So teachers should
then be initiating older children into a tradition of insights, techniques, and concepts that provide them with the wherewithal by
which it becomes possible to transcend that tradition.

The ability to make and grasp statements in the various forms
of knowledge is an acquired ability. Just as children learn the tool of
ordinary language such as English or Zuni at their mother's knee,
and talk and discuss with other people in order to deal with the
common-sense empirical world; just as they learn the epistemologically related but more complex language of science by learning the
ways of the infrastructure of that empirical world, by reading about
it, by experiment, by talking with the science teacher and by attempting to answer practical and scientific problems; so in order to
learn to make and grasp art statements, children must be exposed to
art activity of a sort appropriate to their intellectual level, by doing,
viewing, listening, and so on. It is no accident that those who are not
thus appropriately exposed to the arts in their childhood and teenage
years grow up artistic Philistines, even if they are educated in other
ways.

Thus in developing artistic knowledge there is also a very great
need to talk to children about what they are doing, viewing, listening, or whatever, and to get them to talk about it. This approach will
be informal and chatty with younger children and more structured
and pedagogically deliberate with older ones, who require articulate
verbal communication about their own and other persons' art, of the
kind referred to when concepts were being discussed earlier. The
importance of talk about art at a level appropriate to the child's
artistic development can hardly be overemphasized. It is not that
verbalizing about art should take the place of doing, viewing, and so
on; it is rather that verbalizing helps to make art activity and art
encounter fuller possibilities. It is not intended that high school children should ape the pseudosophistication of the matron at the fashionable art exhibition. The verbalizing is not an end in itself, it is a

way of coming to grasp the nonverbal. Brook puts a tangential point in writing (1978, p. 29):

> The important part of art learning is the learning of appraisal, that is absurdly underrated in pedagogical courses today. The real problem for the teacher is not to get the child to make art in one medium or another but to decide what to do with or say about the art that the child has made. This is appraisal, and it is a wretchedly untended field.

It was said earlier that art statements can be finally specified in no way other than through their own unique instantiations, though they can be alluded to in words. That they can be alluded to in words is the present point, a point that has crucial pedagogical and educational implications. For teachers of art must never assume that pupils and students can develop artistic rationality and cognitive perspective merely by way of a sort of artistic osmosis. As their professional judgment dictates, teachers must talk in detail to children about art statements. In painting they must introduce the conceptual contrast between content and form, and discuss whether they have been successfully integrated. Teachers must help children to see why a particular medium has been chosen, and its benefits and limitations. They should gradually introduce such art concepts as *balance* and *symmetry*, point to particular technical aspects and techniques, compare works of art, place them in cultural contexts, consider the lives of various artists, assess whether in a particular work there is a basic unity or a collocation of discordant elements, and so on. In so doing, talk about art will necessarily range across the other forms of knowledge, from straightforward empirical statements that merely set up the descriptive situation (for example, there are green and red slabs of color running diagonally across the canvas), through other forms of knowledge, for instance the mathematical claim that Cezanne makes use of the Golden Section of lines divided in the proportion of $a : b = b : a + b$, to those that are subtle examples of the statements of philosophical aesthetics (Gombrich's point about representational art, that the artist does not paint what he sees so much as sees what he paints). But the sole artistic point of such teacher talk is to show the pupil or student what is involved in the statement(s)—that is, to give the young person the intellectual tools to enable him to grasp the *art* knowledge itself. This is not a matter of words; it is a matter of, having heard the words, grasping the thing-in-itself.

The view that art can be seen as a distinct form of knowledge, and that works of art make statements about individual things-in-themselves, thus seems to have considerable implications for pedagogy and educational growth.

ART: KEY POINTS

It is not so much that young children do not need to be taught art, but rather that they *ought* not to be taught art. Young children are concerned to state visually problems about themselves and to reach towards psychological solution, not artistic solution. The young child is not an artist for he does not use his gift; his gift uses him.

Young children are not creating art statements in the sense of art that is being used in this book. Rather, they are using art-like activity as a vehicle for making statements of other kinds.

Mature art statements are efforts at becoming cognizant of and of expressing the significance of individual things-in-themselves in their own right. These things-in-themselves may be objects or scenes or ideas or colors or forms. The art of older children and of adults expresses that impulse in persons to take notice of ". . . the things that are real individuals in the world just because they are there and reveal themselves to us."

These various art statements are made by the works of art *themselves.* They are made by *Guernica* and Beethoven's *Fifth Symphony* and *Moby Dick* and *Swan Lake* and *Star Wars* and Shakespeare's *Sonnet CXVI.*

Art teachers must never assume that pupils and students can develop artistic rationality and cognitive perspective merely by way of a sort of artistic osmosis.

The importance of talk about art at a level appropriate to the children's artistic development can hardly be overemphasized if it is to give the young person the intellectual tools to enable him to grasp the *art* knowledge itself. It is a matter of, having heard the words, grasping the thing-in-itself.

So teachers should, then, be initiating older children into a tradition of insight and techniques that provide them with the wherewithal by which it becomes possible to transcend that tradition.

Chapter 4
Control

4.1 RESPECT FOR PERSONS

A. What Is a Person?

First the concept of respect for persons will be considered, and second the principle. But it should be noted that to separate the two is to indulge in conceptual convenience, because analysis of the concept cannot occur without overlapping into consideration of the principle, and consideration of the principle cannot proceed for long without spilling into analysis of the concept.

When philosophers and moralists and the man in the street in his more reflective moments use the word *person* in the phrase "respect for persons," they are pointing to particular crucial features of personhood. As in ordinary usage, they are, of course, contrasting persons with things, and this point is of fundamental importance, but they are doing more than that. For there is a whole cluster of interrelated concepts that, taken together, help to specify and mark out the more specialized concept of a person, either because they relate to features of persons themselves, or because in other complex ways

they interrelate with such features. There are such mentalistic concepts as *mind, rationality, cognitive perspective, creativity, self-con-
scious awareness, identity through time, intention, action, autonomy,* and *free will;* there are such moral concepts as *rights, duties,
responsibility, praise, blame, right, wrong, value;* and so on.

To examine the implications of all these concepts and the arguments connected with them would be to consider just about every
well-known historical and modern philosophical question, each of
which is itself immensely complicated—for example, what it means
to have a mind is itself an enormously complex issue that has become
even more complex in relation to personhood in recent years with
developments in neurophysiology, electronic computers, cyborgs,
and robots, and moral issues of personhood have taken on further
complexities since the invention of prostheses and of modern life-
support systems of cardiac pacemakers and the use of kidney machines, intravenous feeding, heart and kidney transplants, and the
awesome possibilities of cloning (Rorvik, 1978).

It is clear that although all such concepts and questions have
implications for both the concept of a person and the principle of
respect for persons, only one or two ideas can be considered in a short,
practical book such as this. Most writers on this subject emphasize the
mental and rational aspects of personhood, and because I have suggested that education is crucial in giving cognitive perspective and
rationality, I agree with their emphasis. For instance, Walters in an
interesting article, called *Persons and Non-Persons* (1966) asks the
question, What makes something a person? and answers (p. 41),

> It is briefly that having a mind of a certain complexity and being capable
> of rational behaviour are the essential characteristics of persons. Human
> beings have sufficiently complex minds and are capable of rational
> behaviour. They are, thus, recognised as persons and, within the range
> of our ordinary experience of the world, are the only beings recognised
> as persons.

He then goes on to discuss an extended denotation for personhood
(p. 43),

> Suppose now, however, that something like [an] extended kind of per-
> sonification occurred . . . in fact. Suppose . . . to use an example from
> John Locke . . . there were a cat or a parrot that could "discourse, reason,
> and philosophize". We would think at first that there was some trickery;
> but as we became convinced that the animals in question were intelli-
> gent, autonomous and responsible creatures . . . we would come to
> recognise and accept them as persons.[1]

[1] In passing, it may be mentioned that the literary device of personification and the
modern entertainment medium of the animated cartoon are based upon the attribu-
tion of the characteristics of persons to such nonpersons as animals and trees.

This idea of extended personhood is an intriguing one. Folklore of fairies and leprechauns, and the speculations of modern science fiction, involve this notion. Indeed, it seems to be an extremely high mathematical probability that somewhere in the universe there are persons who are not human beings. For example, after having discussed the strong evidence for the existence of a planet revolving around Barnard's Star, one of our nearest galactic neighbors, about six light-years away, Moore (1970, p. 30) says that similar results have been obtained for other close stars and that this would indicate that planet families around stars should be the rule rather than the exception.

If planets are indeed common, then with a Milky Way galaxy of some 100 thousand million stars, which is itself but one galaxy among some 100 thousand million galaxies, it seems unlikely that with the abundance of organic chemicals already found in interstellar space, that our sun is the only star with intelligent and rational life. Indeed, some scientists have suggested that there are perhaps a million advanced civilizations in our Milky Way galaxy alone, though such figures depend upon just how much stress is put on certain aspects of the evidence (Sneath, 1970, p. 124; Bracewell, 1976, p. 59).

This is all quite fascinating speculation. But all the persons we happen to know are also human beings, so we can sum up the known situation by contrasting mankind with animals. We can then point to persons' being self-aware, rule-following, language-using entities, who have emotions, who use their language and rationality to learn, and who make purposeful use of the space-time situation in which they find themselves, through controlling their environment by having points of view, making decisions, laying plans, and deferring gratification.

Personhood is not, of course, a unitary thing. We recognize degrees of understanding, rationality, and self-awareness; we ascribe different amounts of responsibility (lunatics are not held to be morally culpable, for instance); and so on. Because such features as rationality and the ability to be responsible for our actions seem to be so important in the concept of a person, and because these vary in degree, there may be problems of definition with some human beings. For instance, how do we describe the extremely mentally retarded or the catatonic schizophrenic mental patient, newborn babies or extremely senile old people in geriatric institutions, or human beings in a vegetable state such as the comatose Karen Quinlan? Furthermore, I was speculating a moment ago about persons in a form different from the human, so we can envisage persons with generally superior rationality and Kantian degrees of moral responsibility. Such superior entities might have more rapid and complete understanding, might be able to make finer and more appropriate distinctions—that is, might have mastered more of (and more than?) Hirst's seven forms of knowledge, might be more emotionally educated, and so forth.

Personhood, then, is a matter of degree: newborn babies are just potential persons; what turns them into persons is their growing up within a society that socializes, trains, and *educates* them. That we may have difficulty in drawing a line between persons and nonpersons does not mean that the distinction is false. There is a parallel problem with life and death, good and evil, youth and age, but we can still make clear distinctions at each end of such continua. Newborn babies and feral children are not persons; Einstein and Shakespeare clearly were. Most of the human race fits degrees of personhood between these poles. This recognition that personhood is a matter of degree of course makes moral questions about appropriate treatment more complicated. It is because of the extreme complexity, because no simple categorization into persons and nonpersons can be drawn, and because of the difficulty in predicting whether people in an insane or comatose state will regain their faculties, that we agonize over such moral issues as euthanasia.

B. What Is Respect?

So much for the concept of a *person*. What can we say about respect for persons? To quite an extent we have already begun to talk about respect, because to explicate the concept of a person seems at the same time to indicate something about appropriate treatment.

To refer to someone's personhood is to emphasize that he is more than a mere thing. It is a living, feeling, striving entity we are referring to. Even though personhood may be a matter of degree, it is because persons are not mere things that we can argue that they must be treated in the special manner that may be called *respect for persons.*

Putting this another way, we can say that *things* are things that may be used for the purposes of persons. Things take on instrumental or intrinsic value because of the experiences they provide for persons. Because persons do the valuing, things have no value outside the experiences of persons. Presumably, persons may also be used for the purposes of persons. But philosophers and moralists also want to argue that any particular person also has value in his own right, independent of the experiences he may be able to provide for other persons. Robinson Crusoe did not lose his value because there were no other persons about to value him. Persons, unlike the value provided by things, have value in themselves; they are of unconditional worth. To emphasize the difference, Kant says that things have *price,* persons have *worth.* Perhaps the cynic who says that every man has his price is referring to a particular way in which persons are sometimes immorally seen as things that can in a sense be bought.

So, whereas the value of things (books, banks, beer, and bromide) depends upon the quality and quantity of experience that they provide in the pursuit of persons' activities, it may be argued that persons themselves must not be used *merely* as qualities and quantities in the pursuit of other persons' activities. For, in Kant's famous phrase, persons are "ends-in-themselves," or they have intrinsic value. It will be recalled that in 2.1 it was argued that some activities have intrinsic value, but, of course, they have intrinsic value *for* persons, whereas persons themselves have instrinsic value *as* persons.

Though the institution of slavery has varied widely in the actual practices adopted, it seems necessary that there would always have been some aspects of the practice that reduced slaves to things. Whenever slaves were merely means to their owners' ends, we had the degradation of persons to things. Interestingly, also, until recently in our own culture and at the present time in many cultures, although women have not been placed on a par with slaves as *mere* things, there have certainly been aspects of thinghood in their treatment by men, especially in the area of sexual activity (Millett, 1970), though this has often been masked by subtle and believable disguises like mediaeval chivalry or Moslem modesty. I am not taking a stand that Western men today should or should not feel some sort of collective guilt; I am merely indicating something about inappropriate behavior towards women in a Western world that respects persons.

Because persons are ends-in-themselves, then to respect persons is to act in ways that accord others attention and consideration,

which show we agree that they are entitled to their own points of view and values, can choose and have intentions, and have the right to build a life as they see fit. To lack respect for persons is to discount these things, to suppress others' personalities, and to pursue our ends at the expense of theirs.

As it was once put by a member of a class that I tutored on philosophy for technical instructors, we ought still to show respect for persons "even if the apprentice is a small, freckle-faced, unintelligent, dirty, smelly, untidy-looking, long-haired troublemaker." In short, it is important not to ride roughshod over someone's personhood. Even though a person may well be inferior in specific areas—less good at games, less articulate, or whatever—he still retains this essential core of being that is of unconditional worth. Unfortunately, many people do not respect others in this way. Some persons have had the disillusioning experience of thinking that someone's interest in them was genuine, that it was due to personal attractive qualities, when all the time the other person was using them merely for his own ends—they were being used as things only.

But the most intolerable infringement of the principle of respect for persons has been achieved by the state. It is an unfortunate fact that there exist today dozens of nations, at both ends of the political spectrum, in which respect for persons is trampled on almost completely. The writing of Solzhenitsyn is one of the more recent that details the plight of the individual human being who is persecuted by the whole monstrous apparatus of state oppression in the *Gulag*

Archipelago (1963). It should be carefully noted that the Western tradition of political individualism and freedom emphasizes that the state exists to preserve the rights, dignity, and inviolability of the human person, and not vice versa, and that such values are crucial in respecting persons.

The injunction to respect persons is usually taken to be specified in Kant's famous formulation (*Groundwork,* p. 429):

> So act that you treat humanity in your own person and in the person of everyone else always at the same time as an end and never merely as a means.

Kant's use of the word "merely" shows that he was aware of the fact that we must make use of other persons in some ways. However, we are not to use persons as means only, but always with their personhood in mind. Because he develops this statement as an alternative formulation of his categorical imperative (which runs, "Act only on that maxim through which you can at the same time will that it should become a universal law" (*Groundwork,* p. 421)), Kant does not say exactly what we have to do if we are to treat one another as ends as well as means, neither does he provide much help as to how much we can use other persons.

To treat persons merely as a means can perhaps be called *using* them. "You just use people" seems to be a deeply critical judgment of someone. But presumably when we condemn the use of other persons, we are not condemning all use of them; we are not saying that only hermits and Crusoe before the arrival of Friday live moral lives. So what we have to distinguish between is *morally* acceptable and unacceptable ways of using persons. After all, civilized living is only possible through the interrelationships and interdependence of persons. Even to gain an education and *become* a person, it is empirically necessary for children to use other persons in various ways. As Marietta (1972, p. 233) puts it:

> We begin life using the body of a mother, and we never cease using other people. We derive most of the great satisfactions in life from letting other people use us. A refusal to accept the notion of using people is an unjustifiable squeamishness which comes from failure to distinguish between moral and immoral uses of people.

It is to be noted that Kant's injunction forbids the use of persons as means only, it does not forbid their use as means *and* as ends-in-themselves. What we need to establish, then, are criteria for showing when a person is being used as a means and also as an end in himself.

Since I am claiming that the important point about persons is that they are able to formulate intentions, act rationally, and in con-

nection with their actions suffer remorse and feel joy, and so on, the
question of justifiable use of persons by other persons would seem to
be not how much one person uses another, but how that use affects
the realization of the other person's ends. It would seem that we can
use other persons as means to our ends as long as such use does not
obviously restrict the other person's attainment of his own ends. Like
many moral issues, this will involve us in matters of degree.

In the hope of finding some guidelines, let us consider a few
examples. It seems to me that the context of the action helps very
much to show what will be mere using and what will be using and
treating as an end-in-himself.

In his article, Marietta (1972) considers a Mr. X in four contrasting contexts. Mr. X gets a cup of coffee from a railway station vending
machine by inserting the right amount of real money. He then visits
a shop and deals civilly with the counter girl in their brief inter-
change. Later in the day he has an extended encounter at the office
with a younger and more junior executive, in which there is a greater
meeting of minds and a broader sharing of concerns than in the shop
situation, because they are both members of a business team with
common goals and similar wants and needs. At home that night Mr.
X. chats with his wife, who is:

> . . . unhappy because she has learned that he did not share an important
> matter with her. This was not something important to the coffee ma-
> chine owner, the counter girl, or even his business associates, but it is
> important to his marriage. With his wife, Mr. X has a relationship which,
> in our culture at the present time, involves an intense emotional rela-
> tionship between the spouses with the expectation of interpersonal
> fulfillment . . . in marriage, the other person must be recognised and
> related to as an end more completely than in any other formal institu-
> tion. (Ibid., p. 236)

Mr. X is using persons for *his* own ends but in general they are able
to fulfill *their* own ends at the same time. Some of the points made
show where other person's ends might be frustrated—for example,
in X's not telling his wife, or if he had not shared the business concerns with his colleague.

The examples indicate that the conventional behavior dictated
by membership of social institutions is usually very helpful in providing parameters that, if kept within, make it possible for us to use
persons for our own ends while at the same time not frustrating the
attainment of their ends. After all, the individual knowledge and
capacities of most persons to examine adequately what they are
doing is very limited. Ways of life, honed and modified as they have
been over eons of social experience, are generally better guides to

what to do. (The general importance to individual persons of their societal background, discussed in 3.2B, may be recalled here.) In other words, provided we keep generally within the conventions of the various social institutions of our society, we are *likely* to be meeting the requirements of Kant's injunction and so in this philosophical sense respecting the persons involved. It is for the above reasons that I believe that writers are in general incorrect to argue that it is to infringe respect for persons if we treat persons merely as occupants of roles. For if we indeed treat persons merely as role occupants in our sort of culture, then we take into consideration a crucial feature of their existence. I believe also that in the culture of Western liberal democracies there is a particular background of behavior assumptions toward others in their roles. These are such moral procedures and principles as fairness, freedom, and truth telling, and such seemingly mundane matters as saying *Please, Thank you,* and *Have a nice day.* And it is such things that help make possible the attainment of our ends without frustrating theirs.

This is not to condone all our present social institutions, however, for some roles are mentally deadening and destructive. It must nevertheless be pointed out that it is social institutions that not merely make most of our ends possible, but also *make the ends what they are*—for example, the institution of marriage itself makes spouse-type rewards possible, the institution of artistic activity determines what the personal ends of artists will be, clubs makes club-life possible, the institution of the school creates the role of teacher, which at its best is both a profession and a calling, and so on. It is because there is a Western liberal-democratic society with its complex interrelationships of institutional and role expectations, that the lives of persons in our society acquire depth and meaning. Social institutions that make role rewards possible will, of course, be the case whatever the society (even if in some societies roles are more fixed and personally restrictive than in our own) because the defining characteristics of a society are in fact certain basic rules to which all have generally to conform, or else social life is impossible: there must be some shared beliefs, points of view, and ways of living that help to make the rewards of any social life what they are.

Nevertheless, despite its great usefulness, the claim that social institutions alone provide satisfactory guidance on acceptable and unacceptable use of persons does not seem adequate, because *in itself* it does not provide for criticism and development of institutions. Even though I have suggested that it is such principles as fairness, freedom, truth telling, and so on that form background assumptions in Western democratic societies whatever the role, naturally such principles are applied in various degrees by different persons. Presumably, therefore, our social institutions themselves are subject to the normal range of moral criticism that derives from such fundamental moral principles.

C. Why Respect Persons?

But the explication and analysis of a concept do not themselves settle the question about how we should behave. *Should* we respect persons?

This is perhaps the most significant and fundamental moral question of all.

There is a problem here, because we are now dealing with a fundamental issue, and how do we justify something that is itself fundamental, since the very process of justification usually depends upon referring to things that are more fundamental than the thing we are justifying? Perhaps we just intuit respect for persons?

No. This seems not to be the answer, because someone may just intuit *dis*respect for persons. If intuition itself is the justification, one intuition is as good as another. What about the suggestion that we just find respecting persons intrinsically valuable? After all, to find an activity intrinsically valuable is often taken as a justification for doing something. But this will not do, either, because someone may just find disrespecting persons intrinsically valuable. (Presumably such a person will also have to claim that he disagrees with the earlier suggestion that persons are, as persons, intrinsically valuable.) So to find some activity intrinsically valuable will only be a justification, other things being equal.

Let us look for a moment at the situation of providing a justification:

Why is a student putting on jogging shoes at 7:00 A.M.?
    Because he wants to be prepared for his morning jog.
Why does he want to jog?
    Because he wants to get fit.
Why get fit?
    Because it helps him to play football better.
Why does he want to play football better?
    He just enjoys playing well.
    or (it may be possible to take the sequence a little farther),
       for example,
    It gives him added status among his friends and acquaintances.
Why does he want added status?
    Because he enjoys added status.

The logic of this pattern of justification seems to be that either:

We justify an activity because of what it *leads* on to,
> or

We justify it *itself*,
> or

We justify it for what it leads to *and* for itself.

Putting this situation in another way we get,

We find the activity *instrumentally* valuable,
> or

We find it *intrinsically* valuable,
> or

We find the activity *both* instrumentally valuable and intrinsically valuable
(as was claimed in respect to education, in 2.1E, above).

This pattern of justification seems fairly acceptable as long as only oneself is involved. Robinson Crusoe had comparatively uncomplicated value decisions until Friday appeared. But when Friday appeared, some of Crusoe's decisions necessarily took on moral implications. Actions that affect others are usually seen as falling within the realm of moral deliberation. This is why it was said a moment ago that to find something instrinsically valuable will only be a justification other things being equal, for once a situation takes on moral implications other things are no longer equal in the pursuit of value. Something further seems to be required if our actions are to be justified.

Those activities that have instrinsic value for persons are in their own way self-justifying. We can say that they are autonomous in the sense that they require nothing outside themselves. But the problem is often that I like golf and you like swimming, I prefer eating chocolate ice cream and you prefer vanilla. In short, many intrinsically valuable activities, though in a sense self-justifying and autonomous, are subjective. If we can produce a situation in which our values are both self-justifying and *objective,* we seem to be in a much more satisfactory position; though it may not matter with games or ice cream, objectivity is what seems to be needed in moral valuing.

By way of analogy at this point, consider the case of making claims in science and mathematics. How do we justify scientific claims? How do we justify mathematical claims? In science we show claims to be acceptable by showing that they actually describe what occurs in the empirical world. Anyone who understands the meaning of the concepts and their interrelationships within the scientific theory can himself replicate the empirical situation and tests. Similarly,

anyone who understands the mathematical concepts and interrelationships and also the complex logic of mathematical reasoning can
also replicate the mathematical steps and arrive at the same result.
Thus scientific and mathematical claims seem to be autonomous in
that scientific precepts are shown to be acceptable or not by empirical tests, and mathematics by mathematical deduction. They both
seem to be objective also insofar as the results do not depend upon
who is doing the activity, but can be replicated and found acceptable
by other persons.

The interesting question is, can we perform the same trick with
moral claims?

One promising way of demonstrating this kind of a justification
comes about through showing that, at least with the fundamental
moral principles such as freedom, fairness, and benevolence, we are
dealing with logical principles that the search for justification itself
presupposes. This type of justification is sometimes called a *transcendental justification.* A transcendental justification tries to show what
is logically being presupposed by a particular question or action.

To presuppose something in this sense is to act as though we
realized it were the case. We may not know and often do not realise
that it is the case, though we act as though we do; we consciously or
subconsciously take the thing into account in what we do. To presuppose something is to take it for granted, or to involve it as a logically
necessary antecedent. Human life and activity are full of presuppositions that people take completely for granted. Most readers of this
book, for instance, presupposed that their universities and colleges
would still be in existence several years after they commenced their
courses, a presupposition that is not always borne out in practice. A
presupposition, then, is a sort of assumption that persons may or may
not know they are taking into account when they act in particular
ways and when they ask questions of various sorts.

Can some similar sort of logical presupposition be shown to exist
when people ask the question, Why respect persons?

To answer this question, consider the actual empirical situation.
There is a guiding rule or general principle that in fact underlies our
everyday relationships with one another in Western liberal democracies. This is the principle that we tend to treat other persons the
same unless there seems to be some good *reason* for treating them
differently. For example, I give each philosophy paper from my
students the same amount of attention unless a student requests
further help. A schoolteacher gives both offenders in the class a
punishment rather than give one a punishment and send a letter
home to the parents of the other, unless there seems to be good
reason for treating the second offender differently—for example, the

child is new to the school and so does not know the school rules. What is more, this principle or presumption also extends to the consideration that whenever we wish to treat different persons differently, the onus is upon us to show why we see this different treatment as appropriate or justified. Put another way, in our type of society it is generally assumed that the onus is not upon us to show why different persons should be treated the same. For example, it is not generally assumed that we need to show why there should be one person, one vote, or why everyone should have the same right to drive a car or to attend a school supported by public funds, and so on.

Now, I am claiming that this is, as a matter of fact, the principle we tend to work with, but though this is a matter of fact, why should it be raised in an argument about justification? In short, such an approach may be how we actually go about things in our daily lives in Western liberal democracies, but is it justifiable? After all, there are many things that we do in the world that we can generalize about as being the case, but which we find morally reprehensible. So is it justifiable to treat one person the same as another unless there seems to be some reason why we should treat them differently? In short, *should* we treat persons the same unless there are reasons for treating them differently?

It is at this point in the argument that the transcendental justification comes in. This is where we expose the presupposition lying behind our behavior and questioning; we lay bare the logic of the situation. (The argument here closely follows that of Peters [1966] and Griffiths [1967].) For in order sensibly to ask questions about how we should treat persons, we are already, within the question itself, *presupposing that various reasons are going to be supplied* as answers to our questions. We are presupposing that reasons will be given, that differences that seem to be relevant to the treatment will be indicated. These are the sorts of things that we are implicitly looking for in asking this very question, else why ask the question at all?

And what would count as a reason for acting in one way rather than another? It must surely be some sort of difference in one situation compared with another. So we cannot ask how we should behave, or how we should treat persons, or why we should do one thing rather than another, without logically already presupposing that differences will count in getting an answer. In other words, in order to ask such questions at all, we already presuppose that differences will be raised as justifications for distinctions in treatment. These are the very things that we are implicitly looking for in asking our question.

This can be summarized by saying that in order to be logical, we only make distinctions in treatment of persons where differences can be shown to be relevant. So it is not just an empirical generalization that we treat persons the same in our society, unless there are clear reasons for treating them differently, it is also that this is the only logical thing we can do.

Another way we can describe a situation in which we treat persons differently only where there seem to be suitable distinctions is to say that we are *being fair.* So what this transcendental justification shows is that in order to be logical, we must be fair. Fairness or justice is presupposed in asking questions about how we should behave. Again, if we seriously wish to do the right thing in our actions towards other persons, then it seems that we must also be presupposing that we and others ought to be *left free* to act upon the answers that we get to the question, *else why ask the question?* So the principle of freedom seems to be presupposed in the same way that the principle of fairness is presupposed (see 4.2C for a fuller discussion of this justification of freedom). What is more, benevolence (the consideration of interests) must also be presupposed, for how can we seriously and in its fullness of implication ask the question, How shall we treat these persons? if we do not take into proper account the *interests of all?*

And now we can return to the original question, Why respect persons? For in transcendentally justifying the principles of fairness, freedom and benevolence, we have at the same time been justifying respect for persons. After all, what does it mean to be fair, to grant freedom to persons, and to consider their interests, but to respect them as persons?

To the extent that this argument holds good, respect for persons is not just intuited or seen as a principle worthwhile in itself, but is objectively established. Just as claims and statements within mathematics and science can be shown to be true or appropriate, so, it may be said, can *fundamental* claims and statements within morality. (The word *fundamental* is emphasized because there are, of course, complex problems remaining in relation to the application of these principles and of adjudication between then when they conflict.) Anyone who can grasp the moral concepts involved and who can follow the logic of the transcendental argument can replicate the activity of justification.

D. Schooling and Respect for Persons

It has already been suggested that personhood is a matter of degree. In order to simplify the discussion, let us assume that young people by the time they reach eighteen years of age can be viewed as persons in some full sense. Persons, as has been suggested, are living, feeling, striving entities who have intentions and desires, purposes and plans, who can be both happy and sad, who show a degree of rationality, who should be seen as being ends-in-themselves, and so on. On the other hand, newborn babies are merely living, feeling, striving entities who may be seen as being ends-in-themselves (since it is an empirical fact that without the earlier stage of babyhood there could be no later stage of personhood) in whom the further attributes of personhood are yet to be developed. It will be the activities of socialization, training, and, above all, education, that develop them into persons in some fuller sense. So it should be carefully noted, first, that to establish the principle of respect for persons is not thereby to establish something like disrespect for nonpersons such as animals or for potential persons such as human babies, and, second, something like respect for nonpersons and potential persons may be establishable in other ways (e.g., through the deontological principle of reverence for all life, and the teleological principles of the rejection of expediency and the rejection of the moral corrosion of casual attitudes to life). However, the attitude described above as *respect* for non- and potential persons is probably better described as *concern*, because it is not respect in the respect-for-persons sense being used in this book (Reich, 1978).

Whatever the culture, children are socialized and trained in various ways. But here I wish to talk mainly about education.

It was suggested earlier that there can be morally acceptable use of persons by others, that provided we keep generally within the conventions and the roles of the various social institutions of our society, we are likely to be meeting the requirements of morally acceptable use and so respecting the persons involved. The role of teachers in liberal democracies is concerned particularly with education. The teacher is certainly using children for his own ends, as a means of getting his salary, and experiencing the intrinsic value of a worthwhile and challenging job, but also in various ways he is both enabling them to fulfill many of their present ends and, through his teaching, aiding them in learning skills and knowledge that will allow children to fulfill the ends they evolve and strive for in the future.

This suggests that teachers must try to ensure that they really are educating their pupils and students, that they really are widening children's cognitive perspective and making them more rational, which argues for a continually high performance in the way of getting children to understand, through a sensitive adjustment of the teacher's educational content and expectations to the children's judged abilities.

Furthermore, if children's rationality and cognitive perspective are to be developed by way of induction into the various forms of knowledge, then teachers should be continually extending children and encouraging them to reach new standards of attainment. An educational situation is not one in which just "anything goes," and teachers are infringing the principle of respect for persons when they become benign child-minders who allow their charges to do more or less as they like. Even in the area of art education this is the case, for if children are to develop their artistic insights through becoming increasingly aware of the significance of individual things-in-themselves, then they require *instruction* in art that pushes them towards ever more subtle production and construals. And the same point can be made about the other forms of knowledge. As John White has tried to show (1973), if we do not induct children into the various forms of knowledge, then we condemn them to a restricted personhood. Particular importance would seem to attach to education in the moral form of knowledge. This is because moral education not merely shows respect for children as persons, but also helps develop in children the sort of knowledge and understanding that make it possible for children to respect others as persons also. (John Wilson's list of requirements discussed in 3.3F will be germane here.)

Concern with education means that teachers and administrators need to cast a skeptical eye upon the fads and fashions of teaching that from time to time come to the fore to fool us: the fashions that in various subtle ways divert teachers from inducting pupils into the world of human meanings. I have in mind not merely such fashions as open-plan schools and teaching machines, so-called teaching for general creativity and so on, all of which require the most discriminating handling if they are not to waylay the unwary, but also such snares as a misplaced emphasis on present social concerns and a misunderstanding of the concept of "relevance" in education. Concern with education obviously also means careful avoidance of anything that smacks of indoctrination.

It is not being suggested that personhood, rationality, and the educated state are all-or-nothing things, or that by eighteen years of age all humans are equally rational, educated, and fully persons. But enough of them are to the extent that the law in most liberal democracies grants them full adult status. The law does this because it is assumed that they are by then sufficiently discriminating and have sufficient understanding and knowledge of the world to chart a course for their own lives in terms of such knowledge, values, decisions, and viewpoints and can make some sort of meaningful contribution to the society in which they find themselves. The teacher who has done the job properly can look back on his work and see that he has been instrumental in providing a range of concepts, knowledge, habits, attitudes, and so on, and thus in leading children along the continuum from their babyhood to a fuller personhood. The potential importance of the teacher's work for the development of persons can hardly be overestimated.

RESPECT FOR PERSONS: KEY POINTS

Persons are self-aware, rule-following, language-using entities, who have emotions, who use their language and rationality to learn, and who make purposeful use of the space-time situation in which they find themselves, through having points of view, making decisions, laying plans.

Persons, unlike things, have value in themselves, are ends-in-themselves.

We can use other persons as means to our own ends as long as such use does not obviously restrict the other person's attainment of his own ends.

The individual knowledge and capacities of most persons to examine adequately what they are doing is very limited. Ways of life are generally a better guide to what to do, honed and modified as they have been over eons of social experience. Provided we are keeping generally within the conventions of our society, we are likely to be respecting the persons involved.

It must be pointed out that it is social institutions that not merely make most of our ends possible, but also make the ends what they are.

That we treat persons the same unless there are clear reasons for treating them differently is the only logical thing we can do. Another way we can describe this situation is to say that we are *being fair*. Again, if we seriously wish to do the right thing we must also be presupposing that we and others ought to be *left free* to act upon the answers that we get. What is more, how can we seriously and in its fullness of implication ask the question, How shall we treat these persons? if we do not take into proper account the *interests of all?* And in transcendentally justifying the principles of fairness, freedom, and benevolence, we have at the same time been justifying respect for persons.

An educational situation is not one in which just "anything goes," and I believe that teachers are infringing the principle of respect for persons when they become benign child-minders who allow their charges to do more or less as they like.

Concern with education means that teachers need to cast a skeptical eye upon the fads and fashions of teaching that from time to time come to the fore to fool us. The teacher who has done his job properly can look back on his work and see that he has been instrumental in providing a range of concepts, knowledge, habits, attitudes, and so on, and so in leading children along the continuum from their babyhood to a fuller personhood.

4.2 FREEDOM

A. The Meaning of, the Principle of, and Educational Implications of Freedom

A permanent moral problem presents itself to teachers in liberal Western democracies, that of appropriately allowing children freedom at certain times, while at other times authoritatively directing them. This problem is, of course, somewhat different from that facing adults in their dealings with one another, for it is complicated by two interrelated facts: (a) the pupils with whom teachers have to deal are at various levels in their development as persons, and because of this have not yet been socially granted a general autonomy over their activities; (b) schools are the chief institutional transmitters of the culture, and teachers are people paid to develop children's cognitive perspective and rationality and in doing so to initiate them into the public body of knowledge and experience.

Freedom is an important moral-social-political principle that is a crucial aspect of respect for persons. For thousands of years, persons have seen freedom as intrinsically and instrumentally valuable, and as central to the exercise of personhood. Rational beings are able to use the freedom they have in a meaningful way. Rational beings *ought* to have their freedom maximized. But though it is crucial, freedom is only one principle in a gamut of principles that focus on the dignity, inviolability, and integrity of the individual person, others being such principles as fairness and benevolence (and, derivable from these, such lower-level principles as truth telling, noninjury, promise keeping, equality before the law, and so on). And it is clear that respect for persons at various times involves adjudicating conflicts of interests between persons; this means that particular freedoms will then be curtailed for one of the parties. So bearing in mind points (a) and (b) made above, it should be clear that there will be many situations in schools in which one or more of the above principles will be arguably of greater weight than children's freedom.

Principles other than freedom can be seen to have importance in two overlapping contexts: first in the educational activities that occur, and second in the general social control of children (of course, the social control is important only because of its connection with the educational activities). It is in the context of social control that the oft-mentioned "paradox of freedom," comes into importance in the schoolroom, which is, as Popper (1966, p. 265) has put it, "the argument that freedom in the sense of absence of any restraining control must lead to very great restraint." For it is both an historical and a social scientific fact that if human beings are given freedom to do just as they wish, then the strong impose arbitrary restrictions on the weak, and the few have wide freedom while the many have little. A teacher need not have had much classroom experience before becoming convinced of this general point. Some children, even infants, can soon become real tyrants when not restrained by rules (either by rules applied by adults or by rules widely accepted and implemented by the children themselves). As one of my students recently put it: "Without rules at school, class bullies inflict uncalled-for violence, class fools steal the teacher's audience, and the education system becomes grossly distorted." In the social sphere then, in order to have a modicum of freedom for all children, it is necessary for children to accept some restraints on their freedom, which also prevent other children from interfering with them in what they want to do.

But as was said earlier, the social-control rules exist only because children are brought together in large numbers in schools to receive education and training, and in order to get children started on educational activities it is usually the case that certain sorts of restrictions on their freedom are again necessary—education is controlled activity. Contrary to Froebel's own ideas, it is here that Froebel's notion of the "kindergarten" has its real analogical force. For plants in a garden do not just grow. In gardens it is weeds that just grow. In gardens plants are pruned, nurtured, fertilized, repotted, and watered so that they take on desirable form. Likewise (as mentioned in the section on educational growth) no responsible teacher can let children *just* grow. Teachers, in order to do their job properly, have to restrict, channel, guide, help. They have not merely to deal with what children want, they have also to broaden and change these wants and to deal with what children need. They have not merely to be concerned with children's psychological interests; through their acts of vicarious prudence they have both to vet and to develop children's psychological interests.

Just as not just anything is allowable in a garden if it is to remain a garden, so not just anything is allowable in a school if it is to continue to be an educational institution rather than merely a place of entertainment or containment. To put it another way, teachers in general consider that in this area of human activity the principle of benevolence or the consideration of persons' interests must often overrule the principle of freedom, for it is in the children's interests to be educated. Whether or not a child ought to be free from X will depend upon the content of X: talk of freedom in schools can make clear sense only when that which children are being freed from is specified. It can then be decided whether or not such suggestions should be agreed to. Should children be free from the teacher's control? from a required curriculum? from particular school rules? from compulsory attendance? The answers to such questions must vary with the content and the context. In recent years in the schools of the West, there has been some easing of restrictions and compulsions. It is usually agreed that this relaxation has had a generally positive pedagogical effect. But it can be taken too far.

Indeed, a strong case can be made that it is wise for a liberal-democratic society to impose constraints on children now, so that later in their lives children will be able to exercise wider choice among activities, and so that they will become educated and disciplined and develop as persons. For instance, I believe it is advisable to keep children at school for five or six hours a day for many years, even though numbers of them at the time see this as an imposition and restriction on their freedom, because the sort of constraint that often has to be imposed on children in, say, getting them to learn to read leads to wider possibilities for action (e.g., for choosing what they will read and do) when they grow up. Learning to read is, of course, merely one example. The same basic argument applies to many things learned at school: languages, art and craft techniques, tennis and football, scientific understanding, carpentry and cooking, trigonometry and terms of trade. Furthermore, it is necessary that children be constrained in this way not merely to educate them, not merely to widen their own possibilities in the future, but also to help them to be economically and sociably viable as adults and so have a chance to make a meaningful and moral contribution to the greater community. Teachers are therefore placed *in* authority in the schools, because each is to some extent *an* authority who is able to induct children into the understanding of the various forms of knowledge that are necessary for a rational construction of the world (see 4.4). The teacher's suggestion to "Do it this way," neatly shows how knowledge authority and social authority are blended in the job of teaching.

Nevertheless, it must be stressed that although I believe in the necessity of constraints of various sorts and of the importance of children being placed under the control of teachers who are knowledge authorities, freedom will still be an immensely important principle underpinning educational practice. Freedom is to be restricted only for good reason. For the teacher who wishes to be an educator is concerned that whenever possible, in order to provide for children's developing rationality, learners should be left free to make their own choices, to consider different points of view, and to draw conclusions for themselves. Other things being equal, freedom is always an important guiding pedagogical and educational principle, and a necessary one if what goes on is to be different from that desired by an indoctrinator. It goes without saying that to the extent that constraints do not have these good results, then to that extent they are unjustified. But it should also be carefully noticed that to be restrictive and constraining is not the *same* thing as being coercive; though schooling is compulsory, teachers can try to make it pleasant. Within the constraints they impose, they can use all sorts of imaginative, attractive, and challenging methods with various degrees of educationally relevant freedom of choice for the children within these methods.[2]

To my mind persons have freedom *to the extent that* they are not restrained by others from doing the things that they want to do, and are not forced to do things they do not want to do. By the term *others* is meant both literally other persons and also the state and other authorities. The term *freedom* refers to an area of conduct in which a person chooses his own course and is uncompelled and

---

[2]It is the claim that many schools do not achieve these good results that the advocates of deschooling use as their key argument, as do many of the followers of the more extreme progressive pedagogical doctrines. But such claims are complex empirical, conceptual, and moral matters, so in the absence of hard data and cogent argument supporting the deschoolers and the extreme progressives, and because of ambiguity and moral dispute over what counts as progressive practice, the onus surely still rests upon persons who want to engage in utopian pedagogical engineering to show cause why their ideas should be put widely into practice. Deschooling seems to be at the level of slogan shouting rather than at that of serious practical theory (see 4.5 below). And the more extreme progressive doctrines are riddled with conceptual confusion, conflicts, inconsistencies, and sheer ignorance of such fundamental connections as that between child order and discipline, and adult autonomy and achievement (see 4.3).

unrestricted by others. Of course persons may naturally *use* that freedom to bring constraints upon themselves, as occurs when they freely enter into marriage or begin a course of study. Thus one is more or less free; freedom is a matter of particulars and degree. What is more, a person's freedom is as various as the potential particular compulsions and restrictions that may be placed on him by others, though it is usually only after a compulsion or restriction is placed upon him that he becomes especially conscious that he previously had such freedom. Suppose, for instance, that a particular school principal does not interfere in the teaching methods that his staff choose to use; when the principal is replaced by another who believes that principals should in some way dictate teaching methods, the teachers are now made aware that they formerly enjoyed freedom even though they were largely unaware of it at the time.

Freedom, then, is an immensely important principle for considering what should go on in schools. But, as has already been argued, freedom should often be overridden by constraints imposed in the light of other issues and principles that, for the time being, are more important.

B. Freedom Contrasted with Ability

Pedagogical theory is only as good as its concepts and as the precision of the language that carries those concepts; and unfortunately, some theoretical ways of stating things cause confusion rather than clarity. This is mentioned because it is at this point in the discussion of freedom in schools that some teachers and administrators become confused.

Some persons confuse the meaning of freedom and the value of freedom. They say that because freedom is so important an issue, because so many historical struggles have been based upon it, surely it cannot be the absence of things as sketched above, that surely it must be positive, and since it is positive, it must mean doing things to people. But, of course, although freedom *means an absence* of constraints, such *absence is of positive value* to the people who want the freedom: it is the value that is positive, not the meaning. Certainly it is of positive value to be free from restrictions that we do not want and to be allowed to do things that we do want, but if we are to avoid confusion, then the meaning of freedom must be understood as the taking away of or the absence of constraints.[3]

[3]I acknowledge that people sometimes *use* the words *free, freeing,* and so forth to mean doing things to others, but this is a misleading and even morally dangerous usage (see below).

There is a second and slightly more complex confusion between two different descriptions of educational activities. We can, if we wish, say that to educate children is to free them from the constraints of ignorance and inability. But in order to achieve this we have to get them to do things like learning to read, and to stop them from doing things like playing all day in the park. Freeing from ignorance *means* taking the constraints of ignorance from children, and giving an education *means* achieving cognitive perspective and rationality through constraining children in various ways. It is merely that they are alternative descriptions of the same activities, and the important question is, Which is the better description for pedagogical purposes? It seems to me that it is a better description and more purposeful to see education in terms of doing things to children, such as giving better opportunities, maximizing personal development, being benevolent, and developing understanding; as providing children with knowledge, abilities, and ways of seeing the world and *making them more able,* rather than as freeing them.

It is because freedom is such an important feature of civilized life that its meaning should in no way be confused. Indeed, it should be noted that in ordinary language the chief use of the word *freedom* is in connection with an absence of restraints or coercions; it is used in just the way I have used it here. It is also interesting to observe how the key use of the cognate *free* is to indicate the lack of a charge or fee that might act as a constraint that stops a person from enjoying a service or gaining an object. This ordinary-language use has developed for the good reason that it marks a key concept in civilized social and political intercourse and the attempt to make freedom "positive" in the sense described above—that is, in meaning—makes a mockery of this fundamental distinction: it robs the term of its significant and unequivocal function in our English language (Partridge, 1967, p. 222). This distinction between freedom and other valued principles and abilities may be emphasized by some examples.

If I ask, Do I have freedom to walk into the headquarters of the K.G.B. in Moscow? the question can be clearly understood, and the answer is an equally clear No. If I ask, Do I have freedom to walk the oceans? the question seems peculiar, and the appropriate answer seems to be, Yes, you *have freedom to,* but you are *unable to*—that is, if you like to put the question that way, certainly no person or authority is stopping you, but you still cannot do it. However, if I ask the question, Did Jesus have freedom to walk the oceans? the proper answer (given the claimed incident on Galilee) seems to be both, Yes he had freedom to, and He was also able to; but his freedom was not the same thing as his ability. Or consider the example of the intelligent, able, American airman, Duane Bachon, shot down over Vietnam and captured by the Viet Cong. Bachon, who now lives in Brisbane, Australia, is a fresh-food fanatic.

> What you should know to feel at ease when Bachon talks fresh food is that he once spent 517 days in a bamboo cage (six feet square and four feet high) with nothing to eat except rice and cockroaches. This living nightmare, punctuated by daily clubbing with a Viet Cong rifle butt, certainly entitles Bachon to be as crazy as he pleases. (Robson, 1976)

The present point about this example is that Bachon was in possession of various sorts of abilities: he could fly planes, speak three Chinese dialects, play aggressive football, cook all sorts of dishes and so on; but he was not free to do these things—the Viet Cong cage confined him to an animal existence. He was able, but he did not have freedom. The opposite situation is also possible: persons can be free but not able, as would be the case with jurors who paid little attention to the evidence of witnesses or the summing-up of the judge. This seems to be the error made by some progressive teachers and theorists such as A. S. Neill, and by such deschoolers as Illich (see 4.5). Unlike people who confuse *being able* with *having freedom,* they confuse *having freedom* with *being able.*

Further reason for confusion derives from the empirical situation mentioned earlier in connection with the paradox of freedom—it is usually necessary to have some restraints on all so that there can be some measure of freedom for all. "Too much freedom leads to too little" (Peters, 1966, or p. 186). As John Locke has put it, "For liberty is to be free from restraint and violence from others; which cannot be where there is no law" (Ch. 6.57). But these are really claims about how freedom from various constraints is to be maximized; they have little to do with the meaning of freedom. Indeed, we have to know the meaning of freedom before we are able to observe a range of situations of freedom and draw the empirical generalization that "too much freedom leads to too little."

So it seems advisable, as argued above, to keep children constrained in schools and under the authority of teachers. By constraining them and getting them going on educational activities, we are increasing their abilities and powers, we are broadening their cognitive perspective and making them more rational, and we are certainly doing what is in their interests, but the constraining is still constraining.

This point about meaning is being emphasized because it is so important in terms of our moral, social, political, and educational life that it be made. For if we once suppose that to be free or to gain freedom may *mean* to have constraints, then we have opened the way for all sorts of double-talk and confusion that may play and often have played into the hands of the enemies of freedom, such people as indoctrinators and extremists of the political and religious kinds who do not want persons to think for themselves. The point needs to be forcefully made, "otherwise there will be a danger of confusion in theory and justification of oppression in practice, in the name of liberty itself" (Berlin, 1969, p. xxxix). For freedom is a crucially important feature of respect for persons, and it is not without careful consideration that the restrictive position in schools outlined in the first part of this section has been advocated.

C. Transcendental Justification of Freedom

The interesting question now becomes, Is there any way of justifying the principle of freedom, or do we just "take a stand" upon such a fundamental issue? There is something rationally unsatisfactory about the idea that when we reach the fundamental principles of morality we merely intuit them or "see" them as appropriate, and various philosophers have tried to present arguments to show *why* such principles should be supported. When fairness was being justified in the earlier section (4.1C), an attempt at such an argument was made.

Here will be presented in simplified form an approach to the justification of freedom used by Griffiths (1967, p. 177) and Peters (1967, p. 180), one that has its antecedents in the philosophy of Kant, who sought a morality binding on man's rational mind. Peters starts by mentioning that just as there is a presumption to treat people the same, so there is a presumption or presupposition in Western liberal-democratic societies to allow people freedom, other things being equal. In short, the onus is always upon him who wishes to restrict freedom to show why he should do so; the onus is not upon him who wishes to be free to show why he should be left free. (The onus of proof in showing why children's freedom should be restricted was accepted in 4.2A above.) But, as Peters says, this is merely an empirical generalization about our type of society. It may not be a generalization about other types of societies—the military dictatorships of Africa? the Marxist peoples' republics? the feudal societies of the Middle Ages? the cannibal societies of Peking Man of the Palaeolithic Age? So can this presumption in favor of freedom be justified?

Suppose we are asking ourselves about our behavior toward other persons. What should we do in particular circumstances? How should we behave at this juncture? What should our reaction be?

Now, in seriously asking such questions of ourselves, are we taking anything for granted? Are we presupposing particular things? I think we are. First, we are presupposing or taking for granted that we want the very best answers to such questions, else why ask them seriously? Second, we are presupposing that (other things being equal) we should be allowed to take action upon the basis of the best answers. This seems to indicate that prior to the answers being provided, no one should be excluded from the debate (for we cannot know what his contribution will be prior to our hearing it), and that there should be an absence of interference upon what we do as a result of getting the best answers. If we were not presupposing such nonexclusion and such absence of interference, other things being equal, that is, if we were not presupposing freedom to provide answers and to act upon the answers—then there would be no point in our asking such questions, no point in our deliberating.

This questioning occurs in a social situation in which various other persons contribute to the dialogue and make suggestions about what are the best ways of acting and of behaving toward others. It would be inconsistent and arbitrary, therefore, and a philosophical fault, for us to argue that it is a presupposition of such questioning for us to be allowed to take into consideration and to act on what we consider to be good reasons, but that although we have taken the thinking of other persons into account in constructing our own best reasons, others will not be allowed to do the same. Given the social situation in which such questioning occurs, it seems logical that we must also be presupposing general absence of interference with other persons.

The point, then, is that in the very concern that we show to discover the best ways of acting in a social situation, we are already presupposing that freedom of speech and action must be a basic principle: our behavior as rational beings cannot even begin without such a principle. Freedom is thus seen as a principle that is fundamental to any rational activity at all. It is not merely intuited; it is rationally established.

FREEDOM: KEY POINTS

"Freedom" *means* an absence of constraints.

Freedom is an important moral-social-political principle that is a crucial aspect of respect for persons.

Though crucial, freedom is only one principle in a gamut of principles that focus on the dignity, inviolability, and integrity of the individual person, so it should be clear that there will be many situations in schools in which other principles will be of arguably greater weight.

Not just anything is allowable in a school, if it is to continue to be a school rather than a place of entertainment or containment. Teachers in general consider that in this area of human activity, the principle of benevolence must often overrule the principle of freedom.

If human beings are given freedom to do just as they wish, then the strong impose arbitrary restrictions on the weak. A teacher need not have had much classroom experience before becoming convinced of this general point.

People confuse having freedom with being able. This is the error made by some progressive teachers and theorists such as A. S. Neill, and by deschoolers such as Illich.

It is a better description to see education in terms of providing children with knowledge, abilities, and construals, and *making them more able,* rather than as freeing them.

If we once acknowledge that to be free may *mean* to have constraints, then we have opened the way for all sorts of double-talk and confusion that may play into the hands of the enemies of freedom—such people as indoctrinators and extremists of the political and religious kinds.

In the very concern that we show to discover the best ways of acting in a social situation, we are already presupposing that freedom must be a basic principle: our behavior as rational beings cannot even begin without such a principle.

Freedom is a principle that I value highly, and it is not without careful consideration that the restrictive position in schools has been advocated.

4.3 DISCIPLINE

A. Some Significant Constraints

The last section mentioned the importance of social control in schools if education is to go on. It is an unfortunate fact that problems of control are deeply entrenched in some schools, and it does not help matters when educationists pretend that this is not the case.

Paul Francis is correct when he writes (1977, p. 33) that in some teacher education institutions,

> . . . there is a consistent disdain for matters of discipline which goes deeper than personal taste. The established tone of academic discussion precludes too sustained an attention to the control of children, since this is felt to belong to a repressive era now safely past. In some areas a valuable emphasis on positive work and creative relationships has hardened into a dogma, so that extreme devotees refuse to countenance the possibility that a child may be lazy, destructive or rude. As a result, many [teacher education] lecturers are sometimes inhibited from exploring adequately with their students one of the most serious threats to their ultimate effectiveness.

Francis is exposing what has become something of a doctrine in some institutions. But doctrines and dogmas in our approach to the control of children in schools are as vitiating as in any other area of human endeavor. It seems to me that there are many things that teacher-preparation institutions and those in authority in schools can do about discipline, and many things that can be suggested if we approach the situation in an open-minded way.

Let me begin with five important generalizations that should be kept in mind throughout the following discussion:

1. We must recognize that *there will be some problem situations* with pupils and students *for which there is no solution,* just as in other contexts we can ask questions for which there are no answers. Some of the children we meet in schools cannot be controlled in any ordinary way, just as some adult citizens cannot be held within ordinary society under the law. I well remember a difficult class of boys to whom I tried with little success to teach English in a secondary school in Buckinghamshire. Known as "the remove," because they were to leave school without going on to external examinations, they were mostly displaced Londoners from the East End. Our battle of wits dragged on for two terms, and despite long nights of soul-searching and a variety of teaching approaches, I failed to find a consistently successful answer about how to teach those boys.

2. *Pupils and students are,* in their personal characteristics, *a microcosm of the adult world.* There are shy and outgoing pupils, quiet and strident ones, some who live with the saints and heroes and others who are mean and vicious. But teachers have to try to teach them all. Indeed, the needs and wants of any two children in a class at any one time may not merely be conflicting, but perhaps contradictory: if you succeed with the one, you necessarily fail with the other.

3. Most *children are neither all good nor all bad.* Writers who take extreme but opposite positions in relation to methods of control are equally unhelpful in their claims. The strict authoritarian sees children in need of absolute repression. His opponent at the other end of the spectrum pays more heed to his pedagogical doctrine than to the real nature of the living children in front of him, and sees imposed control as an anachronism that can be ignored (Francis, 1977, p. 47). And control can be safely ignored, but after a time of transition and in the sense that the teacher is tending to concentrate on other things because control issues are now "under control." Actual control situations are more complex and ever-changing than absolutists allow for. After all, one way of solving a dilemma is to go between the horns.

4. Talk of control and discipline arouses powerful emotions; implementation does too! Teachers must be *prepared to have to do things they don't want* to do, such as being firm, fearless, and perhaps even unfriendly when they first take charge of a new class.

5. Problems of control and discipline *cannot be reduced to an exhaustive* outline, anymore than can other problems to do with education and teaching, because the teacher is dealing with human beings in all their manifest differences. *But some things can be said.*

B. Discipline and Rules

Let me begin with some ordinary-language examples in order to tease out some ideas:

1. Athlete about clubmate: "To have any chance in the mile, Mike needs to discipline himself more."
2. Teacher to pupil: "History is just one discipline you have to study to judge the world appropriately."
3. Principal to beginning teacher: "Be strict when you first take charge of this class, but relax your discipline as your confidence and experience grow."
4. Ex-sailor to friend: "I'm convinced that naval discipline helped me to become more organized."
5. Lieutenant to Sergeant: "When you find the men who committed this offense, discipline them!"

These examples show that, despite the variety, there is in ordinary-language use of the word *discipline* a common core of meaning—*the idea of submitting to the authority of rules* (Peters, 1966, p. 267). In

1 the athlete will need to lay down his own rules about training. In 2 it is because there are rules of appropriateness, of consistency, of the establishment and validation of facts and arguments, and because learners can submit themselves to such rules and have to submit themselves to such rules if they are to do history, that history is being called a discipline. In 3 the beginner is being enjoined initially to lay down rules and enforce them, but gradually to try to get children to follow them willingly or to follow acceptable rules of their own making. In 4 the navy rules have become internalized after having been externally imposed at the beginning of the man's service. In 5 *discipline* is being used as a rough synonym for *punishment;* punishment is to be applied in this instance, with the idea of getting the offenders to obey the rules in the future.

So the word *discipline* is applied in ordinary-language use when people are referring in various ways to the authority of rules. However, I suggest that the use of the word *discipline* for the word *punishment* or the word *order* be dropped because it confuses several different concepts (punishment is used to *gain order*). In the ordinary-language use of the word, then, one way of describing a situation in which discipline exists is to say either that someone is actually in control in the situation, and/or that the participants have internalized the rules of the situation and its activities. But, refining our vocabulary rather more, we can say that a *disciplined* situation exists only when those in authority are being obeyed largely because the subordinates see the point of the rules, the rights, and the activities. Thus, in this more specialized vocabulary it can be said that it is largely *order* that exists when authority is being followed mainly because of the power it wields. In this more refined usage, examples 3 and 4 above are more accurately called *order,* while 5 may be called *punishment.*

So three different concepts have now been distinguished, falling under the words *order, punishment,* and *discipline.* These are conceptual distinctions; that the actual empirical situation is rarely tidy is to be expected. The conceptual point is nevertheless worth making because of its fundamental importance for the classroom. It is the making of such distinctions that Scriven has in mind when he says that, "In philosophy we lift ourselves up by our bootstraps . . . ; we eventually reach a better understanding of the very concepts used in the original question . . ." (Quoted in full in Chapter 1.)

All too often, of course, teachers have to use power—punishment, bluff, conflict, superior will, assertion, and strength of character—so as to get order in the classroom. Generations of hard experience have demonstrated that new teachers often must *impose* this order on a new class. As Hargreaves puts it (1973, p. 233):

This is a lesson learned the hard way by countless generations of student teachers who, believing that the pupils ought to be treated with respect as mature persons, try to create a definition of the situation that is congruent with their beliefs. Almost always the result is disastrous. The pupils do not respond in the expected way. Soon the teacher finds himself only nominally in charge of a collection of noisy, disobedient, rude and irresponsible children who are quite unwilling either to listen to the teacher or to work.

What Hargreaves has said is basically correct, I believe, but requires comment. He says that student teachers believe in respecting pupils as mature persons. This may be what they think that they are doing, but to the extent that student teachers fail to do the sorts of things mentioned in the latter part of the section on respect for persons, they are in fact failing to conform to that principle. This is because roles and contexts are all-important in respect for persons, and it is necessary for beginning teachers to judge both correctly if they are to have success in control. What some young teachers are doing is not respecting persons, but trying to curry favor with the class or to become "one of them."

A teacher may have a class situation in control, the children may be working because of the teacher's firm presence. But such a situation of control is better described as being orderly—order exists, not discipline. For *order* is a word that describes a state of affairs, whereas *discipline* is a word that describes a state of mind. Where discipline exists there is authority, not power. In a way, as authority is to power, so discipline is to order, or as some writers would put it, self-discipline is to imposed discipline. (The word *self-discipline* may make more explicit what I am in this section calling *discipline*.)

Teachers who wish to maximize educational opportunities strive to develop discipline out of mere order. In this change from order to discipline, there is a change from an external dominance to a personal authority based upon teacherly qualities and the special relationships built up between teacher and taught. In the orderly situation, the adult community grants the teacher the right to train and educate; in the disciplined situation, the children also grant him the right. But

... redefining the situation in this way is, as all experienced, successful teachers know, much more difficult and more an uneven process than it sounds. If it were easy, so many teachers would not become trapped for life in the stage of initial dominance. (Hargreaves, 1973, p. 243)

It must be emphasized that the achievement of discipline is of, course not, a once-and-for-all business. It requires continual attention. (Some suggestions relating to the maintenance of order and discipline are made below [4.3D].) What is more, pupils and students who can be described as generally disciplined in class appreciate various external supports and pressures that keep them to their tasks. This last point is true even of well-disciplined adults in their day-to-day lives. To believe anything different is to promote a false psychology.

C. Discipline and Achievement

A further interesting thing can be said about rules and discipline. Rules, of course, always in some sense impose restrictions, and thus to that extent interfere with freedom, but they also allow for possibilities; for rules form a context within which a challenge of possible achievements is set up. Great artists have always known this, and great sportsmen too. A musical genius like Bach achieved the heights of soaring, intricately woven themes by depending on his understanding of the rules of counterpoint. Great painters like Picasso break some of the conventional rules, but they substitute new rules that form a context of challenge. Great sportsmen adapt within the rules and invent the two-handed backhand in tennis, or the Western Roll in high jumping, and so do marvellous things within the rules. But it is not merely that little is achieved in art or sport or life without discipline, and that this is as true of the classroom as of anywhere else; it is also that the very discipline gained through internalizing the rules of various activities and interests largely *makes the achievements possible.* For there is no creativity without discipline, though there may be whim and fad and novelty and caprice.

It has just been said that it is the internalizing of rules that makes achievements in art and sport possible. Equally, it is the internalizing of the rules of the disciplines and forms of knowledge that makes education possible. The conceptual connection between *discipline* as a form of control and *discipline* as an area of study should be noted at this point. As was indicated above, it is because there are rules of appropriateness, of consistency, of the establishment and validation of facts and arguments, and because learners can submit themselves to such rules, that we call history *a* discipline. For there to be education, there must at least be order, but the amount of education possible where there is mere order is limited. This is because in such situations the children are not doing *their own* cognitive work on the material; for, as argued earlier, it is not by chance that education is maximized when an imaginative teacher encounters a thoughtful child. Education is maximized when the child absorbs the discipline of the disciplines.

In most situations, I suppose, there is a mixture of order and discipline, so that the conscientious and bright are not hindered by the troublemaker and the lazy, so that the teacher's duty to educate all sorts of children can be performed (including the education of the troublemaker and the lazy), so that at least a minimum of achievement is possible by all children. The valuable activities of education can take place smoothly and efficiently only in situations that are governed by rules—situations that provide experiences that broaden children's understanding, that give cognitive perspective and develop rationality, and that are such that children can gradually internalize them.

The corollary is that to the extent that a teacher is unable to achieve order, order and discipline, or discipline, to that extent he is usually failing as an educator. The person will still be a teacher, of course, merely by bringing about some kind of learning, but learning is not synonymous with education; indeed, where there is not even an atmosphere of order (one of disorder? of indiscipline?) the learning is more likely to be of the morally unacceptable social sort such as "always do as the peer-group indicates" and "might is right." So it would seem that part of what it means to say that we have an educational situation, is to say that we have a disciplined situation.

So I want discipline in schools because I want to maximize education in schools. And we do not need to carry out any empirical research to know that discipline is important. We need merely to have clear concepts of *discipline* and *education,* to see the necessary conceptual relationship, and therefore the empirical implications.

D. The Empirical Situation—The Importance of Context

As we well know, the ability to gain a measure of order, of order and discipline, or of discipline, or the lack of this ability, makes or breaks the careers of young teachers. Too many excellent people are lost to the profession through not being able to achieve some kind of control. In a class of thirty to forty children the initial imposition of order and the later inculcation of discipline are, however, a subtle business. Teachers succeed in this task according to their own efforts, their personalities, the amenability and ages and sex of individual children, the physical conditions under which they teach, the children's home backgrounds, the relations between the child and his peers, the time of day or of term, whether there was a "riot" in the previous lesson, whether this child had a fight in the playground at lunchtime or a valuable possession stolen, how the children are spaced in the room, whether it is a rainy day, and so on. Teachers have to try to adjust their teaching techniques in accordance with such varying circumstances.

To say these things is in a sense to talk about *context.* It is the context in which the teacher finds himself that so much affects order and discipline. The teacher is only a small part of a complex living whole that has all sorts of influences on the children and that has had all sorts of influences. Children are products of their pasts —their present abilities to internalize rules and discipline themselves are also products of this past. The content of the particular discipline and/or the particular topic being taught also changes the nature of the context and, therefore, of the rule following that is appropriate. The method used by the teacher affects things, too— one sort of control is appropriate for a lecture, another for discussion. Again, teachers need to be aware of the personal effect they have; what sort of influence in this situation are their voices, accents, clothes, hairstyles having? It is often suggested, with considerable truth, that if a teacher can interest a class, then discipline will take care of itself. But as I have argued (3.1F), the concept of interest should not be naively interpreted. Interest is mentioned at this point because to interest children is itself to construct a particular sort of context.

Good schools have rules and are consistent in their approach to rules. The opposite school situation is shown in the words of the girl who said, "There were so many rules that no one could ever remember them, but no actual discipline as such. No two teachers were alike. This left us in a state of perpetual unbalance" (Newsom Report, 1963, p. 65). This child has provided an interesting example of a school situation that can scarcely be called "rule-governed"—"no two teachers were alike." I am not suggesting that all teachers have to approach their task in the same way—that would be to run counter to much of what I have already written—but I am saying that in a school there should be a general framework of social rules within which individual approaches can operate.

Which leads to the general empirical point that the following approaches have, I believe, been shown to be typical of large numbers of teachers who have fewer control problems. When they first take responsibility for a class, they impose their own "definition" of the situation on it by making quite clear what is expected of the children—that is, they impose a firm order, and recognize the importance of routines. Their plans are well-laid and they show foresight by planning ahead. Individual lessons, too, are planned. They know their subject matter in depth and have carefully analyzed the content of what they are to teach, and they have well worked out ideas on how to get the matter across to children. The work is varied and suited to the ability level of the children, dull or bright, and there is plenty of it. Reasons for a particular piece of work are forthcoming whenever possible. When educationally relevant, the children are given a say in what they do.

Such teachers are firm and meet trouble squarely and consistently, and ensure that the children know that they do—they try, however, to be good humored, adaptable, and just, to keep a sense of proportion, for they show a line of acceptable behavior and stick to it, having thought out their position well beforehand; they avoid expedient solutions, for they realize that situations tend to get worse, not better, when allowed to go unchecked. Their total presented image and role are consistent and convincing ones even to the fine details of their behavior. They praise and criticize when appropriate, and criticism is rarely personal. They show they care by marking work regularly. They try to develop embryonic personal relationships with their pupils as persons, and to respect their individual differences, and they allow time for this to happen; but they do not have favorites. They learn the children's names, even if they teach 200 different children in a high school. They know that the classroom situation is no different in this respect from any other—to learn to work well with someone usually takes time. Good teachers wait for children to get used to them; they change from order to discipline in a very slow-moving way, that they may still keep the "definition" of the control situation in their own hands. They cultivate a sense of humor, acknowledge their mistakes, and laugh when the joke is on them. They practice what they preach (teach!). They know that in a disciplined class the children are, in however embryonic a way, engaged *in* disciplines—it is the disciplined content and material that give point and meaning to the enterprise, that provide the rules that children internalize, and that are still present in a disciplined situation when the teacher is absent and in a disciplined person when his schooldays are over.

What has been said indicates the immense complexity of discipline. But the common thread running through this list of teacher behavior is that most of these techniques are, to some extent, explicit applications of rule setting and rule following, with all that these imply by way of forethought, impartiality, consistency, sense of context, and so on. In short, I believe that *the empirical conditions necessary for the attainment of a disciplined classroom are, at least partly, implementations of the conceptual point that discipline necessarily involves systematic rule following.*

There is a further contextual point worth putting in a paragraph all by itself: teachers should watch the successes and mistakes of other staff and should borrow from the range of control ploys that seem to work *in this particular school.*

What this all amounts to, then, is the importance of knowing the parameters of the organizational context that the teacher has to face in the real world of school, not in some ideal and abstract model of it. This is, of course, a common-sense point, but common sense can be a philosophical virtue, too, and in the case of discipline it is.

E. The Gradual Development of Discipline

Individual teachers can be helped to develop discipline through the general application of a body of rules, if such rules are enforced throughout the school. Rules are then not a matter of the personal fiat of a particular teacher, but become part of the context.

At first, the rule following will have to be enforced from outside. Later it should become a habit; it should be internalized. I am not suggesting that we stick to rules at all costs. For although justice and consistency are fundamental values in any disciplined situation, there may still be times when a teacher's professional judgment tells him to bend a rule, as the lesser of two evils. Discipline is neither a natural inheritance nor an immediately achievable objective; it is therefore both unrealistic and unfair to expect it of individual children or classes early in a school career or course. Children need help and guidance, and, until discipline is self-established, a *given* framework of enforced rules.

Autobiographies of outstanding teachers are thus pregnant ideals, but of little use to beginners, for such high ideals are too often unrelated to the realities of a particular teacher's job and ignore the matter of context. Instant success in discipline matters is as unlikely as it is in life. Young teachers can perhaps emulate the creative adaptations of the great teachers, but only after hard work, caution, much experience, and proper attention to the complex real world of schools (Francis, 1977, p. 50). Furthermore, despite the tradition of teacher independence, to be realistic, some teachers have to realize that they need from some other teachers some control help with some children. Teachers must see things in proportion—loss of face is better than permanent loss of control of a class. Realism is better than innocence and naiveté.

With discipline, as with any other aspect of educational theory, teachers must to do their own thinking and make appropriate adjustments as they go along. There must be continual introspection and analysis of situations, for schools continue, but change; there is no single solution or set of solutions. Teachers should share insights and understanding, but each has still to test all suggestions carefully against the actual classroom world that he knows. In systems-theory terms, teachers must be monitoring continually the feedback that they receive. The point is that there is a dynamic, give-and-take, and ever-changing relationship of discipline.

Order and discipline can thus be seen not as quite different things, but merely as different stages on a continuum of control. An alternative way of putting this whole issue is to say that discipline is the product of a person's education over a time, and not a situation that we can assume at the outset, or *"discipline marks the end of a process, not its beginning"* (Entwistle, 1970, p. 73). Though their ultimate aim for both moral and pedagogical reasons is to diminish their imposed control as much as possible, teachers in liberal-democratic societies need to establish some sort of control when they first take charge of a class.

It is amazing how many educators get wrong this rather common-sense point about the gradual development of discipline. For instance, Paul Francis (1977, p. 47) discusses the case of the teacher who asks how his students can learn discipline if he constantly imposes control. In commenting on this statement Francis correctly says, How naive can a supposedly experienced teacher get? For this teacher is certainly naive about the relationship between order and discipline. Indeed, when approached with a doctrinally clear head the teacher's view can be seen to be wrong on two counts: It is *empirically* untrue to claim that children ever learn discipline in the absence of constraints; what is more, children can only acquire the *concept* of discipline through being exposed to control of one kind or another. A child must have experience of rules and engage in rule following in order to become a rule-following entity. It is therefore just pedagogical nonsense for newly qualified teachers to say such things as, "I am not going to force my own control on the children in my first class; they must learn to control themselves in their own way." One American philosopher of education puts the general point this way,

> Among living things man alone can subordinate his present desires to less immediate ends. If we do not encourage this capacity in the child, we discourage him from making the best of his own resources. We make it harder for him to attain the self-discipline and self-control necessary to the achievement of any worthwhile end. Self-discipline is rarely self-taught; rather it is normally the result of the experience of external discipline. (Kneller, 1964, p. 115)

This is generally sound advice. But Kneller is wrong in saying that self-discipline is *rarely* self-taught. It is *never* self-taught.

F. The Justification of Discipline

That order and discipline are justified has, I believe, been shown in various ways in what has already been said. Specifically, it may be argued that order and discipline are necessary for education, that education is necessary for the proper development of persons, that persons should be developed because of the principle of respect for persons, and that respect for persons can itself be justified transcendentally.

Order and discipline can thus be seen to be important moral issues, and the change from order to discipline is itself justified because a disciplined situation is empirically more efficient (education occurs more easily) and morally a more appropriate way of meeting the principle of respect for persons.

There will always be issues of morality in gaining control over pupils and in achieving discipline, some more difficult than others. The following passage from a short practical guide to new teachers is interesting in this respect.

> So many of these collective actions on the part of high-spirited classes are successful in worrying the teacher because it is difficult to find an individual who can be spoken to, or blamed, or otherwise dealt with. A teacher has to be fair, but not at the expense of his own survival. If you feel that you need to pick out a couple of children and see them individually after school, or send them to a senior member of staff, then do it unhesitatingly and regardless of protests against unfairness. No class can be allowed to go on being obstructionist simply because there are no obvious ringleaders. (Haig, 1972, p. 19)

Despite the possible unfairness, this is generally acceptable advice. Practical situations such as the teaching of children often involve clashes of moral principles. In such situations the teacher's only recourse is to quick, clear comparison of principles to find that one which seems overriding in that situation. In the present context, it is the principle of respect for persons for all the children in the class, and the claim that respecting persons in schools involves sincere attempts to educate, that in the above sort of situation together make it necessary for the teacher to be less than scrupulously fair to all.

In short, the fundamental point in this part of the book is that by thinking systematically about the concept of *discipline* we can tease out some very useful practical principles.

DISCIPLINE: KEY POINTS

Order is a word that describes a state of affairs, whereas *discipline* is a word that describes a state of mind. In the orderly situation the adult community grants the teacher the right to educate; in the disciplined situation the children also grant him the right.

We can say that a disciplined situation exists only when those in authority are being obeyed largely because the subordinates see the point of the rules, the rights, and the activities.

A child must have experience of rules and engage in rule following in order to become a rule-following entity.

Pupils and students who can be described as generally disciplined in class appreciate various external supports and pressures that keep them to their tasks. This last point is true even of well-disciplined adults in their daily lives. To believe anything else is to promote a false psychology.

It is not merely that little is achieved in art or sport or life without discipline, and this is as true of the classroom as of anywhere else, it is also that the very discipline gained through internalizing the rules of the various activities and interests largely *makes the achievements possible.*

Education is maximized when the child absorbs the discipline of the disciplines.

Discipline is the product of a person's education over a time, and not a situation that we can assume at the outset, or "discipline marks the end of the process not its beginning."

It is amazing how many educators get wrong this common-sense point about the gradual development of discipline.

The empirical conditions necessary for the attainment of a disciplined classroom are at least partly implementations of the conceptual point that discipline necessarily involves systematic rule following. One does not need to carry out any empirical research to know that discipline is important, one merely needs to have clear concepts of *discipline* and *education.*

Common sense can be a philosophical virtue too, and it is in the case of discipline.

4.4 RIGHTS

A. The Logic of Rights Talk

Heated discussions are conducted and vigorous claims are made in terms of *rights.* But what is the logical status of rights? For rights are not things of the world in the way that hills and houses are; rather, they are ways in which particular situations are construed and viewed. People are giving particular interpretations to situations when they describe them in terms of rights. A particular sort of personal importance is being indicated in rights talk. We naturally raise issues of rights in areas of social relations that are potentially highly contentious, are already highly contentious, or in which there is danger of crass lack of consideration for the interests of one of the parties. I am worried, therefore, about a growing tendency in social and political discussion by which almost any claim tends to be phrased in terms of rights (from children's "right to play" to an adolescent's "right to sexual intercourse"), because such a plethora is likely to make rights talk trivial. The concept of a "right" is an important one, and rights talk has an important part to play in human relations. Yet surely it is not every human activity or need that merits enshrining as a right; this is so because rights focus on the fundamental and irreducible value of the individual person and also because they involve duties by other persons (see 4.4Cii below). Clearly enough, *things* do not possess rights; some would claim that the higher animals have rights, but rights are most meaningfully applied in relation to persons.

The verbs that go naturally with rights talk are revealing. We talk of rights being *conferred, accorded, possessed, involved, demanded, asserted, waived, revoked*—that is, there are particular *contexts* in which rights talk makes sense.

What are these contexts? In spite of the variety, rights talk makes sense when such talk is referring to *rules* that apply or ought to apply in certain situations of human relationships. To say that someone actually has a right to something is to imply that a rule exists which entitles the someone to the something; rights talk, that is, has a clear sense in rule-governed contexts. When persons use rights talk in contexts that are not actually rule-governed, they seem to be implying that there ought to be rules that would affect the situations in particular ways. The first sort of right may be called a *granted right*, the second sort a *claimed right*.

So, as with other social control concepts such as the concept of *authority* and the concept of *discipline*, the concept of *rights* presupposes the concept of *rules*. Because of this connection with rules, various rights will be classifiable in accordance with classifications of rules, and because there are different *sorts of rules* there will be different *sorts of rights*. There will be, on one level or categorization, legal rights, customary rights, political rights, economic rights, moral rights; and on another level or categorization there will be rights as freedoms, rights as entitlements, rights as deriving from special relations [Ringe, 1973, p. 104], and so on. Any granted or claimed children's rights will also be of such various sorts as have just been listed, and the questions relating to such rights will therefore be as broad-ranging and complex.

B. The Existence of Granted Rights and the Justification of Granted and Claimed Rights

The existence of rights and the justification of rights are two different issues. However, many persons use claimed-rights talk in such a way that merely by saying that something is a right, they believe that it exists (is a granted right) and that they have justified it. But, as should be clear, merely to *say* that something is a right is to achieve neither of these things. Rather, with both claimed and granted rights, it is really a tactical move, or an aggressive way of handling a situation.

That granted rights do exist we show by pointing to an existing rule, but this is not the same thing as *justifying* the right through justifying the rule that the granted right falls under. For the justification of the rule itself will depend upon the *sort of argument* that can be produced in favor of having such a rule. Consider this example from a book about running to keep fit,

> A few years ago I had some bad moments with a Great Dane in a public park near my house. In alarm, I picked up a stick in order to hold the beast at bay. Its owner rushed over and ordered me to drop the stick. "You're frightening my dog," he said. "Your dog is frightening me," I replied none too pleasantly. I was not at my cheerful best. "Well, do your practicing somewhere else," he said. "Tiny has as much right to be here as you have." (Fixx, 1977, p. 156)

Whether the right claimed for the dog exists will depend upon whether in that park there is a rule that gives equal entitlement to dogs and persons; and whether such a rule can be justified depends on its moral basis. On both these counts of existence and justification, the right claimed by the dog owner will fail.

Because rules are justified in various ways, granted rights will be justified in various ways. That there is a granted legal right is shown by pointing to the legal rule (which may, of course, be a very complex business). That the legal right is justified will be shown by producing an argument in favor of such a rule. The argument will be implicitly or explicitly of the moral sort. Granted moral rights, such as to being told the truth or to being respected as a person, will be justified in the ways used to justify morality (see, for example, 4.1C, 4.2B). So-called civil rights are granted when communities actually observe them, and will be justified by indicating the pointfulness and morality of the complex interrelationships between customs, political traditions, and social rules. Rights as freedoms, rights as entitlements, and rights as deriving from special relations will also be granted when persons accord them to others, and will also be justified in various ways. The first will be in connection with the justification of the fundamental moral principle of freedom, the second in relation to the arguments for fairness and the consideration of what is in persons' interests, the third through showing that the parties to the special relationship have acceptable reasons for sustaining it, and so on.

Granted legal rights provide the most straightforward examples of existence and justification, for existence is demonstrated by showing that there is indeed a law; and justification for that law, though often complicated, can nevertheless be explained and appraised. Indeed, granted legal rights are clear to such an extent that when they are infringed or unacknowledged, it is appropriate for the legal authority to bring various sorts of compulsion to bear, in order to make certain persons accord others such rights. Children's right to schooling is an example of this.

Claimed rights become granted rights when rules covering them actually come into existence. That claimed rights are justified (and ought therefore to be granted rights) will be demonstrated in the same ways as with granted rights. It is worth pointing out in this discussion of justification that if we do not want rights talk to become trivialized, then we must keep in mind that rights seem to have something to do with the *fundamentals* of personhood.

It should be clear now why it was said in the first paragraph that rights are not things of the world in the way that hills and houses are, but are ways in which situations are construed by persons in relation to themselves and others. For rights are made possible by contexts and rules, and contexts and rules are provided by human societies. Without a particular society, with its variety of rules, there are no rights, granted or claimed.

C. Granted Rights and Duties

(i) THE CONCEPTUAL CORRELATION

Granted rights come into existence because of rules, and rules affect persons in various ways—for instance, there are those who follow the rule and those who benefit from the rule. Thus, granted rights, and duties, will be correlative; in normal circumstances, one cannot exist without the other. I say "in normal circumstances" because, although no granted rights actually exist without corresponding duties, some persons (such as saints and heroes) may believe that they have duties toward others, but we do not normally think that the beneficiaries of their dutiful acts have a right to such acts.

In countries where children have the granted right to schooling, such a right is made possible because teachers and administrators acknowledge and act upon their duty to teach and organize. If the teachers and administrators do not do their duty, there is no way in which the children have the right. To say that someone has the granted right to something is therefore to imply that there is a rule that, when applied, *imposes on someone else the duty* either to allow the something, or actively to provide it—without the possibility of this correlative duty resting on someone, there is no granted right. Indeed, granted rights are precious precisely because of their connection with the duties of other persons. Reasons may exist for wishing that there were granted rights, but reasons for wishing that there were are not the same thing as having the rights.

A granted right may entail merely *noninterference* on the part of others—for example, the moral-customary-legal-political right to free speech in liberal democracies entails that the other ordinary citizens in those communities and lawyers and policemen and so on do not interfere when persons write letters to the editor, or speak in the corner shop or at political rallies, or whatever. On the other hand, while all granted rights entail noninterference on the part of some persons, they may also entail *active performance* on the part of others; the granted legal right to hospitalization, for example, entails various duties on such community members as ambulance men and nurses, and the moral-legal right to schooling just mentioned entails various duties on teachers and parents. Some co-called "welfare rights," such as claimed rights to shelter, to choice of employment, to rest and leisure, to enjoy the arts, and so on (as listed in the United Nations Universal Declaration of Human Rights) seem to be problematical for precisely the reason that it is not easy to see on whom the correlative duty to active performance actually lies, and so remain merely claimed rights rather than granted rights.

So, depending upon the point of view taken, granted right and duty are two different ways of seeing the same normative relationship that has been set up by the existence of a rule.

(ii) THE MORAL CORRELATION

I have been talking about the conceptual correlation between granted rights and duties, but there is usually thought to be a further, moral correlation on the part of the person who points to his granted right or argues for his claimed right. This is because the enjoyment of rights is, at least for adults, morally conditional upon their own performance of duties—that is, no one can be morally reasonable in expecting his interests to be safeguarded by society in general unless he recognizes and respects the corresponding rights of other persons and, therefore, his corresponding duties to them. I wrote "at least for adults" because to a certain extent we do grant rights to children, especially to young children, without expecting them to perform correlative duties.

Because of the conceptual and moral correlations, and because rights are possible only in the context of a society, granted rights will have interrelationships with one another, and these interrelationships will be in a state of change. The fact that in recent years persons have begun to use the phrase "children's rights" points to this state of change in granted rights and rights talk in children's affairs. There is pressure for claimed rights to become granted rights and, in some special cases, for granted rights to be withdrawn.[4]

D. Children's Rights

As some of the general conceptual and justificatory questions have been sorted out, arguments about children's rights should now be considered. For instance, 1979 was designated by the United Nations the Year of the Child, and various claims about the rights of children were raised during that year. But just what are we to make of such claims, how should we deal with them, and which should we accept?

It is because of the fundamental moral principle of respect for persons, and its subordinate principle of benevolence (or consideration of interests), and because children have interests, in the normative sense (3.1F), that we can attribute rights to them. Newborn infants are entirely dependent upon other human beings for consideration of their interests. In most liberal-democratic societies, 18-year-olds are allowed the full entitlement of adulthood to look after their own interests and to choose and direct their own lives. Children are presumably at various stages on a continuum between infants and adults.

In recent years the more vociferous and aggressive protagonists of claimed children's rights have been attempting to shift the status of children in general much nearer to the adult end of the continuum. John Holt, in typically extravagant mood, writes (1974, p. 18),

> I propose . . . that the rights, privileges, duties, responsibilities of adult citizens be made available to any young person, of whatever age, who wants to make use of them.

At first sight this desire may seem to some persons to be admirable. My own contention is that it is largely misconceived and that our present situation, with some minor adjustments, is in children's best interests. There might not be adverse effects if the children's-rights movement represented the utterances of an extreme fringe, but now its literature and ideas are increasingly being seen and heard in schools and teacher-preparation institutions. My purpose in the rest of this section is, therefore, to expose the confusion in some of

[4]For some granted rights to be withdrawn is what Holt and Illich are in part arguing for, though they may not realize this fact. See references to Holt, below, and to Illich in 4.5.

the writing that has argued for this sort of extension of children's rights.

To begin with, as indicated in 4.4A, rights talk is not all of a kind. That we use the one word *rights* cloaks the fact that there are vastly different sorts of rights. As was also said a moment ago, just as there are different sorts of rights so there will need to be different sorts of arguments in support of any claims made.

As was indicated above, rights can for convenience be categorized in various ways. One helpful way, for present purposes, is to divide rights into three sorts mentioned earlier. First, there are rights that may be regarded as *freedom* or *liberties* (freedom from restraints on doing what we want to do, or from compulsions to do what we do not want to do)—the right to choose our own leisure activities, for example. Second, there are rights that may be viewed as *entitlements* to help from other people—such as, in liberal-democratic societies, the right to attend a state school. Third, some rights may be seen as deriving from special *undertakings* that have been contracted or from *special relationships* in which persons find themselves—for instance, the right to receive the appropriate remuneration when we have performed an agreed task, or the right of teachers to teach the children in their classes.

I have made this threefold division because most of the rights that have been proposed in recent years by the children's rights advocates in Western liberal democracies also seem to me to fall easily into such categories, though they do not differentiate them in this way. The rights claims that I now list are representative of the thinking of children's rights advocates, although they by no means exhaust the multitude of rights that have been proposed. One immediate and significant point to notice is that there may be clashes between these three sorts of rights—someone's granted right of entitlement may be made possible only by taking away someone else's granted right of freedom. A second point rests on the distinction drawn earlier, between freedom and ability. Some people make the mistake of assimilating too many rights into the category of rights as freedoms from constraints; whereas it should be clear that many rights will be rights to the acquisition of abilities. In category one (rights as freedoms) the following are typical of the claims that have been made:

1. that children have a right to inquire (Bandman, 1980, p. 4)
2. that the family ought not to interfere with the adolescent's right of association (Ollendorf, 1975, p. 120)
3. that children should have the right to their own political and religious beliefs, independently of their parents' wishes

4. that children ought to have the right to freedom of expression, written and verbal (National Council for Civil Liberties, no date, p. 2)
5. that children should have the right to choose their own curriculum (National Council for Civil Liberties, no date, p. 3)
6. that children should have the right to participate in the administration of their schools
7. that order and discipline should be relaxed
8. that because compulsory schooling from 5 to 16 and more does little to help children to become self-regulating persons, and because such compulsion would be totally unacceptable for adults, children should have the right to reject it also (Berger, 1975, p. 158)

There is a range of questions that may be raised in respect to this list. First, there are complex problems of meaning: just what interpretation is being given to concepts such as inquire, expression, curriculum, participation, administration, discipline, and so on? Second, many of the other chapters and sections of this book (on education, interests, growth, freedom, discipline, etc.) have shown specifically why such suggestions, with the exception of the first, either must be severely modified or else entirely rejected, whatever meaning is carried by the concepts. Third, the initial part of 8 is factually incorrect, even if schooling does at times leave much to be desired. In relation to 8, I would suggest that although schooling should be compulsory for young children, it is quite a different matter to make it compulsory for 15 year olds who would rather be doing other things. These comments help to show just how complicated these matters are, and how unhelpful it is to propose simple solutions to questions relating to the good of children.

In general, such claims seem to boil down to two broad suggestions: that children ought to be allowed much more control over and less interference in their lives at home and in their leisure time, control approximating that enjoyed by adults; and that children ought to be given much more say in the schooling they receive. While such claims need to be considered on their merits, the short reply is that they generally appear to be forgetting that children are, indeed, children and that we do have a concept of *childhood*. Surely we would not have such a concept and have used it for so long if it did no meaningful work in our type of society (Ariès, 1973). It is because children are at various stages of immaturity that they cannot be granted many of the freedoms or liberties appropriate for adults. It is because they are children that they *are* subjected to compulsions that "would be totally unacceptable for adults." Children, because of their incapacities, cannot be granted the *same* rights and duties as adults.

The coming of maturity and wisdom and the getting of an *education* are in late-twentieth-century democracies very gradual things —we are not dealing with the lives of children in a peasant culture in Mediaeval Europe or the nomad Bakhtiari of present-day Iran, where "The only habits that survive are the old habits. The only ambition of the son is to be like the father" (Bronowski, 1973, p. 62). And in the meantime children in our society require not freedom from adult restrictions, but care and attention from adults. As Aristotle remarked many years ago, it is as unfair to treat unequals equally as it is to treat equals unequally (*Nichomachean Ethics*, 5.2, 1131a). If we consider the situation of schooling, while infants are at one end of an educational ladder, graduate students are at the other, and to the extent that graduate students are allowed to choose their curricular content this is because they have relevant understanding —they have mastered some part of a form of knowledge. Children are somewhere in the middle of this ladder. It is in the very nature of the situation that pupils cannot, at the beginning, understand the point of many of the activities in which they have to engage if they are to develop into educated human persons. No doubt the writers who make the claims just listed would argue that children should be able to develop into autonomous, independently thinking adults. I agree heartily with them, but I largely disagree about how to achieve such an end. For, as was argued in an earlier section (3.1F), when children do not know what is in their interests, adults such as teachers must use vicarious prudence on behalf of the children.

It is sometimes suggested, as a counter to what has just been written, that unless children are allowed to choose and allowed to control their lives, then they never will learn to choose wisely. This retort is mischievous. For I am not saying that children should be given no choice; I am merely saying that the amount of freedom of choice must bear some relation to the children's present experience and knowledge. Only on such a basis can choices be both meaningful and worthwhile. Freedom to develop their own approaches is a necessary condition for children to develop in and master an area of human endeavor, but it is never a sufficient condition.[5]

It is probable that children's rights advocates, if asked to classify

---

[5]It is puzzling how many persons who concern themselves with children's development get this and similar points wrong. It was only as late as 1974 that Dr. Benjamin Spock, the famous child-rearing specialist, repented his earlier permissive convictions in order to say such things as: "the inability to be firm is to my mind the commonest problem of parents in America" (*Los Angeles Times*, January 23, 1974).

the above list, would place them under rights as freedoms (from adults). From their point of view this makes sense. But I want to argue that the actually important issues that they touch upon have really to do with rights as *entitlements* (to *help* from adults).

Within this second category of rights, namely, rights as entitlements to help from other persons, the following are representative of the claims that have actually been made by rights protagonists:

9. the right to grow up nurtured by affectionate parents (Kohler, 1977, p. 224)
10. the right to remain at home with their parents during their formative years, until they are old enough to go out into the world on their own (and not be bundled off to boarding school) (Adams, 1975, p. 87)
11. that children ought to have access to suitably trained and appointed people to whom they can take complaints and grievances (National Council for Civil Liberties, no date, p. 2)
12. that there should be established youth groups that have no connection with organizations such as churches or schools and that are to implement children's rights (Ollendorf, 1975, 123)
13. that children ought to be protected from excessive claims made on them by parents and others in authority
14. that sex education must include the teaching of methods of contraception until such methods become second nature to civilized people (Ollendorf, 1975, p. 121)
15. the claim from Holt, quoted earlier, "that the rights, privileges, duties, responsibilities of adult citizens be made available to any young person, of whatever age, who wants to make use of them"
16. that current classification procedures in schools violate the child's right to be evaluated within a culturally appropriate normative framework, and their right to be fully educated (Mercer, 1977, p. 125)

Such claims seem to reduce to the recommendation that children are entitled to greater help, from their parents, from other adults, and from the community, in the protection of granted rights and the establishment of claimed rights, and in their development as autonomous human beings who can live full and happy lives.

But whether adults should give help in establishing children's claimed rights and what this help should consist in will surely depend upon just what those claimed rights are. Of those listed above, I would in general support 9 and 10 (though it is difficult to see how they could be enforced), but 11 to 15 are questionable, and 16 may even be a paradox.

The claim to greater help toward children's development as autonomous persons is, of course, uncontentious. It is how we promote this development of children, however, that will be contentious, and which can lead to the sort of contradiction existing between claims 9 and 10 on the one hand and claims 11, 12, and 13 on the other. In the first case it is advocated that children remain at home to receive the benefits of the home; in the second case it is said that children should have access to people to whom they can take complaints and grievances, yet a number of these complaints would according to these particular rights advocates, be against the parents. Claims 11, 12, and 13 seem to be socially simple-minded. They underestimate the crucial formative influence of the family and the subtle balance of interpersonal relationships within it. They also show how such people forget the important place the family normally plays in the preservation of both freedom and democracy; the family has this crucial role because it provides a context of ideas and beliefs different from those provided by the state. It removes from the state the authority, influence, and power to mold minds. Indeed, it should be noticed how totalitarian societies usually interfere in what families do. The word *normally* was used above, because in some circumstances the family itself is capable of the most extreme indoctrination of its children. At that point, it is the duty of the school to *educate* children out of this indoctrination, by providing alternative points of view.

Again, how are the youth groups with no connection with churches or schools to be run, and who is supposed to control them? On a point of detail, perhaps contraception should become second nature to civilized people, but there are delicate matters of human development to be considered here, for civilized persons do not deal with contraception without considering the crucial aspects of personal relationships and respect for persons: talk of contraception is cant, without real education. And the suggestion made by Holt in 15 is complete nonsense. If children were granted the right to make contracts, there would be a duty to keep them. If they had the right to sit on juries, we should expect that they themselves would be liable to criminal prosecution as adults are. While these features are consonant with the principle of fairness, they are manifestly inappropriate for children (Schrag, 1978, p. 63). Claim 16 may be paradoxical, because (deriving from what has been said in other parts of this book, about the complexities of real education) it may be suggested that a "culturally appropriate normative framework" may trap children in one way of regarding the world, and actually hinder them from "their right to be fully educated."

The third category of rights suggested above, was that of rights that derive from special relationships. In this category can be listed:

17. the right to treatment under the juvenile justice system (*Harvard Educational Review*, 1974, p. 481)
18. that children should have the right to the same amount of respect from teachers as have the clients of any other profession (National Council for Civil Liberties, no date, p. 3)

Claim 17 is important and appropriate, but 18 is to say the least, superficial, for the analogy is unsuitable. Children certainly have a granted right to respect as persons, but it seems peculiar to claim a right to respect as clients of a profession in any normal meaning of client respect. Children in school are not like divorce petitioners consulting their lawyer. It has been argued earlier that what teachers do is not merely to be taken or left by pupils, in accordance with pupils' present psychological interests and wants; teaching that educates actually changes pupils. Children in schools are, indeed, in a special relationship with their teachers, with their parents, and with the community in general, but the rights that can be seen as deriving from this special relationship are of a unique sort and will only be confused by false analogies. Claim 18 refers to a client relationship, but the relationship underpinning the *actual* granted right to schooling involves a delicate balance of consideration and constraint, freedom and force, inspiration and instruction. It is the attainment of an education that is aimed at, not the elimination of a problem.

In short, my criticisms of the children's rights movement as it has evolved in recent years are thus that its proponents have been:

1. working with a distressingly naive view of educational situations and activities, and the nature of children's intellectual growth
2. arguing for largely unnecessary social engineering
3. claiming rights that are in many instances inappropriate for children's level of intellectual and social maturity and that conflict with their needs

What such advocates fail to see is that children already possess a granted *right to childhood.*

E. The Right to Education

This book continually emphasizes the importance of developing children into autonomous, educated, and rational persons. The activities by which this achievement occurs are to some extent socialization and training, but, of course, most fundamentally, education itself.

I want to suggest, therefore, that the most important of all the rights that can be claimed for children is the right to education. It is important to stress that I am not talking about socialization, for socialization is merely the fitting of a human being into a particular society. Cannibals, Communists, Cro-Magnon man, and Conquistadores have all been socialized. They have all enjoyed the granted right to socialization to the extent that their type of society has taken responsibility for socializing them. But only in a society such as that of a late-twentieth-century liberal democracy that makes great play of rationality and of broadening a person's views of the world does socialization begin to become education in the sense intended here. It may be that socialization and education overlap considerably in this type of society—that is, we need to be educated to be properly socialized, but it should be manifest that this situation is very much the exception in the history of the world.

It has been suggested that rights may be categorized in numerous ways. What sort of right is the claimed right to education? It is interesting, and an indication of its significance, to note that it seems to fall under various categories. For instance, it would seem to be at least a claimed right to freedom from constraints and coercions that interfere with its attainment. It must also be a claimed right as entitlement to special help, and the duty to provide such help will have to fall on someone. It also seems that it will have to be a right deriving from a special relationship. Furthermore, it is also of the moral and social right sort (see below).

However, can the claimed right to education be justified? I mentioned earlier how persons often imagine that merely in stating a right they believe that they have justified it, which, of course, they have not. The claimed right to education, like any other claim, needs rational justification. Although the United Nations and other august bodies may state a universal right to education, the claim still needs an argument. Of course, it is easy to see why the mere claim seems to convince. After all, there is a world of difference in mental effect between saying, Education is a universal human right, and, Education is something we should aim at for everyone. The first has direct moral force; the second is comparatively anaemic.

Earlier, it was argued that human beings are entitled to respect as persons, and an attempt was made to justify respect for persons transcendentally. It was also argued that giving an education was crucial in providing such respect. It seems to me that these arguments make a case that the claimed right to education is, indeed, justified.

But it is also useful to attempt a justification that is more context-based and less formal, which helps to bring the right to earth in particular circumstances (Olafson, 1973). This justification argues that the right is implicitly taken for granted within the points of view and contexts that form the background to an actual system of action. It suggests that there exists in the society the sort of special relationship mentioned above, an actual relationship between parents and children, schools and pupils, teachers and children, younger and older, junior citizens and the adult community, and so on. Such persons do in fact take cognizance of and agree about the moral importance of the relationship. In so doing, they provide a justification and a granted right. To point to such an existing and on-going situation as a basis for both the justification and the granting of the right is also interesting in view of the suggestion in 4.1B that the best way of being reasonably certain of acting in accordance with respect for persons was to follow the general mores, roles, and practices of our society. To point to actual and continuing relationships also helps to indicate the moral inconsistency of those persons in the society who wish to withdraw from their duty to support the schooling of the young, for they themselves have benefited in the past from just these on-going relationships. What I am trying to show in this paragraph is that in liberal democracies there actually exists a set of continuing relationships under which children are accorded various justified and granted rights, and that one of these rights is certainly the right to schooling, and perhaps the right to education.

So important do liberal democracies take schooling to be that their legislatures enshrine it in acts that make the provision of schooling for children a legal duty encumbent upon the state and the parent, including laws that compel parents who, because of ignorance or economics, are uninterested in schooling to send their offspring to school.

It is, however, only some 200 years since the idea of schooling as a right of all, even in democracies, was suggested. Tom Paine, that lover of liberty, mentions it in his *The Rights of Man,* and Edmund Burke, who more than most realized the telling function of tradition, talks of the right to instruction in his *Reflections on the Revolution in France.* There are possibilities of abuse here, of course, when states get into the act, as occurs in totalitarian countries with the propagation of the official line on dogma and doctrine, which turns that part of their schooling into indoctrination rather than education. This is why liberal democracies spread the responsibility for schooling decisions and actions across a variety of persons and organizations. In doing so, they are drawing the crucial distinction between state-compelled schooling and state-controlled schooling.

There is a further crucial point to be made by looking at the actual situation in democracies, for in such societies it is expected that ordinary citizens will be able to play a proper part in the running of local and national affairs. Citizens are expected to be able to vote intelligently, to contribute to the development of policy, to hold democratic office, to serve on jury duty. Such expectations may be categorized as democratic duties, but it is unreasonable to expect duties unless particular abilities are actual. That such abilities may become actual seems to indicate the need for granted rights, in democratic societies, to the wherewithal by which the abilities may be gained. I think that it can be generally agreed that this intricate relationship between granted rights and duties exists in significant degree in such societies.

As has been suggested, there is clearly a granted right to schooling. The statutes of parliaments and legislatures provide such a right. But it is still education that educated people hope will be achieved as a result of the schooling. Furthermore, some of the competencies needed in a democratic society would seem to have to draw upon abilities that only schooling that is also education can produce. Yet, because of the subtleties of educational situations, it seems to be a conceptual impossibility that legislatures could *legislate* for education—it will be recalled, for instance, that education is maximized when an imaginative teacher encounters a thoughtful child. It is the belief that all too often what happens is merely schooling, and not education, that is at the base of the complaints laid by deschoolers; but, as argued below (4.5), a deschooled society is likely to achieve even less education, not more.

Thus, although it may be said that education is fundamental in the development of personhood, and therefore is a claimed right of persons, the degree to which the claimed right is enjoyed—that is, becomes a granted right—necessarily remains somewhat fortuitous.

RIGHTS: KEY POINTS

Rights are ways in which particular situations are viewed.

Rights are most meaningfully applied in relation to persons.

I am worried about a growing tendency by which almost any claim tends to be phrased in terms of rights, because such a plethora is likely to make rights talk trivial. We must keep in mind that rights seem to have something to do with the *fundamentals of personhood*.

To say that something is a right is a tactical move or an aggressive way of handling a situation.

Rights talk makes sense when such talk is referring to rules that apply or ought to apply in certain situations. The first sort of right may be called a *granted right*, the second sort a *claimed right*.

That granted rights do exist we show by pointing to an existing rule. The justification of the rule itself will depend upon the *sort of argument* that can be produced.

Various rights will be classifiable in accordance with classifications of rules, and because there are different *sorts of rules* there will be different *sorts of rights:* on one level or categorization, legal rights, customary rights, political rights, economic rights, moral rights; and on another level. rights as freedoms, rights as entitlements, rights as deriving from special relations, and so on.

The enjoyment of rights is, at least for adults, morally conditional upon their own performance of duties.

To say that someone has the granted right to something is therefore to imply that *someone else has the duty* to allow the something or actively to provide it.

Granted rights will have interrelationships with one another and be in a state of change. There is pressure for claimed rights to become granted rights and, in some special cases, for granted rights to be withdrawn.

Protagonists of claimed children's rights have been attempting to shift the status of children much nearer to the adult end of the continuum. My own contention is that this is largely misconceived, for they have been:
1. working with a distressingly naive view of educational situations and activities, and of the nature of children's intellectual growth.
2. arguing for largely unnecessary social engineering.
3. claiming rights that are in most instances inappropriate for children's level of intellectual and social maturity.

They fail to see that children already possess a granted *right to childhood.*

The most important of all the rights that can be claimed for children is the right to education.

Education is crucial in providing respect for persons. Such arguments make a case that the claimed right to education is indeed justified.

The degree to which the claimed right (to education) is enjoyed—that is, becomes a granted right—necessarily remains somewhat fortuitous.

4.5 SCHOOL

A. The Utopianism of Deschooling

I believe that what has already been written in this book demonstrates the need for schools and for considerable years of compulsory school attendance. Not all those who claim a concern for education agree with this view, however. For instance, Ivan Illich, in his book *Deschooling Society,* proposes a radical and relatively simple solution for what he diagnoses as the ills of present-day schooling: close the schools and replace them with a web of more "convivial" organizations that are not compulsory. He believes that he will thereby not merely make for the better education of society, but also solve most of the problems of the morality of control that I have been considering in this chapter.

I have chosen to challenge his ideas at this point in the book because such a challenge nicely lists some of the central arguments in favor of schools and exposes several fallacies related to the acquisition of an education. If we believe in the principle of respect for persons and are concerned for the development and rationality of all children as autonomous persons, and therefore wish to maximize real educational opportunities, then Illich's suggestions must be rejected.

His more general target is institutions and what he considers to be their debilitating and paradoxical effects on persons. He thus sees schools in much the same way as he sees prisons and hospitals, which to him are manipulative institutions that create an artificial demand for their own services and an artificial valuation of such services. He therefore wants to replace such institutions with a new group of noncompulsory institutions that he calls *convivial institutions.* Convivial institutions are, in his definition, any institutions that promote real human values and are used "spontaneously" by persons who do not have to be institutionally convinced that the institution promotes their advantage (Illich, 1973, p. 44).

What he proposes in place of formal and compulsory schooling is the provision of four interrelated networks or *learning webs,* which, he suggests, will be convivial in the way just described. Such webs are to be based upon *things* (books, computers, television studios, libraries, etc), upon *skill models* (people with particular skills from guitar playing, to Sanskrit, to keeping fit), upon pupils' and students' own *peers* (contracts being made by way of "peer matching" through a communications network that links learners who have similar interests), and upon *elders or professional educators,* who would help set up the networks just mentioned, who would give advice when asked about the best sources of learning, and some of whom would function as intellectual gurus who might even attract groups of learners to them. He encapsulates the idea behind the four learning webs when he writes (ibid., p. 26),

> The most radical alternative to school would be a network or service which gave each man the same opportunity to share his current concern with others motivated by the same concern.

My argument with Illich is not so much with his view of the deficiencies of our present system (though it is partly with that), as with his misdescription of it and his recommendations for its improvement. While his general suggestions about interrelated learning webs is sound enough, why does he suggest that these should *replace* compulsory schooling? Indeed, enlightened school systems already make use of such approaches, but they also make use of serious, systematic, and sustained learning *in* school. Again, what leads him to believe that what he calls "conviviality" is so missing from schools?

The philosophical and scientific naiveté of Illich and his deschooling colleagues (Goodman, Reimer, etc.) amazes me. I have looked in vain for any detailed and "hard" educational theory of a philosophical or empirical kind in Illich's work.[6] Instead, as Bowen and Hobson say (1974, p. 395), "he develops it from an intuitive description of man and society" and thereby brings with his writing all the sorts of faults that intuitive leaping necessarily carries. What Illich is advocating seems to me to be utopian social engineering at its most extreme (Popper, 1957, p. 64), with all that implies for unanticipated pitfalls. Popper points out (p. 68) that the larger in scale the changes that we attempt to bring about (holistic changes he calls them), the greater are the unintended and unexpected repercussions. Such a situation then forces upon the holistic social planner the invidious expedient of piecemeal *improvisation*—which is, of course, very different from piecemeal social planning. The holistic or utopian social planner has continually to do that which he did not intend to do. This point has particular relevance for pedagogical developments, which is why it is mentioned here. Dispassionate analysis of most large-scale pedagogical plans in many countries shows its force. Consider, for example, the movement towards teacher accountability in the United States in recent years, which has brought with it a whole range of unanticipated complications. Or look at the 1944 Education Act in England, which with the best of intentions produced the massive changes of the tri-partite grammar, technical, and modern school system, and which had such completely unexpected and unintended results during the following years that large numbers of educationists and politicians fought fiercely to dismantle it and also were forced to adopt piecemeal improvisation. Or examine the repercussions in various Australian states of the large changes in external examination policies, which in the last few years have led to brand-new unfairnesses. In short, the more complex the pedagogical goal is, the less likely is it to be achieved in the expected way.

Postman is making my point precisely when he writes (1973, pp. 141–142),

---

[6]This does not mean that his views are not worthy of challenge. They are, after all, influential despite their faults.

... there is a vast qualitative difference between what Illich has in mind and some education experiment such as a university without walls or a school within a school. Most innovations are an attempt to correct a specific evil. One tries them, criticizes them, and then determines how much good they do. If they do not work one tries something else, and then something else again if that does not work. Experimentation also occurs within a reasonably stable framework, which presumably remains intact if the experiment fails.

But Illich is arguing for destroying the whole framework and context! What would make so much more sense would be the retention but piecemeal modification of schools as we know them (with better teachers? a lowered leaving age? better curricula?) together with the trying of some of Illich's "convivial" institutions. But instead of repairing the schools or adding to them, he calls for their wholesale removal. Doing away with schools merely avoids any problem and removes a granted right; it does not solve any problem.

Illich makes the classical mistake of the intellectual who thinks that what would be good for him would be good for everyone. He forgets that if someone is to make voluntary use of educational and training facilities, he must already be educated sufficiently to understand them so that he can fit in at an appropriate place. But for many persons it is only compulsory schooling that drags them even partially from ignorance into light. Illich imagines that all the good things that we now have in the system will continue when we are without the system. He typifies the revolutionary who thinks that he can have present goods *and* his own brand of revolutionary goods after the revolution. This again is utopian. For what tends to happen is that even if the revolutionary good things are established by the revolution (most revolutions do not in fact achieve their aims), many of the original goods are lost in the revolution, never to reappear. Illich seems to forget that the process of change is crucial; he takes no cognizance of how the process of getting where he wants society to be will affect where society ends up.

I believe that his voluntary system would tend to heap cumulative disadvantages upon children already disadvantaged through their home background. It is rather the opposite of what Illich says: for one hundred years now in Western liberal democracies, compulsion has made possible the achievements of many children who without compulsion would never even have seen the inside of an educational institution, but would have been slaving in "Satanic mills." What is more, a high value is put upon education only by those who know something about it. Surely it cannot be expected that all families will be able to make proper use of a voluntary system. Human nature being what it is, structures enforced by law seem to be empiri-

cally necessary, if individual (but especially, young) human beings
are to have their rights protected. I think education is no exception.
It is only by having compulsory schooling that the poor and the
deprived get anything like their fair share. Indeed, starting from
basically the same premises as Illich, John Wilson has recently argued
(1977, p. 23) for the opposite of the Illich approach—namely, that
what is required are more specifically *well-defended* and well-organ-
ized school *enclaves*.

Michael Oakeshott (1972, p. 223) makes a similar point in describing schools and teaching at their best:

> "School" is a place apart in which the heir may encounter his moral and
> intellectual inheritance, not in the terms in which it is being used in the
> current engagements and occupations of the world outside (where
> much of it is forgotten, neglected, obscured, vulgarized or abridged,
> and where it appears only in scraps and as investments in immediate
> enterprizes) but as an estate, entire unqualified and unencumbered.
> "School" is an emancipation achieved in a continuous redirection of
> attention . . . here he may acquire new interests and pursue them
> uncorrupted by the need for immediate results; there he may learn to
> seek satisfactions he has never yet imagined or wished for. . . . In short,
> "school" is monastic in respect of being a place apart where excellences
> may be heard because the din of worldly laxities and partialities is
> silenced or abated.

What is more, if children are allowed to grow up without schooling
they may go past the point at which they can ever fully develop their
personhood. One cannot just leave educational development until
children are interested or until some adult is moved to encourage
them. If children do not receive requisite stimuli at the right time,
they may fail to develop to higher stages of understanding at all.
Older children who have not received cultural and educational stimulation may no longer be in that pristine state from which education
to their full potential is possible, but may instead be permanently
stunted. An extreme example of this sort of situation is provided by
feral children, who in the absence of early human stimulation never
achieve personhood when placed in a human environment. It is not
beside the point to discuss feral children, because they represent one
end of a continuum of developmental retardation that can result
from lack of stimulus. The fundamental misconception of Illich is
perhaps that whereas mature and educated minds may choose wisely
and well in a situation of no compulsion, such is not the case with the
immature.

Like too many other revolutionaries, Illich shows little interest
in consulting those whom his proposals would most affect. "Ask [the
poor] if they want to do away with schools; if they want instead a

network of peers, and skill models, and educational resources; if the institution of school has lost all its legitimacy. They will tell you that what they want is better schools and better teachers, and control over both. . . ." (Postman, 1973, p. 144). Indeed, for many of the schools of liberal democracies, Illich's generalizations are entirely wrong, and I believe Beck (1974, p. 74) is correct when he says that "A remarkably high proportion of students in contemporary Western schools and universities will say, when questioned, that 'school is O.K.,' and that with several fairly obvious modifications it could be 'pretty good.' "

In the fashion that is typical of utopian writers, much of Illich's account does not concern itself with the real world of education, training, and schools as we have them, but with a false idealization of it. What is more, he generalizes from some situations to all situations; he generalizes from big-city U.S.A. and Latin American cases to all cases; he says, for example (p. 74), "other basic institutions may differ from one country to another . . . [but] everywhere the school curriculum has the same structure, and everywhere its hidden curriculum has the same effect." But such an assertion is clearly incorrect. Common sense refutes it and various empirical studies by Bronfenbrenner, Spiro, Foster, and Clignet (Musgrave, 1975, p. 75) show it to be false. What goes on in the one-teacher Australian bush school at Dingo Ponds is altogether different from the action in the downtown Detroit slum school of 6000 children, run by a bankrupt school board. This example is merely a specific case of Illich's more pervading general fault, for he makes the error of viewing a part as a whole. His whole thesis commits a variation of the fallacy of composition, of mistaking features of part of a system for features of the whole system. He clearly indicates disadvantages of part of the schooling system and then suggests that these disadvantages apply to the whole system, believing that he thereby has an argument for dismantling the whole system.

B. Epistemological Naiveté and the Necessity of Instruction

Illich does make some allowance for the importance of teachers in his new order. As I have mentioned, he talks about "learning webs" that make possible the pursuit of knowledge when the learner so desires it. But in arguing for a completely free approach to taking or leaving what such teachers have to offer, Illich seriously misunderstands the nature of knowledge and the ways in which it can be acquired. I referred earlier to his lack of firm theory, and it is this epistemological and pedagogical lack as much as anything that vitiates his major proposals.

Unfortunately for the Illich approach, knowledge is not all of a kind. People who are unsophisticated in a discipline just cannot see the problems the sophisticate ponders. They cannot even ask the right questions, let alone get the right answers. Often, they cannot see that there are any questions. The differentiated sort of understanding of the world that twentieth-century philosophers like Wittgenstein and Hirst and their predecessors have shown to exist cannot be acquired in a random manner or just when the mood takes us. Such understanding is acquired only by application and induction into a world of concepts by others who have already been inducted into the living tradition and progressive refinements of the particular disciplines and forms of knowledge. The sort of casual approach to learning and understanding that Illich envisages is a sad misrepresentation of possibilities. People who understand by way of a discipline do not come to understand in just any chance way. Their understanding has a *history* of progressive evolution and incrementation. To put it in Piaget's terms, it is a process of assimilation *and* accommodation—that is, the learner not merely acquires more of the same kind, but at various stages in his learning has to make qualitative shifts; his learning does not just increase in volume, it changes in kind; and these changes in kind are unlikely to occur without both appropriate stimulation from someone who has mastered ideas at the higher level, and continual pressures and motivation towards mastering the changes. It is as though deschoolers like Illich had never heard of Popper and Peters and Chomsky and Kohlberg, who in their different ways emphasize both the independence and activity of persons' minds and also the necessary *history* to such an independence and activity, a history that includes continual encouragement from other minds and from a culture and society of educated people who make such activity possible. The necessity of a whole context of this sort for moral education is one particularly obvious curriculum area in which Illich's inadequacy is exposed.

It appears that deschoolers like Illich are working with what Popper calls "the bucket theory of mind" (1974, p. 341). On this approach all a child has to do is open his senses to experience, and knowledge will come slopping in like water into a bucket and at any time the child desires. But their view is too simple, being a variety of the doctrine of learning from experience criticized in Chapter 1. For the experiences we have depend upon our present conceptual schemes, and our concepts *make* the experiences what they are. A similar way of putting the point is to say that experience is made possible through our expectations or conjunctions in a context. As Popper says (1974, p. 345), "We are living in the center of what I usually call a 'horizon of expectation' . . . only their setting in this frame confers meaning or significance on our experiences, actions and observations."

For Popper (and I agree with him) the point of education is to *induct* children into this frame of expectations by which we approach, modify, interpret, and change our experiences. "The incredible thing about life, evolution and mental growth, is just this method of give-and-take, this interaction between our actions and their results by which we constantly transcend ourselves, our talents, our gifts" (1974, p. 147). Illich's lack of understanding of the complex nature of knowledge and of the real difficulties in the acquisition of it is continually revealed. For instance, his examples of where knowledge is locked away (in industrial plants, police stations, railway offices) are not examples of where knowledge is locked away, but only of where *information* is stored.

C. Truths and Half-Truths about Schooling

There are, nevertheless, some things that can be learned from Illich. Some of his criticisms of contemporary schooling are quite to the point—for example, he attacks unimaginative teaching, inert ideas, lack of participation, and dogmatism. And some substantive recommendations, such as that of "edu-credit cards" that can be used later when persons feel that they need instruction, are interesting.

At times he perceives real sources of difficulties, such as unions that protect their trade interests and so discourage the sharing of skills, but he seems to underestimate the difficulties to be encountered in counteracting such restrictive practices. And one of our present faults is indeed that "The non-specialist is discouraged from figuring out what makes a watch tick, or a telephone ring. . . . This type of design tends to reinforce a non-inventive society in which the experts find it progressively easier to hide behind their expertise and beyond evaluation" (p. 82). Certainly we lose insights and useful experience if we automatically discredit the importance of the self-taught man or woman (p. 44). But the present situation is by no means as negative as Illich suggests, and it is also difficult to see how any of his suggestions would make the situation in general better.

Illich puts his finger on several important half-truths about the inefficiency of much schooling. "The pupil is thereby 'schooled' to confuse teaching with learning, grade advancement with education, a diploma with competence, and fluency with the ability to say something new" (this last point may apply to much of Illich himself) (p. 9). The preposterous phenomenon of American high school *graduates* who are illiterate makes his point nicely. But once again this is merely to point to inefficiency and waste in those schools and school systems; I can see no logical connection between these premises and Illich's conclusion to close the schools. There is also insight in his claim that after a certain point increased educational expenditure is either proportionately less helpful or even counterproductive (p. 15). And it is true that, at its worst, "increased expenditure [on schools] escalates their destructiveness at home and abroad" (p. 17). Unfortunately, all too many schools, in what they do, do give "unlimited opportunity for legitimated waste" (p. 51); some of the lunatic-fringe of school-based curriculum innovation funded by the U.S. government and the various states in recent years bears this out (and a similar point could be made of other countries, such as Australia). But though these claims are valid and though they may at times be arguments for *less* schooling, they are hardly arguments for *de*-schooling.

Illich also seems to be correct when he attributes growing bureaucratic problems to schooling because of its similar organizational patterns to other such large-scale institutions as labor unions, the churches, and social security (p. 65), and when he points an analogy at schools. But once again, I cannot see this as an argument for deschooling, though it may be an argument for making schools smaller.

In passing, he properly points out that the free-school movement confuses discipline and indoctrination (p. 69). This mistake of free-schoolers is a most mischievous one, as some sort of initial external order is an empirical and conceptual necessity for the attainment of eventual discipline, as was pointed out when discipline was discussed earlier (4.3). Order or discipline of some sort is necessary if the intellectual tools for *combating* indoctrination are to be acquired by children.

But although he discusses numerous half-truths that are valuable because of their half of truth, Illich also parades many others that are dangerous because of the half that is false:

> A second major illusion on which the school system rests is that most learning is the result of teaching. Teaching, it is true, may contribute to certain kinds of learning under certain circumstances. But most people acquire most of their knowledge outside school, and in school only in so far as school, in a few rich countries has become their place of confinement during an increasing part of their lives. Most learning happens casually.... Normal children learn their first language casually. ... (p. 20)

But just how much learning is connected with teaching depends upon which concept of *teaching* we are working with. If by the word *teaching* he means direct instruction, with the pupils sitting quietly and watching and listening to the teacher, then most learning probably is not the result of such teaching. But if we take teaching to be any act the intention of which is to bring learning about, then plainly he is wrong, for teaching then includes the writing of textbooks, the organizing of programs to be used in teaching machines, the structuring of a laboratory for scientific discovery learning, the setting of precise passages of textbooks to be read, the casual leading question to a child as the teacher goes about helping individuals, the encouragement, the stimulation, and so on. Most of the learning of the medical doctor who diagnosed my latest illness, of the civil engineer whose bridge I drove across this morning, and of the lawyer who defended the latest local delinquent, was the result of teaching in this wider sense. Illich can win this particular point only by using a most naive concept of teaching.

Since most of the world does not go to school for more than a few years, it is undoubtedly true that "most people acquire most of their knowledge outside school"; but why is that supposed to be relevant reason for deschooling in societies that do send their children to school?

Again, his claim that "most learning happens casually" is either false or, if true, is true only because the word "most" is ambiguous as to designation. It may be true if it refers to trivia, but not to serious varieties of knowledge and understanding, or to the acquisition of a measure of rationality. The statement will also be true if it is a tautology—most casual learning happens casually. And though it may be true that most persons spend more time in situations in which casual learning is occurring than in situations in which they are positively attempting to learn, are they indeed learning all that time? Illich completely underestimates the importance of external incentive, for there are many times when even the person who is highly interested in his discipline appreciates some external pressure that can get him through the less exciting and more mundane technicalities. While children certainly gain interests outside schools, they also certainly gain them in schools; indeed, many such interests last a lifetime.

It is also massively misleading to draw an analogy for learning in general from his claim that "Normal children learn their first language casually." Learning a native language is a very different business from learning the disciplines and forms of knowledge that are built up later by using that language as a tool. The learning of a native language is of a unique kind. Indeed, Chomsky (1972) suggests that the only way of explaining the ease with which children acquire their native language in all its depth and variety is on the postulation of *innate* structures of mind that make possible the construction of broad systems of knowledge and experience on a basis of restricted evidence. But there are no such innate structures that can help with the acquisition of disciplines and forms of knowledge. These have been built to the stage we have them now only through slowly developing and painful intellectual increments by the great minds of the human race over thousands of years. Even the learning of a second language is a very different thing from the learning of one's native tongue.

Illich writes:

> Or shall we set up only those institutional arrangements that protect the autonomy of the learner—his private initiative to decide what he will learn and his inalienable right to learn what he likes rather than what is useful to somebody else? (Gartner, 1973, p. 2)

How many questions are begged here? As I have tried to show elsewhere in this book, a real autonomy is not likely to develop when persons are left to learn what they like:

> To learn what one likes is to learn prejudices. If there is one thing we know about human beings it is that they do not want to know what they do not want to know. Education self-selected will be no education currently available to us (it comes to us on half a dozen simultaneous channels on television), and there we find a Gresham's law of culture: bad drives out good, and the frivolous outdraws the serious. (Pearl, 1973, p. 115)

Where children are left so to learn by themselves, their interests are developed from the particular social set-up they have so far experienced, and are limited by its limits. It is only by being educated out of these limits that they can develop into fully functioning autonomous adult persons. Again, how is such a claimed inalienable right to learn what one likes to be justified? What about the moral duty of helping others? And is the only alternative "what is useful to somebody else"? After all, we can be made to learn many things that are useful to ourselves.

The claimed right of *all* children to be educated into a fuller personhood, argued for in 4.4E, makes talk of deschooling an absurdity. There must continue to be schools. (Smaller schools, more-personal schools, schools run by educated parents, and so on, are all acceptable within this general model.) But teachers must strive always to make that schooling education. This is necessary for the moral well-being of individual persons, and for the preservation and development of the liberal democracy.

SCHOOL: KEY POINTS

The holistic or utopian social planner has continually to do that which he did not intend to do. This point has particular relevance for pedagogical developments. Dispassionate analysis of most large-scale pedagogical plans shows its force. In short, the more complex the goal is, the less likely is it to be achieved in the expected way.

Illich makes the classical mistake of the intellectual who thinks that what would be good for him would be good for everyone. But for many persons it is only compulsory schooling that drags them even partially from ignorance into light. In arguing for a completely free approach to taking or leaving what teachers have to offer, Illich seriously misunderstands the nature of knowledge and the ways in which it can be acquired.

There are no innate structures that can help with the acquisition of disciplines and forms of knowledge. These have been built to the stage we now have them only through minute and painful intellectual increments by the great minds of the human race over thousands of years.

The learner not merely acquires more of the same kind, but at various stages in his learning has to make qualitative shifts; his learning does not just increase in volume, it changes in kind; and these changes in kind are unlikely to occur without both appropriate stimulation from someone who has mastered ideas at the higher level, and continual pressures and motivation. Illich completely underestimates the importance of external incentive.

Illich's voluntary system would tend to heap cumulative disadvantages upon children already disadvantaged through their home background.

The fundamental misconception of Illich is perhaps that whereas mature and educated minds may choose wisely and well in a situation of no compulsion, such is not the case with the immature.

Illich can win his point only by using a most naive concept of teaching.

There must continue to be schools, but teachers must strive always to make that schooling education. This is necessary for the moral well-being of individual persons, and for the preservation and development of the liberal democracy.

Epilogue

This book has argued that persons will not have particular experiences if they lack the appropriate conceptual background, and that it is education that makes possible the attainment of such a conceptual background. It has also tried to indicate the crucial place of philosophical thinking for teachers and school administrators, and indeed for anyone who is interested in providing the best schooling for the children of a liberal democracy. Of course, features other than philosophical ones affect the quality of schooling and the provision of education, and these have to be tackled, too. But without rigorous philosophical analysis, pedagogical practice will continue to suffer far more than it should from inappropriate theoretical guidelines and concomitant actual inadequacies.

There are, of course, many other issues that could have been examined in a book of this sort, issues such as open education, the doctrine of behavioral objectives in curriculum planning, moves into teacher accountability, equality of opportunity, and so on. The list is legion. But the aim has been merely to consider a range of issues representative of the sorts that occur.

Indeed, if the history of actual school practices is a reliable guide, then each new decade will continue to present people who work in schools with challenges that will themselves require the most discriminating analysis. As I wrote in the section on schooling and respect for persons, "Concern with education means that teachers and administrators need to cast a skeptical eye upon the fads and fashions of teaching that from time to time come to the fore to fool us." Fortunately, most new pedagogical fashions contain a core of good sense. However, this core can be separated from the husk of delusion only if we take the time to philosophically analyze all new suggestions.

Bibliography

Action, H. B., 1973. *The Illusion of the Epoch: Marxism-Leninism as a Philosophical Creed*. London: Routledge and Kegan Paul.

Archambault, R. D. (ed.), 1965. *Philosophical Analysis and Education*. London: Routledge and Kegan Paul.

Ariès, P., 1973. *Centuries of Childhood*. Harmondsworth: Penguin.

Aristotle. *Nichomachean Ethics*, (any edition).

Australian Schools Commission, 1979. *Issues in Teacher Education: A Discussion Paper*. Canberra: Australian Schools Commission.

Bandman, B., 1980. "The Child's Right to Inquire." *Thinking*. vol. 2, 4–11.

Bantock, G. H., 1970. "Discovery Methods," in Cox, C. B., and Dyson, A. E., (eds.), *Black Paper Two*. London: The Critical Quarterly Society.

Barrow, R., 1975. *Moral Philosophy for Education*. London: George Allen & Unwin.

——, 1976. *Commonsense and the Curriculum*. London: George Allen & Unwin.

Beck, C., 1974. *Educational Philosophy and Theory*. Boston: Little, Brown.

Bell, D. R., 1971. "Authority," in *The Proper Study*, Royal Institute of Philosophy, London: Macmillan.

Benn, S. I., and Peters, R. S., 1959. *Social Principles and the Democratic State*. New York: Macmillan.

183

Berger, N., 1975. "The Child, the Law and the State," in Hall, J. (ed.), *Children's Rights.* London: Elek Books.

Berger, P., and Luckman, T., 1966. *The Social Construction of Reality.* London: Allen Lane.

Berlin, I., 1969. *Four Essays on Liberty.* London: Oxford University Press.

Bowen, J. and Hobson, P. R., 1974, *Theories of Education.* Sydney: Wiley.

Bracewell, R. N., 1976. *The Galactic Club.* San Francisco: San Francisco Book Company.

Bradley, A. C., 1965, "Poetry for Poetry's sake," in Rader, M. (ed.), *A Modern Book of Esthetics.* New York: Holt, Rinehart and Winston.

Brent, A., 1978. *Philosophical Foundations for the Curriculum.* London: George Allen & Unwin.

Bronowski, J., 1973. *The Ascent of Man.* London: B. B. C.; Boston: Little, Brown.

Brook, D., 1974. "Children's art and people's art." Keynote address to the first South Australian State Art Teachers' Conference, Adelaide. Reprinted with modifications. *Educational Philosophy and Theory,* 10, no. 1: 19–30.

Cape Times, 1972. "Toddlers Glorify Red Leader." Associated Press dispatch.

Chomsky, N., 1972. *Problems of Knowledge and Freedom.* London: George Allen & Unwin.

Collis, K., and Biggs, J. B., 1981. *Evaluating the Quality of Student Learning: The Solo Taxonomy,* New York: Academic Press.

Corbett, P., 1965. *Ideologies.* London: Hutchinson.

Dearden, R. F., 1968. *The Philosophy of Primary Education,* London: Routledge and Kegan Paul.

Dearden, R. F., 1972. "Needs in Education," in Dearden, R. F., Hirst, P. H., and Peters, R. S., *Education and the Development of Reason.* London: Routledge and Kegan Paul.

Dearden, R. F., Hirst, P. H., and Peters, R. S., 1972. *Education and the Development of Reason.* London: Routledge and Kegan Paul.

Degenhardt, M. A. B., 1976. "Indoctrination," in Lloyd, D. I. (ed.), *Philosophy and the Teacher.* London: Routledge and Kegan Paul.

Dray, W. H., 1964. *Philosophy of History.* Englewood Cliffs, N.J.: Prentice-Hall.

Dingle, H., 1972. *Science at the Crossroads.* London: Martin, Brian & O'Keefe.

Elvin, L., 1977. *The Place of Commonsense in Educational Thought.* London: George Allen & Unwin.

Field, D., 1970. *Change in Art Education.* London: Routledge and Kegan Paul.

Fixx, J. T., 1977. *The Complete Book of Running.* New York: Random House.

Flew, A., 1973. *Crime or Disease?* London: Macmillan.

———, 1976. *Sociology, Equality and Education.* London: Macmillan.

Flew, A., and MacIntyre, A. (eds.), 1963. *New Essays in Philosophical Theology.* London: S.C.M. Press.

Francis, P., 1977. *Beyond Control.* London: George Allen & Unwin.

Gartner, A. (ed.), 1973. *After Deschooling, What?* New York: Harper & Row.

Gombrich, E. H., 1962. *Art and Illusion.* London: Phaidon Press.

Gribble, J., 1969. *Introduction to Philosophy of Education.* Boston: Allyn & Bacon.

Griffiths, A. P., 1967. "Ultimate Moral Principles: Their Justification," in *The Encyclopedia of Philosophy,* vol. 8. New York: The Free Press.

Haig, G., 1972. *Beginning Teaching.* London: Pitman.

Hamlyn, D., 1967. "The Logical and Psychological Aspects of Teaching," in Peters, R. S. (ed.), *The Concept of Education.* London: Routledge and Kegan Paul.

Hare, R. M., 1964. "Adolescents into Adults," in Hollins, T. H. B., (ed.) *Aims in Education: The Philosophic Approach.* Manchester: Manchester University Press.

Hargreaves, G., 1972. *Interpersonal Relations and Education.* London: Routledge and Kegan Paul.

Harris, A., 1976. *Teaching Morality and Religion.* London: George Allen and Unwin.

Hilgard, E. R., Atkinson, R. C., and Atkinson, R. L., 1971. *Introduction to Psychology.* New York: Harcourt Brace Jovanovich.

Hirst, P. H., 1965. "Liberal Education and the Nature of Knowledge," in Archambault, R. D. (ed.), *Philosophical Analysis and Education.* London: Routledge and Kegan Paul.

————, 1966. "Educational Theory," in Tibble, J. W. (ed.), *The Study of Education,* London: Routledge and Kegan Paul.

————, 1974. *Knowledge and the Curriculum.* London: Routledge and Kegan Paul.

Hirst, P. H., and Peters, R. S., 1970. *The Logic of Education.* London: Routledge and Kegan Paul.

Holt, J., 1974. *Escape from Childhood: The Needs and Rights of Youth.* New York: Dutton.

Hook, S., 1973. *Education and the Taming of Power.* La Salle, Ill.: Open Court.

Hull, C. L., 1943. *The Principles of Behavior.* New York: Appleton-Century-Crofts.

Huxley, A., 1965. *Brave New World and Brave New World Revisited.* New York: Harper & Row.

Illich, I., 1972. *Deschooling Society.* London: Penguin.

Jacka, K., Cox, C., and Marks, J., 1975. *Rape of Reason.* London: Churchill Press Limited.

Kant, I. *Groundwork of the Metaphysic of Morals,* (any edition).

Kelmer-Pringle, M. L., and Edwards, J. B., 1964. "Some Moral Concepts and Judgments of Junior School Children," in *Journal of Social and Clinical Psychology.* vol. 12:14–28.

Kenny, A., 1963. *Action, Emotion and Will.* London: Routledge and Kegan Paul.

Kneller, G. F., 1964. *Introduction to Philosophy of Education.* New York: Wiley.

Kohlberg, L., 1970. "The Child as Moral Philosopher," in *Readings in Educational Psychology Today*. Del Mar, Calif.: C. R. M. Books.

Kohler, M., 1977. "To What are Children Entitled?" in Gross, B. and Gross, R., (eds.), *The Children's Rights Movement*. New York: Anchor Press Doubleday.

Komisar, B. P., and Macmillan, C. B. J., 1976. *Psychological Concepts in Education*. Chicago: Rand McNally.

Lewis, G. C., 1849. *On the Influence of Authority in Matters of Opinion*. London.

Lifton, R. J., 1961. *Thought Reform and the Psychology of Totalism*. New York: Norton.

Lipper, E., 1971. *Eleven Years in Soviet Prison Camps*. Heron Books, by arrangement with Zurich: Europa-Verlag A.G. and Henry Regnery Co.

Locke, J. *Second Treatise on Civil Government*, (any edition).

Lucas, C. J. (ed.), 1969. *What is Philosophy of Education?* London: Macmillan. Collier-Macmillan.

McKinnon, A., 1970. *Falsification and Belief*. The Hague and Paris: Mouton.

Macmurray, J., 1972. *Reason and Emotion*. London: Faber & Faber.

McPherson, T., 1970. *Social Philosophy*. London: Van Nostrand-Reinhold.

———, 1974. *Philosophy and Religious Belief*. London: Hutchinson.

Magee, J.B., 1971. *Philosophical Analysis in Education*. New York: Harper & Row.

Malraux, A., 1974. *The Voices of Silence*. St. Albans, England: Granada/Paladin.

Marietta, D. E., 1972. "On Using People," in *Ethics*, 83, 232–238.

Martin, J. R., (ed.), 1970. *Readings in the Philosophy of Education: A Study of Curriculum*. Boston: Allyn and Bacon.

Mercer, J. R., 1977. "A Policy Statement on Assessment Procedures and the Rights of Children," in Gross, B., and Gross, R., *The Children's Rights Movement*. New York: Anchor Press Doubleday.

Marx, K., and Engels, F., 1962. *Selected Works*. Moscow: Foreign Languages Publishing House.

Millett, K., 1970. *Sexual Politics*. London: Abacus/Sphere.

Ministry of Education, 1959, *Primary Education*, London: Her Majesty's Stationery Office.

Moore, P., 1970. *The Atlas of the Universe*. London: Hamlyn.

Mouly, G. J., 1972. *Psychology for Effective Teaching*. New York: Holt, Rinehart & Winston.

Murray, H. A., and others, 1938. *Explorations in Personality*. London: Oxford University Press.

Musgrave, P. W., 1975. "The Educational Illusions of Illich," in Musgrave D.W., and Selleck, R.J.W., (eds.), *Alternative Schools*. Sydney: Wiley.

National Council for Civil Liberties (no date). *Discussion Paper No. 1— Children in School*, London.

Neill, A. S., 1937. *That Dreadful School*. London: Herbert Jenkins.

———, 1974. *Summerhill*. Harmondsworth: Penguin.

Newsom, J., 1964. *Half our Future: Report of the Central Advisory Council for Education*. London: H.M.S.O.

Oakeshott, M., 1962. *Rationalism in Politics.* London: Methuen.

———, 1972. "Education: The Engagement and its Frustration," in Dearden, R. F., and others (eds.), above.

Olafson, F. A., 1973. "Rights and Duties in Education," in Doyle, J. F. (ed.), *Educational Judgments.* London: Routledge and Kegan Paul.

Ollendorf, R., 1975. "The Rights of Adolescents," in Hall, J. (ed.), *Children's Rights.* London: Elek Books.

Olson, R.G. 1978, *Ethics: A Short Introduction.* Random House, New York.

Ostrowski, W., 1961. *Russia the Suburb of Hell.* London: Byelorussian Central Council.

Partridge, P. H., 1967, "Freedom," in *The Encyclopedia of Philosophy,* New York: The Free Press.

Pearl, A., 1973. "The Case for Schooling America," in Gartner, A. (ed.), above.

Peters, R.S., 1963, "Reason and Habit: the Paradox of Moral Education," in Niblett, W. R. (ed.), *Moral Education in a Changing Society.* London: Faber & Faber.

———, 1964. "Mental Health as an Educational Aim," in Hollins, T. H. B., (ed.), *Aims in Education: The Philosophic Approach.* Manchester: Manchester University Press.

———, 1966. *Ethics and Education.* London: George Allen & Unwin.

———, (ed.), 1967. *The Concept of Education.* London: Routledge and Kegan Paul; New York: The Humanities Press.

———, 1973a. *Authority, Responsibility and Education.* 3d ed. London: George Allen and Unwin.

———, 1973b. *Reason and Compassion.* London: Routledge and Kegan Paul.

———, 1974. *Psychology and Ethical Development.* London: George Allen and Unwin.

———, 1977. *Education and the Education of Teachers.* London: Routledge and Kegan Paul.

Piaget, J., 1932. *The Moral Judgment of the Child.* London: Routledge and Kegan Paul.

Plowden, Lady Bridget (chairman), 1967. *Children and their Primary Schools.* London: H.M.S.O.

Popper, K. R., 1957. *The Poverty of Historicism.* London: Routledge and Kegan Paul.

———, 1966. *The Open Society and Its Enemies.* London: Routledge and Kegan Paul.

———, 1968. *The Logic of Scientific Discovery.* 3d ed. London: Hutchinson.

———, 1969. *Conjectures and Refutations.* London: Routledge and Kegan Paul.

———, 1974. *Objective Knowledge.* London: Oxford University Press.

Postman, N., 1973. "My Ivan Illich Problem," in Gartner, A. (ed.), above.

Ramsay, I. T., 1974. *Religious Language.* London: SCM Press.

Reich, W. T. (ed.), 1978. *Encyclopedia of Bioethics.* New York: The Free Press; London: Collier Macmillan.

Riley, W., 1967, "Mormonism," in Hastings, J., (ed.), *Encyclopedia of Religion and Ethics,* vol. 11. Edinburgh: T. and T. Clark.

Ringe, C.A., 1973. "Pupils rights." In the proceedings of the philosophy of education. Society of Great Britain Vol. 7, no. 1, pp. 103–115.

Robson, F., 1977, "Duane is a Fresh Food Fanatic." *Sunday Sun* (Brisbane), November 2, 1977.

Rorvik, D. M., 1978. *In His Image: The Cloning of a Man.* London: Sphere Books.

Schrag, F., 1978. "From Childhood to Adulthood: Assigning Rights and Responsibilities," in Strike, K., and Egan, K., (eds.), *Ethics and Educational Policy.* London: Routledge and Kegan Paul.

Scriven, M., 1966. *Primary Philosophy.* New York: McGraw-Hill.

Shakespeare, W. *King Lear.*

Simons, M., 1978. "Marxism, Magic and Metalanguages." *Educational Philosophy and Theory* Vol. 10, no. 1., 31–44.

Sneath, P. H. A., 1970. *Planets and Life.* London: Thames and Hudson.

Solzhenitsyn, A., 1973. *The Gulag Archipelago.* New York: Harper & Row.

Snook, I., 1973. "Indoctrination and the Indoctrinated Society." *Studies in Philosophy and Education.* vol. 8, no. 1, Summer 1973, 36–47.

Thomson, D., 1969. *The Aims of History.* London: Thames & Hudson.

Trigg, R., 1973. *Reason and Commitment.* Cambridge: Cambridge University Press.

von Daniken, E., 1965. *Chariots of the Gods.* New York: Bantam Books.

Walters, R. S., 1966. "Persons and Non-Persons." *Cogito.* vol. 1, no. 1. p 40–50.

Warnock, M., 1977. *Schools of Thought.* London: Faber & Faber.

Wertenbaker, L., 1980. *The World of Picasso.* Amsterdam: Time-Life International.

White, A. R., 1967. *The Philosophy of Mind.* New York: Random House.

White, J. P., 1967. "Indoctrination," in Peters, R.S. (ed.), *The Concept of Education.* London: Routledge and Kegan Paul.

——, 1973. *Towards a Compulsory Curriculum.* London: Routledge and Kegan Paul.

Whitley, C. H., 1979. "Love, Hate and Emotion." *Philosophy.* vol. 54, no. 208, April.

Wilson, J., 1968. *Education and the Concept of Mental Health.* London: Routledge and Kegan Paul.

——, 1970. *Moral Thinking.* London: Heinemann.

——, 1971. *Education in Religion and the Emotions.* London: Heinemann.

——, 1977. *Philosophy and Practical Education.* London: Routledge and Kegan Paul.

Wilson, J., Williams, N., and Sugarman, B., 1967. *Introduction to Moral Education.* Harmondsworth Penguin.

Wilson, P. S., 1971. *Interest and Discipline in Education.* London: Routledge and Kegan Paul.

Woods, R. G., and Barrow, R. St. C., 1975, *An Introduction to Philosophy of Education.* London: Methuen.

Young, M. F. D. (ed.), 1971. *Knowledge and Control.* London: Collier-Macmillan.

Index

Ability, 137–140
Accommodation and assimilation, 175
Achievement, 147
Adulthood, 131
Aristotle, 162
Art, 101–115, 131
Australia, 30, 45
    changes in examination policies, 171
    curriculum innovation in, 177
Authority, 81, 135–136
    of rules, 145

Balance, 107–108, 114
Benevolence, 73, 129
Brainwashing, 44
Britain, 30, 45

Child-centered approaches, 56
Childhood, 161
Children's rights, 159–165
Cognitive perspective, 18–23, 25, 30
    in art, 101–108
Collis, K., 83
Compulsory schooling, 167, 173
Concepts, 50, 84, 106–108, 175
    conceptual analysis, 70, 181
    conceptual issues, 23, 54–55, 150
Creativity, 147
Curriculum, 73, 84, 91–94, 96–101, 177

Dearden, R. F., 9, 64, 79, 81
Degenhardt, M.A.B., 44
Democracy, 52–57
Deschooling, 136, 169–182

Discipline, 24, 34, 142–154, 177
Disciplines, 89–94, 97, 147, 150
Duties, 157–159

Educated guesses, 19–20
Education, 15–34
    difficulty of legislating for, 168
    as growth, 78–84
    justification of right to, 166–168
    moral, 34, 54, 93, 131, 175
    as a need, 66
    right to, 162–168
    and socialization, 166
Emotions, 25–30
England
    1944 Education Act, 171

Fairness, 125–129
Fallacy of perfect obviousness, 9
Family, 164
Feral children, 80, 173
Fields of knowledge, 94–96
Forms of knowledge, 48, 83–86, 91–93,
    175–176
Francis, P., 143, 144
Freedom, 129, 133–142
    compared with ability, 160
    presupposition of, 72
    as a right, 160–161
Froebel, F., 134

Galaxies, 118
Geography, 23, 96
Growth, 78–87, 134

Hirst, P. H., 83–87, 93, 96, 102–105, 175
History, 4–5, 23, 94–96
Holistic change, 171

Illich, I., 139, 169–180
Indoctrination, 27, 29, 30, 34–47, 131, 136, 167, 177
Interdisciplinary curricula, 87–100
Integration, 87–100
    and art, 109
Interests, 70–78, 134, 149, 159, 178
Irrational fears, 29

Justification of moral principles, 125–129, 140–142
Justification of right to education, 166–168

Kant, I., 121–124, 140
Kindergartens, 73, 111, 134
Knowledge, 83–87, 92, 174, 176
    in art, 101–107
    of minds, 84, 102, 106
Kohlberg, L., 53–56, 82–83, 175

Learning, 47–58, 177–179
    from experience, 8–9, 175
    from interest, 75–76
    a native language, 178
    and teaching, 56, 57, 177–178

MacMurray, J., 28, 103
Marietta, D. E., 122–123
Marxism, 21, 39, 42–43
Maslow, A., 62
Mathematics, 126–127
Moral education, 98–99, 131, 175
Morality, 27, 125, 126
    correlation between rights and duties, 158
    stages of, 53–54
Mormonism, 21, 35–37, 39
Motivation, 67–69, 75, 147, 178

Nazis, 29
Needs, 59–71, 77, 134
Neill, A. S., 39, 139
Newsom Report, 149

Oakeshott, M., 86, 173
Olson, R. G., 22

Paine, T., 167
Pedagogical issues, 2, 10
    in art, 108–114
Persons, 32–33, 37, 116–119
Peters, R. S., 20, 21, 63, 69, 128, 139, 140, 175
Piaget, J., 82, 175

Picasso, P., 105, 111, 113
Play therapy, 112
Popper, K. R., 22, 25, 133, 171, 175–176
Practical theories of knowledge, 94

Rationality, 18–23, 26, 30, 32
    in art, 101–108
    and morality, 25
Relativism, 86, 93
Religion, 37, 39–42, 102
Research, 50
Respect for persons, 32, 116–132, 133
    contraception and, 164
    and schooling and education, 129–132, 173, 179
Revolutionary change, 172
Rights, 154–169
    granted right to schooling, 172
    of teachers, 146
Roles, 146
Rules, 144–145, 147–151

Schools, 56, 169–180
Science, 24, 110, 126–127
Self-discipline, 146
Socialization as education, 166
Social planning, 171
Solzhenitsyn, A., 121

Teaching, 56, 97, 135–136, 148, 149–150, 173–174, 177–178
Things-in-themselves, in art, 103–106
Training, 18, 24–25
    of emotions, 29–30
Transcendental justification, 125–129, 140–142
Truth, 23

United States, 30, 45, 174
    school-based curriculum innovation in, 177
    teacher accountability in, 171

Value
    of human life, 82–83
    instrumental, 16–18, 30, 31, 120, 125–126
    intrinsic, 16–18, 31, 33, 120, 125–126
    of persons, 120
Vicarious prudence, 73–74, 76

White, J. P., 131
Wilson, J., 98–99
Wilson, P. S., 60, 75
Wittgenstein, L., 175
Women, respect for, 120

Zuni, 113